ALLIED MASTER STRATEGISTS

ALLIED MASTER STRATEGISTS

THE COMBINED CHIEFS OF STAFF IN WORLD WAR II

DAVID RIGBY

Naval Institute Press • Annapolis, Maryland

Naval Institute Press
291 Wood Road
Annapolis, MD 21402

Library of Congress Cataloging-in-Publication Data
Rigby, David.
    Allied master strategists : the Combined Chiefs of Staff in World War II / David
Rigby.
        p. cm.
    Includes bibliographical references and index.
    ISBN 978-1-61251-081-1 (hardcover : alk. paper) 1. Combined Chiefs of Staff
(U.S. and Great Britain) 2. World War, 1939-1945—United States. 3. World War,
1939-1945—Great Britain. 4. Military planning—United States—History—20th
century. 5. Military planning—Great Britain—History—20th century. 6. United
States—Military relations—Great Britain. 7. Great Britain—Military relations—
United States. 8. Strategy—History—20th century. I. Title.
    D769.25.R54 2012
    940.54'12—dc23
                                                                2012025617

∞ This paper meets the requirements of ANSI/NISO z39.48-1992 (Permanence
of Paper).
Printed in the United States of America.

20 19 18 17 16 15 14 13 12   9 8 7 6 5 4 3 2 1

First printing

For Anne

CONTENTS

ILLUSTRATIONS

Tables

Figure

PREFACE

I was motivated to write about the Combined Chiefs of Staff because this organization, particularly its principal members, contributed tremendously to the success of the British-American alliance in World War II. The Combined Chiefs are mentioned and discussed in many histories of that war. However, I felt that the Combined Chiefs of Staff deserved a book of their own. As regards the principal members of the Combined Chiefs of Staff, these were great men. They are my heroes. I only wish that God had given them a better writer to tell their story. For now, however, they are stuck with me.

—David Rigby, December 2011

ACKNOWLEDGMENTS

I would like to thank my adviser, Professor Bernard Wasserstein, for his support, wise guidance, and careful editing. I would also like to thank Ms. Carolyn Locke, who was the associate dean of the Graduate School of Arts and Sciences at Brandeis University during my time there. I am indebted to Professors Paul Jankowski and Pierre-Henri Laurent. I am grateful to Chris Warren and Tom Wilson for helping me to focus and for reminding me of the importance of emphasizing my strengths.

I would like to thank Admiral Sir Jock Slater, GCB LVO DL, who said that his family would be happy for me to quote from the papers of his great-uncle, Admiral Lord Cunningham. I would also like to thank Kevin Smith and Mr. Sebastian Cox.

Evelyn M. Cherpak, PhD, the archivist and curator of Special Collections at the U.S. Naval War College, in Newport, Rhode Island, provided indispensable assistance to me. I am grateful to the staffs of the U.S. National Archives and of the Manuscript Division of the Library of Congress, respectively, for their assistance. I would like to thank the staff of the George C. Marshall Research Center. The staff of the Government Documents department of the Lamont Library at Harvard University was also very helpful to me.

While in England, I encountered many helpful people. The efficiency displayed by the staff of The National Archives (formerly the Public Record Office) made working there a pleasure. The staffs of the British Library and Christ Church, Oxford, were very helpful to me. I would particularly like to thank the Trustees of the Liddell Hart Centre for Military Archives, as well as the Master, Fellows, and Scholars of Churchill College in the University of Cambridge.

I am deeply indebted to my late father, without whose support this book never would have been written. All of these people contributed mightily to whatever is good in this manuscript. Any mistakes belong to me alone.

ABBREVIATIONS

BAD	British Admiralty Delegation (to British Joint Staff Mission in Washington)
BAS	British Army Staff (attached to British Joint Staff Mission in Washington)
BL	British Library
CAS	Chief of the Air Staff (British)
CCS	Combined Chiefs of Staff
CIGS	Chief of the Imperial General Staff (British)
CNO	Chief of Naval Operations (U.S.)
CNS	Chief of the Naval Staff (British)
COMINCH	Commander in Chief, U.S. Fleet
COS	British Chiefs of Staff Committee
COSSAC	Chief of Staff of the Supreme Allied Commander
CPRB	Combined Production and Resources Board
CV	fleet aircraft carrier
CVE	escort aircraft carrier
ETOUSA	European Theater of Operations of the United States Army
FRUS	*Foreign Relations of the United States*
JCS	U.S. Joint Chiefs of Staff
JPS	Joint Planning Staff (one British, one American)
JSM	British Joint Staff Mission in Washington
JWPS	Joint War Production Staff (British)
LC	Library of Congress
LHC	Liddell Hart Centre for Military Archives, King's College London
MAP	Ministry of Aircraft Production (British)
NA	National Archives (U.S.)

OPM	Office of Production Management (U.S.)
POW	prisoner of war
RAF	Royal Air Force
RAFDEL	Royal Air Force Delegation to the British Joint Staff Mission in Washington
RN	Royal Navy
SEAC	Southeast Asia Command
TNA	The National Archives (of the UK, Kew)
USN	U.S. Navy
VMI	Virginia Military Institute
WPB	War Production Board (U.S.)
WSA	War Shipping Administration (U.S.)

INTRODUCTION

Only nine American military officers, five generals and four admirals, have ever earned the right to wear five stars on their uniforms. It is telling that almost half of that very select group made up the American contingent of the Combined Chiefs of Staff (CCS) in World War II. The British members of the Combined Chiefs of Staff likewise attained the highest military ranks that Britain could offer. In addition, the three British Combined Chiefs of Staff members who survived the war were all elevated to peerages. None of these men have household names, which is a pity, because famous Allied World War II leaders who are household names in the United States and Britain, such as Eisenhower, MacArthur, Nimitz, Montgomery, Alexander, and Slim, all worked for the Combined Chiefs of Staff.

The Combined Chiefs of Staff was set up in January 1942 in Washington, D.C., as the supreme uniformed military command for the Western Allies. The CCS became the nerve center of the most highly integrated effort at coalition warfare in history, namely, the British-American alliance in World War II. The Combined Chiefs of Staff had as their task the formulation of military and logistical strategies that seemed best suited to bring about Allied victory in World War II as quickly as possible. The Combined Chiefs of Staff incorporated as its principal membership the American Joint Chiefs of Staff (JCS) and the British Chiefs of Staff (COS) Committee, the military advisory bodies to President Franklin Roosevelt and Prime Minister Winston Churchill, respectively. Making Washington, D.C., the home base for the Combined Chiefs of Staff presented an obvious problem for the British. Because the British Chiefs of Staff were forced to spend most of their time in London, they designated a high-ranking officer from each of the three British military services—air, army, and navy—to represent them in Washington on a day-to-day basis and at regular weekly meetings of the Combined Chiefs of Staff. At the eight major wartime conferences involving Britain and the United States, the British Chiefs of Staff themselves were always in attendance. The Washington-based representatives of the British Chiefs of Staff were known as the Joint Staff Mission (JSM), an organization that operated in Washington under the direction of Field Marshal Sir John Dill from January 1942 until his death in November 1944 and continued until the end of the war under Dill's successor, Field Marshal Sir Henry Maitland Wilson. Sir John Dill was also the senior British representative on the Combined Chiefs of Staff.[1]

Never before or since in history has one military staff been responsible for the planning and ongoing supervision of as many simultaneous, large-scale military operations as was the Combined Chiefs of Staff in World War II. Although it was arguably the most important international organization of the twentieth century, the Combined Chiefs of Staff and its contribution to Allied victory were frequently overlooked in the literature on World War II written in the immediate postwar period.[2]

At the time of the Pearl Harbor attack, the British Chiefs of Staff Committee consisted of General Sir Alan Brooke, chief of the Imperial General Staff; Admiral of the Fleet Sir Dudley Pound, chief of the Naval Staff and First Sea Lord; and Air Chief Marshal Sir Charles Portal, chief of the Air Staff. The British Chiefs of Staff had two high-ranking deputies who were not quite subordinates but also not quite equals. Lieutenant General Sir Hastings Ismay, as military adviser to the Minister of Defence (Churchill), sat with the COS Committee but was not technically a member (although some would argue the point). Vice Admiral Lord Louis Mountbatten, as Chief of Combined Operations, participated in COS discussions only when combined operations were being debated. In September 1943, a gravely ill Admiral Pound resigned from the COS Committee, dying shortly thereafter. He was replaced in October by Admiral of the Fleet Sir Andrew B. Cunningham. At the time of Pound's resignation, Mountbatten too left the COS organization, to take up his appointment as Supreme Allied Commander of the new Southeast Asia Command. Mountbatten's place as Chief of Combined Operations was taken by Major General Robert E. Laycock.

The American Joint Chiefs of Staff organization was created in February 1942, modeled on the British COS Committee. The initial members of the Joint Chiefs of Staff were General George C. Marshall, U.S. Army Chief of Staff; Admiral Ernest J. King, Commander in Chief, U.S. Fleet; Admiral

Harold R. Stark, Chief of Naval Operations; and Lieutenant General Henry H. Arnold, commanding general of the U.S. Army Air Forces. In March 1942, President Roosevelt decided that Admiral King would thenceforward hold down the two positions of Commander in Chief, U.S. Fleet, and Chief of Naval Operations. Admiral Stark therefore left the Joint Chiefs of Staff in order to become Commander in Chief, U.S. Naval Forces in Europe. In July 1942, Admiral William D. Leahy, who had recently returned from serving as U.S. ambassador to Vichy France, joined the Joint Chiefs of Staff. Leahy was the president's representative on the Joint Chiefs of Staff and became the presiding member of that body. Admiral Leahy was given the complicated title of Chief of Staff to the Commander in Chief of the Army and Navy of the United States.[3]

There was a great deal more turnover in the personnel of the British Joint Staff Mission in Washington than there was among either the U.S. Joint Chiefs of Staff or the British Chiefs of Staff Committee. However, in the British Joint Staff Mission in Washington served some very impressive figures. These included Air Chief Marshal Sir Arthur Harris, who later went on to command RAF Bomber Command during the combined bomber offensive against German industrial cities, and Admiral Sir James Somerville, who had previously commanded the British Force H based on Gibraltar and then the British Far Eastern Fleet—the latter in operations against the Japanese.

The most important figure among the British Joint Staff Mission was its leader, the aforementioned Field Marshal Sir John Dill, who became very popular in Washington. Because he was on bad terms with the prime minister, Dill was free to give the Americans his own views, not Churchill's. This made Dill very useful to the Americans, who came to trust him more than any other British military officer. This statement requires some qualification, in that Dill was not without his critics. For instance, the memoirs of American general Albert C. Wedemeyer, a key planner for the Combined Chiefs of Staff, make clear that Wedemeyer had a deep distrust of Dill, as well as of every other British national he met during the war. Wedemeyer was an isolationist and an admirer of Charles Lindbergh in the latter's capacity as a spokesman for the Committee for America First. There was, then, at least one high-ranking American army officer in Washington during the war who was not enamored of Sir John Dill.[4] Nevertheless, Dill frequently adopted the American point of view in inter-Allied debates over strategy. When he did not, American planners (because most of them trusted him) realized that they might be wrong and became more open to compromise. To Dill is owed a great deal of the credit for making the Combined Chiefs of Staff function effectively.[5]

The two biggest headaches for members of the Combined Chiefs of Staff were heated disputes among themselves over strategy and collective disputes with their civilian overlords, President Franklin Roosevelt and Prime Minister Winston Churchill. Examining the activities, and the headaches, of the Combined Chiefs of Staff is vital in order to gain an understanding of how Britain and the United States managed to put up with each other as allies during the war.

Speaking of allies, by far the greatest limitation on the influence wielded by the Combined Chiefs of Staff was the fact that it was the Russian army, not that of the Americans or the British, that destroyed the German army as an effective fighting force in World War II. Indeed, so high were German casualties on the Russian front (80 percent of all Wehrmacht losses during the war) that, as Omer Bartov has pointed out, "it was in the Soviet Union that the Wehrmacht's back was broken long before the Western Allies landed in France, and even after June 1944 it was in the East that the Germans continued to commit and lose far more men."[6] Thus, as we shall see, perhaps it is accurate to say that the cross-channel attack of June 6, 1944 (Operation Overlord), and the Combined Chiefs of Staff debates and planning that preceded it were critical in determining the *extent* of the victory that would be won over Germany, not whether Germany would be defeated.

Another limitation on the power of the Combined Chiefs of Staff was that thankfully neither Britain nor the United States was or is a military dictatorship. Consequently, civilian political leaders, in this case Churchill and Roosevelt, had to approve any Combined Chiefs of Staff plan before it could be put into action. The prime minister and the president could also give advice and orders to the Combined Chiefs of Staff. As we shall see, however, the politicians gave plenty of advice but were extremely reluctant to issue direct orders to the Combined Chiefs of Staff.

Despite these limitations, the Combined Chiefs of Staff wielded tremendous power. In addition to the task of planning global strategy, the Combined Chiefs of Staff were forced to grapple on an everyday basis with issues that in their young days as officer cadets none of them could ever have imagined would be part of a military career. Demands upon the judgment of CCS members came from all directions. Some of these were outgrowths of the responsibility for strategic planning, such as planning the production of munitions, supervising the development of new weapons, and seeing that the finished goods arrived at the appropriate fighting fronts on schedule. Others were not. For example, there were requests from the U.S. State Department for guidance on how to respond to complaints from the Japanese government, routed through Spain and Switzerland, that American submarines were attacking Japanese hospital ships.[7] There was also the perennial need to balance the sacred principle of civilian control of the military with the need to quash the half-baked pet schemes regarding strategic decision making that were put forth from time to time by politicians. CCS members also had to contend with requests from the press for war information, as well as requests from private citizens for everything from their autographs to their physical presence at countless speeches, fund-raisers, and other war-related events. This is an indication that members of the Combined Chiefs of Staff were quite well known to the public during the war but have been largely forgotten now, at least in the United States. Indicative of this is that Andrew Roberts had to change the subtitle of his wonderful book *Masters and Commanders* when it was published in the United States in 2009. The British edition had included the name "Alanbrooke" in the subtitle. When he had been made a peer shortly after the war, Field Marshal Brooke had been consulted as to what he would like his title to be. He simply combined his first and last names and was thus created "1st Viscount Alanbrooke." Everyone in England recognizes the name "Alanbrooke," but Americans do not. This book is, in part, an effort to do something about that.

Despite the vast array of subjects that required their attention during the war, the members of the Combined Chiefs were able to adhere to the primary task—the defeat of the Axis powers. They handled their responsibilities so well that, as stated above, each achieved the highest military rank their respective nations could bestow. In December 1944, a grateful U.S. Congress awarded five-star rank to each of the U.S. Joint Chiefs of Staff (and to three American CCS theater commanders—Admiral Chester W. Nimitz, General Dwight D. Eisenhower, and General Douglas MacArthur). By that time, British Combined Chiefs of Staff members had already achieved equivalent ranks. Brooke was a field marshal, Cunningham an admiral of the fleet, and Portal a marshal of the Royal Air Force.

The British-American alliance during World War II was a complex phenomenon. The Combined Chiefs of Staff played a crucial role in permitting this alliance to work by serving as a forum where various tensions could be sorted out and dealt with. Some of these strategy-related tensions were interservice in nature. For example, there was controversy between the American Army Air Forces and the U.S. Navy as to which service would operate the long-range, land-based maritime patrol aircraft that hunted for German submarines off the East Coast of the United States. (The Navy won. These aircraft were under naval control from March 26, 1942, onward.)[8] The most important tensions within the British-American alliance, however, were international rather than interservice. They involved questions regarding broad issues of strategy, such as the importance of keeping China in the war, the proportion of Allied resources that could be devoted to the war against Japan, and which locale—France or Italy—would prove to be a better place from which to launch the Western Allies' main assault against the German army. On such questions as these, the American and British military high commands held views that differed profoundly.

Field Marshal Sir John Dill's role of mediator among the Combined Chiefs of Staff was made much easier by the fact that he was a close personal friend of American army chief of staff, General George C. Marshall.[9] Prior to his arrival in Washington in December 1941, Dill had been Brooke's predecessor as chief of the Imperial General Staff. Dill's tenure as CIGS had been a tumultuous one, due to military disasters, such as the British defeats in Greece and on Crete, and the difficulties of working in close proximity to Winston Churchill on a daily basis. While his services in Washington would prove to be invaluable to the alliance, Dill had never been able to forge an effective working relationship with Churchill (admittedly, no easy task for anyone). Fortunately for the alliance, the fact that Dill and Churchill did not get along very well was to prove a source of delight to the Americans, who, as suggested above, were always suspicious of Churchill's attempts to interfere in strategic planning. The U.S. Joint Chiefs of Staff trusted Dill to act as a British counterweight to the prime minister.[10] Churchill's dislike of Dill stemmed in part, ironically, from the latter's impeccable good manners. Churchill wanted a CIGS who (like Brooke) was willing to argue vehemently. Churchill needed a sparring partner, and he knew it.[11]

There were several factors that were conducive to a close wartime transatlantic relationship between London and Washington. A common language is the most obvious. Another was the experience of having fought on the same side (and against one of the same enemies) in World War I. There was also, of course, the famous friendship between President Roosevelt and Prime Minister Churchill. Their voluminous correspondence leaves no doubt that the two men regarded each other highly. The most important factor, however, for the success of the Western alliance was the supremely high quality of military advice provided by the Combined Chiefs of Staff to the president and the prime minister.[12]

On a chapter-by-chapter basis, this book proceeds in the following manner. I begin with a biographical chapter on the Combined Chiefs of Staff in which I include a thumbnail sketch of each member. Chapter 2 is an attempt to focus on the workings of the CCS as an integral whole and as a modern bureaucracy. I give a detailed view here of the Casablanca Conference, as well as some information about wartime Washington, D.C., as the home base for the Combined Chiefs of Staff organization. I then describe the Combined Chiefs at work in regard to the war in the Pacific. Next, I have attempted to demonstrate that during the war the Allies proved to be incomparably superior to the Axis nations when it came to the art of working together as a coalition. This chapter represents an attempt to prove, first, that the difference between the manners in which the two sides approached the question of coalition warfare was crucial to Allied victory, and second, that the Combined Chiefs were central to this process of coalition building. Attention is given here to the strains between the Western Allies and the Russians, with a view toward demonstrating that while these strains made effective cooperation difficult, the level of cooperation between the British/American component and the Russian component of the alliance was still vastly superior to that demonstrated by Germany, Japan, and Italy. The chapter dealing with Overlord is, like that dealing with the war in the Pacific, an attempt to show the relative effectiveness of the Combined Chiefs of Staff format in reducing inter-Allied friction regarding questions of great strategic significance. These two campaigns represented the two most contentious issues with which the Combined Chiefs had to grapple during the war. In the chapter on "armchair strategy," it is my intention to prove that it was the Combined Chiefs of Staff organization, not politicians, diplomats, or bureaucrats, that was the most important planning agency behind the military victories achieved by the Western Allies during the war. Chapter 7 outlines the method by which the Combined Chiefs of Staff supervised the activities of their subordinate commanders in the field. The purpose of the final chapter is to explain the manner in which the Combined Chiefs of Staff were drawn into dealing with issues of production and diplomacy that had not previously been regarded as areas with which high-ranking military officers needed to concern themselves.

Throughout this work, I have been guided by the following goal—to prove that through its ability to resolve serious disputes the Combined Chiefs of Staff held the Anglo-American alliance together and was the most important organization for the formulation of British-American military strategy during World War II.

ONE

The Combined Chiefs of Staff

Principals

The first task in creating a biographical sketch of the Combined Chiefs of Staff is to determine just who was included in the principal membership of that organization. There is some debate on this issue. On the British side, everyone agrees that Field Marshal Sir Alan Brooke, Marshal of the Royal Air Force Sir Charles Portal, and respective Admirals of the Fleet Sir Dudley Pound and his successor Sir Andrew B. Cunningham were full members of the Combined Chiefs of Staff. For the Americans, Generals George C. Marshall and Henry H. Arnold and Admirals William D. Leahy and Ernest J. King were, of course, full members. The problem lies in how to define the exact status of five high-ranking British officers: Lieutenant General Sir Hastings Ismay, chief of staff to the minister of defence (Churchill); Vice Admiral Lord Louis Mountbatten, chief of Combined Operations—and his successor in that post Major General Robert E. Laycock; Field Marshal Sir John Dill, head of the British Joint Staff Mission in Washington; and Field Marshal Sir Henry Maitland Wilson, Dill's successor. Also problematic is the exact status of American admiral Harold R. Stark, King's immediate predecessor as Chief of Naval Operations.

Andrew Roberts claims that both Ismay and Mountbatten were full members of the British Chiefs of Staff Committee and therefore also of the Combined Chiefs of Staff, while Mark Stoler argues that Ismay was a full member and Mountbatten "a de facto member."[1] Both of these scenarios are perfectly plausible, and either may well be correct. Personally, the view I favor as regards full membership in the Combined Chiefs of Staff is: Dill, yes; Mountbatten, Laycock, Ismay, Wilson, and Stark, no. My plan of campaign is to first provide thumbnail sketches providing basic biographical information for each of the principal members of the Combined Chiefs of Staff and then to briefly explain why I left out those I have omitted.

Table 1-1 provides a brief outline, in national rather than combined format, of the rank and age (in early 1942) as well as the date of appointment to the head of their respective service for each of the Combined Chiefs of Staff principals.

Table 1-1. Rank, Age, and Appointment Date of CCS Principals

	Age (in January 1942)	Appointed
British Chiefs of Staff		
General Sir Alan Brooke	58	November 1941
Air Chief Marshal Sir Charles Portal	48	October 1940
Admiral of the Fleet Sir Dudley Pound	64	June 1939
Adm. of the Fleet Sir A. B. Cunningham	58	October 1943
British Joint Staff Mission in Washington		
Field Marshal Sir John Dill	61	January 20, 1942*
U.S. Joint Chiefs of Staff		
General George C. Marshall	61	September 1939
Lieutenant General Henry H. Arnold	55	September 1938
Admiral Ernest J. King	63	December 1941
Admiral William D. Leahy	66	July 1942**

* In the case of Dill, this is the date on which he was appointed head of the British Joint Staff Mission.
** Leahy was a retired CNO. This date is his appointment to the Joint and Combined Chiefs of Staff.

Personalities
In this section, in contrast to table 1-1, I have listed the members of the Combined Chiefs of Staff in alphabetical order rather than by nationality, in keeping with the combined nature of the organization and of this account.

General of the Army Henry H. Arnold,
Commanding General of the U.S. Army Air Forces

Hap Arnold prior to Pearl Harbor as a major general. *U.S. Naval Institute Photo Archive*

American. Born: June 25, 1886, Gladwyne, Pennsylvania. Died: January 15, 1950, near Sonoma, California. While it is true that General Arnold was a lieutenant general at the inception of the Combined Chiefs of Staff and that he was technically General Marshall's subordinate, any doubts as to "Hap" Arnold's status as a full member of the Combined Chiefs of Staff were removed in December 1944, when Arnold and the other three American members of the Combined Chiefs of Staff were promoted to five-star rank.[2] Well before then, in March 1943, General Marshall, in recommending Arnold for promotion to four-star rank, had reminded President Roosevelt of Arnold's status, writing that General Arnold "sits as a member of the United States Chiefs of Staff."[3]

Henry H. (Hap) Arnold graduated from West Point in 1907, after which he served a tour of duty as an infantry officer in the Philippines. One of America's first military aviators, Arnold learned to fly in 1911 in Dayton,

Ohio. His instructor, Al Welsh, was employed by the Wright brothers them-selves. Arnold's tour of duty as a fledgling pilot in Dayton regularly included Sunday dinners at the Wright brothers' home.[4] He married Eleanor "Bee" Pool in September 1913; they would have three sons and one daughter.[5] As his nickname "Hap" indicates, Arnold was friendly, gregarious, and easygo-ing—what today would be called a "people person." But the strain of World War II would take a terrible toll on General Arnold. His constant travels during the war and his workaholic nature put a great strain on his marriage; the marital trouble was exacerbated by the fact that Mrs. Arnold was simul-taneously driving herself much too hard, doing volunteer Army Air Forces relief work.[6] At just under six feet in height and with a muscular frame, Hap Arnold looked fit. In actuality, he was anything but, suffering a number of serious heart attacks during and after the war, including the one that killed him in 1950.[7] The strain of preparing for big wartime conferences greatly exacerbated Arnold's heart troubles. Indeed, General Arnold missed both the Trident Conference in Washington in May 1943 and the Yalta Confer-ence of February 1945, because on each occasion he was in hospital recover-ing from a heart attack. Arnold suffered at least four heart attacks during the war years alone—all before he had reached the age of sixty. Arnold was intensely loyal to General Marshall; he was a humble man who was not at all certain that he deserved a fifth star when he was promoted to that exceed-ingly rare rank in December 1944.[8]

Arnold gave his active and enthusiastic support to the first Ameri-can program to train female pilots to fly military aircraft—the WASPs, Women's Airforce Service Pilots. However, Arnold's then-progressive view of gender roles did have its limits. While female pilots logged thousands of flying hours during the war ferrying combat aircraft, by Arnold's personal order WASP activity was confined to the continental United States. Ameri-ca's female pilots were prohibited from serving overseas during World War II, even in noncombat roles.[9]

Arnold's membership in the Joint Chiefs of Staff from the outset had been Marshall's idea.[10] Marshall and Arnold trusted each other implicitly and were good friends. Marshall was farsighted enough to recognize the importance of airpower and sensible enough to realize that Hap Arnold, as commanding general of the U.S. Army Air Forces, knew how to mobilize that power.[11] Arnold's efficiency in managing the air war was greatly appre-ciated by the Chief of Staff. In his 1942 Christmas greeting, Marshall wrote to Arnold that "the tremendous problems of expansion, together with the complications of the ferry service and air operations in various corners of the world, have been met with efficient direction. You have taken these colossal problems in your stride but still have managed to retain some remnants of a golden disposition."[12]

Hap Arnold has sometimes been unfairly branded as a lightweight in terms of his abilities as a strategist. (See below for Admiral King's dismissive attitude regarding Arnold's intellect.) Airpower truly came of age as a decisive weapon during World War II. General Arnold realized its potential very early in his career—much earlier than King did. When Hap Arnold qualified as a pilot, in 1911, the U.S. Navy did not even have an aircraft carrier. Admiral King, on the other hand, and for all his obvious brilliance, learned to fly only in 1927, almost as an afterthought, when he was forty-eight years old. Indeed, Arnold's biographer has suggested that King's sensitivity over his own tardiness in realizing the importance of airpower was one reason why King tended to belittle Arnold.[13]

Arnold understood aircraft design, and he was heavily involved in production issues. Arnold knew the directors of aircraft manufacturers like Boeing and Douglas, and he visited their factories frequently. Aviation tycoon Donald Douglas admired Arnold for always looking ahead and seeing the big picture. In his untiring efforts to get the giant Boeing B-29 bomber into service during World War II, Arnold learned a lot about engines—which on the B-29 were particularly troublesome. Admiral King's assertion that, unlike Portal, Arnold knew nothing about engineering was almost certainly unfair and wrong.[14]

Recognizing talent is a form of genius in itself. In that regard, General Arnold's deep respect for Marshall shows that Arnold was not at all lacking in intellectual ability.[15] In his efforts to be of service to General Marshall, Arnold seems to have felt guilty about his own heart trouble. Indeed, Arnold felt that by suffering a heart attack just before Trident he had failed Marshall badly. Arnold wrote from his bed at Walter Reed Army Hospital to General Marshall, on May 10, 1943, "This is one Hell of a time for this to happen. My engine started turning over at 160 when it should have been doing 74 to 76. For this I am sorry. Back to normal now."[16]

Some who met the genial, always smiling Arnold underestimated his willpower. Most people didn't know that the man who as his biographer writes is "universally acknowledged as the father of the modern American Air Force" had to overcome an overwhelming fear of flying. That fear had taken hold after he was almost killed early in his career when a plane he was piloting at Fort Riley, Kansas, suddenly and inexplicably became uncontrollable, causing Arnold to make a terrifying and risky forced landing.[17] The experience left him deeply shaken—so shaken that it would be four years after his near-death experience of November 4, 1912, before Arnold would again take the controls of an airplane. So deep was Arnold's sudden-onset fear of flying that he actually rejoined the infantry, doing a second tour of duty in the Philippines—where, incidentally, he met a young officer named George C. Marshall for the first time.[18] With the approach of American entry into World War I and the concomitant need to train aviators, Arnold was coaxed back into the air service in 1916 by William "Billy" Mitchell, then a major, who would become an important influence on Arnold. Sent to an army airfield at San Diego that year, Arnold went as a supply officer, not a pilot, because he was still not over the trauma of his near-fatal 1912 flight and was not ready to take to the air again even as a passenger. Being stationed at an airfield, however, soon had the effect desired by his superiors, and Arnold became determined to overcome his fear of flying. By the end of 1916 he was not only flying again but was back in the cockpit, taking up planes on his own.[19]

A lieutenant general when the Combined Chiefs of Staff was inaugurated in January 1942, Arnold was promoted at General Marshall's instigation to four-star rank on March 19, 1943.[20] Hap Arnold respected General Marshall so much that he said, "If George Marshall ever took a position contrary to mine, I would know I was wrong."[21]

General Arnold and Admiral King were on friendly terms overall but sparred over certain issues. As he did with Marshall, King did not feel that Arnold knew much about the navy and resented the fact that Arnold automatically backed Marshall on all major issues. The Chief of Naval Operations felt that the requests put forth by the Army Air Forces in terms of budget, personnel, and equipment were not based upon what was really needed but represented instead arbitrary and unnecessary maximums.[22] The subject of land-based aircraft for submarine hunting was a contentious issue for Arnold and King. In early 1942 King endeavored to put Army Air Forces aircraft that were operating in coastal areas of the United States under the control of the navy for the purposes of maritime patrol.[23] This was an especially urgent question in the first half of 1942, because German submarines were then scoring their greatest successes against American merchant shipping along the eastern coast of the United States. A few weeks later, King was able to report with satisfaction in a letter to one of his sea frontier commanders, "You now know that we have had success in attaining 'unity of command' in the sea frontiers which can be expected to improve matters in that you can now *tell* the army air units what to do instead of *asking* them to do it."[24]

Despite their differences, the views of King and Arnold had, by the spring of 1944, converged upon the issue of the Mariana Islands in the western Pacific. King wanted to seize Guam, Saipan, and Tinian as the lynchpin of his Central Pacific drive. General Arnold came to support this idea, because the Marianas could provide bases for the hundreds of B-29 Superfortress bombers that he was planning to use for the strategic bombing campaign against Japan. The Army Air Forces high command had come to appreciate the difficulties involved with basing the B-29s in China or India. The Marianas were within relatively easy B-29 striking distance of Tokyo and were much easier to supply than was any base on the Asian mainland.[25] In September 1947 the U.S. Air Force was officially separated from the army. On June 3, 1949, Arnold's official title was formally changed from "General of the Army" to "General of the Air Force."[26] Hap Arnold remains the only American air force officer ever to attain five-star rank.

Field Marshal Sir Alan Brooke, Chief of the Imperial General Staff

The recently promoted Field Marshal Brooke in Italy, January 1944. *U.S. National Archives and Records Administration*

British. Born: July 23, 1883, Bagnères-de-Bigorre. Died: June 17, 1963, Hartley Wintney, Hampshire. Born in France, Brooke's permanent family home and heritage was Northern Ireland. General Brooke became Field Marshal Brooke effective January 1, 1944. In this account I have tried to use the title for him appropriate to when he is being cited or mentioned.

General Sir Alan Brooke was appointed Chief of the Imperial General Staff (CIGS) in November 1941, when Admiral Pound was chairman of the British Chiefs of Staff Committee. In March 1942, Brooke became chairman of the British Chiefs of Staff Committee, although Pound remained on the COS Committee as First Sea Lord and chief of the Naval Staff, posts that Pound had held since the summer of 1939.[27] Field Marshal Dill, who had been Brooke's predecessor as army chief, was technically the senior British member of the Combined Chiefs of Staff. Dill may well have exercised more influence overall in the British-American alliance than did Brooke.[28] However, in day-to-day dealings in London with Winston Churchill, Brooke was clearly the most influential member of the British Chiefs of Staff Committee. Brooke, like Pound and Portal, harbored no resentment over Dill's unique position in Washington. As Sally Lister Parker points out, "the British Chiefs trusted Dill implicitly as their representative."[29]

Brooke's personality—his brusque and rather dour mannerisms—earned him the instant and lasting enmity of the Americans, particularly General Marshall. What was most responsible for that reaction was aptly articulated by the CIGS himself: in correspondence with J. R. M. Butler and Sir Michael Howard during the preparation of the *Grand Strategy* series, Brooke wrote that in his opinion, "Any idea of a cross Channel operation was completely out of the picture during 1942 and 43 except in the event of the German forces beginning to crack up, which is very unlikely."[30]

Brooke had served heroically in battle in both world wars, never displaying the slightest concern for his own personal safety.[31] How then, does one explain the attribute for which Brooke is most known during World War II, his deep reluctance to undertake Operation Overlord, the cross-channel invasion? Why would a fighter shy away from a fight? Brooke, of course, had terrible memories of the slaughter on the western front during World War I. Also, historians have noted that there was a feeling in the British army in World War II, particularly early, when defeats were common, that Britain's soldiers in this war were simply not as good as those who had served in the British Expeditionary Force during World War I.[32] For instance, Alex Danchev has noted that in World War II "there were deep reservations in the British high command about the capacity of their own soldiers pitted against the Germans, and in particular about the quality of British military leadership."[33] General Brooke fully shared this pessimism and lack of confidence. For example, in March 1942 Brooke confided to his diary that he felt that British forces in general were not currently fighting with enough determination:[34] "Half our Corps & Divisional Commanders are totally unfit for their appointments, and yet if I were to sack them I could find no better! They lack character, imagination, drive & power of leadership."[35] Here Brooke is talking about lieutenant generals and major generals. Thus, if his comment was accurate, the British army really was in trouble. Brooke's biographer has written that early in World War II, Brooke was convinced that the British army as a whole, both officer corps and enlisted ranks, was not up to Great War standards.[36]

Brooke was an expert ornithologist and avid trout fisherman. Yet despite his love of watching and studying birds, Brooke was not above killing a few on occasion. For instance, Brooke and Churchill spent a day hunting partridge just after the Casablanca Conference.[37] A parallel between Brooke and Marshall is that both men lost a beloved first wife but remarried happily shortly thereafter. Brooke's first wife, Janey, was killed in 1925 in a car accident in which Brooke was driving—a circumstance that undoubtedly left him with lasting feelings of guilt as well as grief. He married Benita Lees in 1929, which happened to be less than a year before Marshall's second marriage. Brooke was more fortunate than Marshall in one respect—that both of his wives were capable of bearing children. Brooke had two children by each of his wives.[38]

One of the major stressors on Brooke during World War II was, of course, the person of Winston Churchill. A September 1944 entry in Brooke's diary amply demonstrates how difficult it was for the orderly and extremely self-disciplined Brooke to work for a loose cannon like Churchill. Of his boss Brooke wrote, "Three quarters of the population of the world imagine that Winston Churchill is one of the strategists of history, a second Marlborough, and the other quarter have no conception of what a public menace he is, and has been throughout this war. . . . Without him England was lost for a certainty. . . . [W]ith him England has been on the verge of disaster time and again. . . . Never have I admired and despised a man simultaneously to the same extent."[39] The dual challenges of keeping the prime minister "on the rails" and of the increasingly bitter debate in regard to the cross-channel versus Mediterranean controversy between Brooke and Marshall ensured that Brooke had a very difficult and unpleasant job during World War II.[40]

Developing strategic ideas and plans and setting them down on paper were never Brooke's strong points. He was more apt to refine and champion those submitted to the Combined Chiefs by the planning staffs that he thought had merit.[41] One of Brooke's greatest contributions to the smooth functioning of the Combined Chiefs of Staff was his ability to handle effectively some of the difficult personalities, both civilian and military, with whom he was forced to consort. Brooke's role in this regard has been spelled out accurately by Sir James "P. J." Grigg, the British secretary of state for war: "Above all [Brooke] was the man who managed to restrain Mr. Churchill from embarking on fruitless and costly operations. This was no easy task."[42] Similarly, after the war Mountbatten claimed that one of Brooke's great contributions as CIGS was that Brooke had seemed to be the only person in the Allied high command whom the vainglorious General Bernard Montgomery respected. Despite his reputation for tactlessness in formal conference, Brooke was apparently quite skillful in resolving the disputes that grew out of Montgomery's insulting manner toward Churchill, thereby preventing Montgomery from being fired. One such episode occurred in early January 1945, during the Battle of the Bulge, when Montgomery attempted (unsuccessfully) to prevent Churchill from visiting Allied troops at the front.[43]

One of Brooke's wartime aides has pointed out that one reason for Brooke's success as CIGS is that he understood how to delegate, which is of course an essential skill for effective management. He did not get caught up in the details of day-to-day military operations (something which could *not* be said of the prime minister). Therefore, Brooke was able to concentrate on the larger issues being discussed by the Combined Chiefs of Staff.[44]

Brooke made a poor first impression upon his COS colleague Sir Charles Portal when the two first met in 1940, owing to Brooke's abruptness and lack of interpersonal skills. Portal noticed that whether dealing with politicians such as Churchill or with other members of the

Combined Chiefs of Staff, Brooke expressed his views forcefully, loudly, and frequently without any sense of tact. Nonetheless, in spite of initial doubts about whether Brooke would be effective as Chief of the Imperial General Staff, Portal quickly came to admire Brooke, and the two became good friends.[45]

The same could never be said for Brooke's relations with his American CCS counterparts. Portal felt that "right to the end of the war . . . Brooke 'jarred' on the U.S. Chiefs of Staff. They did not understand him and disliked his abrupt manner and aloofness."[46] The chief of the Air Staff also felt that the Americans were getting under Brooke's skin.[47] Portal could see that without the good offices of Sir John Dill, "who smoothed things out and interpreted Brooke to the Americans," the work of the Combined Chiefs of Staff would have been much more difficult and much less productive.[48]

Just how much Brooke "jarred" on the Americans was made clear by General Joseph Stilwell, who recorded in his diary a contretemps between General Brooke and Admiral King at the Cairo (Sextant) Conference in November 1943. Stillwell recorded, "Brooke got nasty and King got good and sore. King almost climbed over the table at Brooke. God he was mad. I wish he had socked him."[49]

Brooke's first visit to Washington, in June 1942, allowed him to get to know General Marshall (whom he had met for the first time the previous April) a little better. While in Washington Brooke had his first meeting with Admiral King. From that interview Brooke formed a clear impression that General Marshall was primarily concerned with an early second front in Europe but that Admiral King was focused on shifting the war against Japan into high gear. Brooke did not feel that the Americans had at this time reached a very high level of interservice cooperation.[50] (As we will see, he was right about that.) In the light of these observations, Brooke noted in his diary, "There is no doubt that Dill is doing wonderful work and that we owe him a deep debt of gratitude."[51]

Admiral of the Fleet Sir Andrew B. Cunningham, First Sea Lord and Chief of the Naval Staff

British. Born: January 7, 1883, Dublin. Died: June 12, 1963, London. Great Britain has had many great admirals in its history, but only one, Sir Andrew B. Cunningham, is considered to have been in the same league with Lord Nel-

Sir Andrew Cunningham foreground, with American vice admiral H. Kent Hewitt. *U.S. Naval Institute Photo Archive*

son. While commanding the British Mediterranean Fleet early in World War II, Admiral Cunningham was to the Italian navy what Sir Francis Drake had been to the New World settlements of Philip II's Spain—that is, its worst nightmare. Cunningham was without peer as a seagoing commander. He disliked the periodic spells ashore in which he was required to do staff work; however, his performance as a staff officer was better than is sometimes realized.[52]

Cunningham was a fighter—literally. As a young naval cadet, he had never been shy about engaging in fistfights. As a cadet, Cunningham was on hand during the Diamond Jubilee naval review held in honor of Queen Victoria in the Spithead channel between Portsmouth and the Isle of Wight on June 27, 1897.[53] While there Cunningham undoubtedly witnessed, or at least heard about, what is perhaps the greatest public relations coup of all time, namely, the demonstration staged by one Charles Parsons, a brilliant engineer who charged through the anchored fleet in his specially designed steam launch *Turbinia*, a vessel built to prove the superiority of the new steam-turbine engine Parsons had developed. Parsons was hugely successful. British and foreign naval dignitaries were astounded to see *Turbinia*'s slender hull sprinting across the roadstead at well over thirty knots, an unheard-of speed for any seagoing vessel of the 1890s.[54] The advent of the steam turbine and its undoubted superiority over piston engines marked one of many changes the world's leading navies were undergoing at the close of the nineteenth century. The Royal Navy that Cunningham would lead as an Admiral of the Fleet in World War II would be heavily reliant on steam-turbine technology.

As Cunningham's biographer has noted, all was not well with the Royal Navy at the end of the nineteenth century. Lord Nelson a century before had encouraged junior officers to think for themselves. However, by the time of Cunningham's formative years as a young midshipman, "the essence of Nelson's success had been forgotten."[55] By 1900 and well into World War I at least, officers in the Royal Navy, even officers at the rank of rear admiral, waited to be told what to do by senior admirals in charge. For instance, late at night on May 31, 1916, during the closing stages of the battle of Jutland, the crew of the British battleship HMS *Malaya* actually saw elements of the German battle fleet passing astern of the British fleet. The *Malaya*'s captain, Algernon Boyle, did not open fire, because, not expecting the Germans to try such a move, the British fleet commander, Admiral Sir John Jellicoe, had given no orders for the battleships bringing up the rear of his formation to be on the lookout for and if possible engage German battleships in a night action. In 1916, captains of British warships were reluctant to open fire unless an admiral ordered them to do so. But Jellicoe had no idea that the enemy fleet was passing astern of his formation; he thought the bulk of the German forces were out in front of him somewhere, and he intended to renew the battle the next day. Nobody bothered to inform Jellicoe that the German fleet was not where it was supposed to be. The *Malaya*'s captain informed the commander of the division to which his ship belonged, Rear Admiral Sir Hugh Evan-Thomas, but the latter not only refrained from ordering an attack but also failed to relay the report to Jellicoe.[56] Everyone assumed that the senior admiral was fully aware of everything that was going on and that there was no need for any subordinate to make a decision.[57] Nelson would have been appalled. The aggressive leadership that Admiral Cunningham would display during World War II in his assignments afloat and ashore would do much to show the world that the Royal Navy had by then fully regained its aggressive spirit.

Early in his naval career, Cunningham became expert in the handling of destroyers (and their steam-turbine engines) and commanded one, HMS *Scorpion,* in the Mediterranean during World War I. Later, he served as captain of the battleship HMS *Rodney.* He was an avid golfer, gardener, and fisherman. Cunningham married Nona Byatt in December 1929; they were both in their forties at the time and would have no children.[58]

During World War II, under Cunningham's command, the British Mediterranean Fleet carried out the daring November 1940 raid on the

Italian fleet anchorage at Taranto in which British torpedo planes flying from the aircraft carrier HMS *Illustrious* sank three Italian battleships (although two of these were subsequently raised from the harbor bottom, pumped out, repaired, and eventually put back into service). In March 1941, at the battle of Cape Matapan, Cunningham struck again, and hard. A Royal Navy pilot flying from the aircraft carrier HMS *Formidable* dropped a torpedo that damaged the *Vittorio Veneto,* one of Italy's newest battleships. Then Cunningham led his three battleships and a squadron of cruisers in a night action in which three Italian heavy cruisers were sunk. Later that spring, Admiral Cunningham won the undying admiration of the British army by ignoring intense German air attacks in order to evacuate over 20,000 British and New Zealand troops from Crete.[59]

Admiral Cunningham served a brief tour of duty as the leader of the British Admiralty Delegation element of the British Joint Staff Mission in Washington in 1942. In that posting, Cunningham proved to be quite equal to the task of arguing with the volatile Chief of Naval Operations, Admiral King. In arguments that usually revolved around trying to get King to relent enough in his obsession with the war against Japan to devote more American resources to the Battle of the Atlantic, King recognized the fighter in Cunningham and grew to respect him for it.[60]

General Marshall too thought highly of Cunningham. Indeed, Marshall's biographer has written that "Marshall spoke for himself as well as for his colleagues, when he wrote, 'he enjoys our complete confidence.'"[61] Admiral Cunningham had without complaint accepted his posting as Dwight D. Eisenhower's subordinate in the billet of commander of Allied naval forces in the Mediterranean during Operation Torch and subsequently during Husky (the invasion of Sicily), as well as in the beginning of the Allied campaign in Italy. This showed character and forbearance, because it could be argued that Cunningham's brilliant combat performance in the Mediterranean in 1940–41, coupled with his highly successful tour of duty with the British Joint Staff Mission in Washington, made him far more qualified than Eisenhower to be the supreme commander of Torch and Husky. In fact, however, Eisenhower and Cunningham became good friends and worked extremely well together.

For the purposes of this study, Cunningham's most important characteristic was the fact that he was a vigorous proponent of operations in the Central Pacific. He shared Admiral King's view that the Central Pacific drive was the key to defeating Japan. Cunningham had no sympathy for retaking Hong Kong or Singapore, which Britain would get back automatically when Japan surrendered anyway. This position put Cunningham deeply at odds with Churchill, who was very eager to restore British prestige in the Far East through such means as marching British troops back into Hong Kong and Singapore before Japan surrendered. For Cunningham, unlike Churchill, it did not matter *how* the Japanese were defeated, as long as they *were* defeated.[62]

Field Marshal Sir John Dill, Head of the British Joint Staff Mission in Washington

Sir John Dill being honored at Yale University, February 1944. *U.S. National Archives and Records Administration*

British. Born: December 25, 1881, Lurgan (near Galway, Ireland). Died: November 4, 1944, Washington, D.C. Great friend of General Marshall and Brooke's immediate predecessor as Chief of the Imperial General Staff, it was probably a blessing in disguise that Field Marshal Sir John Dill's tenure as CIGS early in the war was unsuccessful. Otherwise, he would not have been cashiered from the position and could not have taken up the post of head of the British Joint Staff Mission in Washington. Churchill neither liked nor respected Dill. Churchill probably did not "like" Brooke either, but the prime minister respected Brooke far more than he did Dill. Appointed by Churchill as CIGS in May 1940, Dill served in that post until December 1941. Part of the reason that Dill's tenure as uniformed head of the British army was a torment that probably shortened his life is that Dill took over command of the army at a time when Britain's military situation appeared hopeless.[63]

Dill's efforts to keep the prime minister grounded in reality incurred Churchill's wrath, but as Alex Danchev has noted, Dill's tenure as Chief of the Imperial General Staff was actually more successful than is sometimes realized: "It was above all Dill who responded to the imperative of the moment and established the wearying but constructive adversarial relationship between Churchill and the Chiefs of Staff on which Brooke, blessed with new allies and augmented resources, so successfully built in 1942 for the duration of the war."[64]

General Brooke certainly did inherit the task of short-circuiting the prime minister's wilder ideas. The unending conflict that characterized Dill's relations with Churchill in London inevitably made his tenure relatively short. In November 1941, it was announced that Field Marshal Dill would retire as CIGS the following month, to be given the sinecure post of governor of Bombay. World events changed all that—Dill never made it to India. The turnover of his duties as army chief to the new CIGS, General Sir Alan Brooke, coincided with American entry into the war. Dill therefore accompanied Winston Churchill to the Arcadia Conference in Washington in December 1941 as a lame-duck CIGS. Dill had by then struck up a friendship and correspondence with General Marshall, whom he had met at the Atlantic Charter Conference at Argentia, Newfoundland, in August 1941.[65]

After the Arcadia discussions in Washington wrapped up in January 1942, Churchill left Dill in Washington, an idea that had originated with General Brooke, to head up the British Joint Staff Mission there. This was undoubtedly one of the best decisions Churchill made during the war. In Washington, Dill's close friendship with General Marshall contributed greatly to reducing, although certainly not eliminating, turmoil in the Western alliance.[66] In addition to being the head of the British Joint Staff Mission, Dill was instructed by Churchill, in a memorandum written on February 6, 1942, to consider himself Churchill's personal representative in day-to-day dealings in Washington with the Americans. Interestingly, in regard to the "personal representative" part, Churchill had apparently needed to be prodded by President Franklin D. Roosevelt (FDR) before he agreed to grant this much power to Dill, undoubtedly due to lingering bad feelings.[67] The misunderstandings that already existed between Churchill and Dill, and those that were just beginning between Generals Brooke and Marshall, would persist. However, as Danchev writes, "The change wrought by Dill's removal to Washington was that the tensions became creative."[68]

The importance to the Anglo-American alliance of the close friendship between Field Marshal Dill and General Marshall has been thoroughly chronicled by others.[69] There is ample evidence in the archives to support the contention that with the possible exception of Arnold, Dill was Marshall's closest colleague among the Combined Chiefs of Staff.[70] In an address he gave at an award ceremony honoring Dill at Yale University, General Marshall paid warm tribute to his good friend, characterizing him as "single-minded in the sincerity of [his] efforts to promote the unity of our two great nations."[71] Dill in fact got on very well with all the U.S. chiefs. He called Arnold by his nickname "Hap." Even Admiral King, whose relations with his British allies were sometimes rocky, was on excellent terms with Dill. King visited Dill frequently when the field marshal was lying ill at Walter Reed and served as an honorary pallbearer at his funeral in November 1944.[72] Dill explained his recipe for successful Anglo-American relations: "To have different views even on major questions of policy need not embitter relations. The great thing on both sides is to be completely frank and when we or Americans have political as opposed to purely military factors influencing action to explain that they are."[73]

As mentioned earlier, Dill was the senior British representative on the Combined Chiefs of Staff. A bit of qualification is called for here. General Brooke, as chairman of the British Chiefs of Staff Committee from March 1942, was certainly Churchill's closest military adviser, while Dill was three thousand miles away in Washington, D.C. Perhaps it could be said that just as Admiral Leahy was nominally the senior member of the U.S. Joint Chiefs of Staff, where he was completely overshadowed as a strategist by Marshall and King; so Dill was nominally the senior British member of the Combined Chiefs of Staff, even though General Brooke clearly had greater influence with Churchill. Where Field Marshal Dill did have plenty of influence was in Washington with the Americans. Indeed, Brooke's proportionately greater influence with Churchill and Dill's proportionally greater influence with the Americans made not only Dill and Marshall a good team but also Dill and Brooke.[74]

Field Marshal Dill was posthumously awarded the Distinguished Service Medal by the United States. His efforts in Washington were also praised in a joint resolution issued by Congress on December 20, 1944. The latter was an honor never before bestowed upon a person who was not an American citizen.[75] Also unusual, but entirely fitting, was that Dill was buried in Arlington National Cemetery, just across the Potomac from Washington, D.C., the city where he had achieved his greatest successes as a soldier and a diplomat.

Fleet Admiral Ernest J. King, Commander in Chief, U.S. Fleet and Chief of Naval Operations

Ernest J. King late in the war as a fleet admiral. *U.S. Naval Institute Photo Archive*

American. Born: November 23, 1878, Lorain, Ohio. Died: June 25, 1956, Portsmouth, New Hampshire. Ernest Joseph King commanded in World War II the largest and most powerful navy the world is ever likely to see. That and Admiral King's global strategy-making responsibilities as a member of the Combined Chiefs of Staff make him the most powerful naval officer in American history.[76] After graduating from the Naval Academy in 1901, King became known, as he would be throughout his career, to be extremely ambitious and extremely bright. He was also arrogant, competitive, and stubborn. King made many enemies, but few doubted his brilliance. Married in October 1905 to Martha "Mattie" Egerton, King had six daughters and one son. While he was harsh with naval personnel who served under him, King appears to have been a somewhat indulgent father. His marriage proved to be a mismatch, however, and by the time he became a member of the Combined Chiefs of Staff, King and Mattie were living very separate lives. A renowned philanderer, King enjoyed parties, and when he went to one he was always on the lookout for attractive women he might seduce.[77]

For all of his adult life Admiral King was a heavy drinker. Misbehavior while drunk had resulted in reprimands by his superiors on several occasions as a young officer.[78] Aware of the trouble that alcohol was causing him, King shifted from hard liquor to beer, wine, and sherry as his drinks of choice during World War II. That may not have solved his problem, however, which seemed to be volume consumed rather than type. For instance, during the war King could easily knock back six glasses of beer in one evening. Therefore, the label of "functional alcoholic" is probably appropriate for King both before and during the war. He also smoked. Probably the only thing King had in common with FDR other than a love of the navy was that both men used old-fashioned cigarette holders. King's other hobbies included reading and crossword puzzles.[79] He was thought to be humorless, but not by those who knew him well. For instance, King was highly amused to hear that even before Pearl Harbor many thought him "so tough that he had to shave with a blowtorch."[80]

In his rise to the top of the navy, King's intelligence and ambition led him to be always on the lookout for new challenges. He was versatile, having served in destroyers, a cruiser, and battleships. During World War I, King served in Europe on the staff of Vice Admiral Henry T. Mayo. After the war, he served in submarines and commanded the submarine base at New London, Connecticut. This position led to some of the most challenging work of King's pre–World War II career, when he was called upon to oversee the salvage of the wrecks of two submarines, the *S-51* and the *S-4*, which had sunk as the result of training accidents in New England waters.

After qualifying as a naval aviator in 1927, King was given command of the aircraft carrier USS *Lexington* in 1930. The *Lexington* always enjoyed the reputation of being a happy ship. The men who served on board the *Lexington* loved their ship deeply. King was no exception. When the *Lexington* was sunk by air attack in the battle of the Coral Sea in May 1942, King took the loss of his old command personally. Indeed, King seemed to blame Rear Admiral Frank Jack Fletcher, the American commander on the scene, more than the Japanese naval aviators who had launched the bombs and torpedoes. Many of the men serving on the *Lexington* at the time she was sunk had served under King. Indeed, so popular was the *Lexington* that many members of her crew during the Coral Sea battle were "plank owners," who had been with the ship since it joined the fleet back in 1927. The loss of the *Lexington* and King's dissatisfaction with the way Fletcher later handled other carriers during the Guadalcanal campaign brought out King's mean streak. King, now the fleet commander and in a position to send admirals wherever he wanted them, was largely responsible for Admiral Fletcher's being "beached" in late 1942 to fly a desk in Seattle as commander of the Northwestern Sea Frontier for a year. Fletcher was eventually given command of the North Pacific Area, but by that time, the autumn of 1943, the area was a quiet backwater, and the job was still at a desk—this time on the windswept, bleak island of Adak in the Aleutians chain off Alaska rather than in Seattle. True, Admirals Nimitz and King also had desk jobs, but theirs were highly influential and interesting postings.[81]

King certainly required efficiency from his staff. He himself always got to the point quickly in discussions and in memoranda and expected the same from others. Still, he was, as stated previously, not without a sense of humor.[82] One of his former aides wrote that "to those who worked directly for him [King] was thoughtful and kindly—but you had to produce."[83] Nevertheless, it is safe to say that many of the personnel working in the Navy Department building on Constitution Avenue in Washington greatly preferred dealing with Admiral King's chief of staff, Rear Admiral Richard S. Edwards, instead of King if at all possible. Edwards' efficiency and kindness were greatly appreciated by King's staff, and by Admiral King as well. Edwards had been hand-picked for the job of chief of staff by King himself, but his billet was not an easy one.[84] King's biographer amply sums up the volatility of working conditions under Ernest J. King: "Despite King's dependence upon Edwards, King could still be a bastard. After weeks of work Edwards once submitted a plan to King for approval. King returned it with a red-penciled notation, 'Take this to the head with you.'"[85] The contradiction between King's volatile personality and the consummate gentlemanliness of General Marshall could not have been more apparent. Indeed, Admiral King was a study in contrasts. He too could be a perfect gentleman when he wanted to be, but the *enfant terrible* mode suited him just as well.[86]

Admiral King was highly confident of his own abilities. He considered himself to be the brightest member of the U.S. Joint Chiefs of Staff. King's ranking system placed the other members of the Joint Chiefs of Staff in the following descending order of ability after himself: Marshall, Leahy, Arnold.[87]

For Admiral Raymond Spruance, who commanded most of the campaigns involved with the Central Pacific drive, Admiral King would always be associated with the idea of seizing the initiative early and never relinquishing it.[88] Spruance wrote King, "It seemed to me that this was always uppermost in your mind whenever you were considering operations in the Pacific."[89]

Although they worked together very effectively during the war, King and Marshall did have a few differences of opinion. For example, King felt that Marshall had been slow to realize the value of seizing the Mariana Islands, while the navy had been discussing the possibility of such an operation as far back as the 1920s. King also felt that the reasoning behind Admiral Leahy's appointment as senior member of the U.S. Joint Chiefs of Staff was that the president had not felt that General Marshall knew enough about sea power.[90] King appreciated Marshall's courteous nature, however, and the latter's sincere efforts to learn more about the navy. In July 1943, General Marshall was King's guest during a brief shakedown cruise aboard the brand-new *Essex*-class aircraft carrier *Lexington*. King was later pleased to report that "Marshall inspected all parts of the ship from engine room to gun turrets and bridge."[91]

Like Marshall, King found General Brooke a difficult person to deal with. King respected Brooke, however, and perhaps for the very stubbornness that Marshall found so exasperating. In addition to finding a good friend in Admiral Pound, King also thought highly of Air Chief Marshal Portal (as did the Americans in general). He rated Portal ahead of Cunningham and Brooke as regarded the abilities of the British Chiefs of Staff Committee;[92] King in fact offered praise for the British Chief of the Air Staff at the expense of King's American colleague Hap Arnold: "Portal, the air man on the British Chiefs, had real brains, and understood strategy and engineering. He was very much broader in his views than Arnold. Portal would talk about anything that was important or interesting. . . . Arnold was not in the same class as Portal as to brains or abilities."[93]

Fleet Admiral William D. Leahy, Chief of Staff to the Commander in Chief of the Army and Navy of the United States

American. Born: May 6, 1875, Hampton, Iowa. Died: July 20, 1959, Bethesda, Maryland. A retired Chief of Naval Operations who had served as American ambassador to Vichy France, William D. Leahy assumed a role as a member of the Combined Chiefs of Staff that was half political, half military. Leahy graduated from the Naval Academy in 1897 and gained experience in destroyers, ordnance, and battleships.[94] Leahy married Louise Tennent Harrington in February 1904. The couple had one son. Louise died in 1942, shortly before

William D. Leahy. *U.S. Naval Institute Photo Archive*

Admiral Leahy departed Vichy to return to the United States; Leahy brought his wife's remains home to the United States for burial. The death of Louise was one of several reasons why the post of U.S. ambassador to Vichy France was a very difficult assignment for Leahy. The other main reason was the collaborationist nature of that regime and the question as to whether America should have had any relations at all with it.[95]

Both the president and General Marshall had wanted Leahy to join the new U.S. Joint Chiefs of Staff organization when he returned from France in mid-1942. The president had been quite happy with Leahy's tenure as Chief of Naval Operations in the late 1930s and trusted his judgment implicitly. General Marshall hoped that Admiral Leahy would be a neutral referee who could mediate disputes between Marshall and King. He feared that once Admiral Stark left Washington for London in March 1942, Admiral King might feel outnumbered on the Joint Chiefs of Staff by the two army generals, Arnold and himself. By suggesting Admiral Leahy to the president as a chairman, Marshall thought he had hit on the perfect solution—King was sure to have no objection to a fourth member being added to the U.S. Joint Chiefs if that member was another admiral.[96]

Unfortunately for General Marshall, the president threw a wrench into the gears of the plan. Instead of being an impartial chairman of the Joint Chiefs, the president seemed to want Admiral Leahy to serve as his personal liaison to the Joint Chiefs of Staff, much as General Ismay served as Winston Churchill's liaison to the British Chiefs of Staff Committee. The result was that Admiral Leahy was unable to devote all his attention to military matters.[97] With an office in the White House, Leahy, who had no political ambitions whatsoever, found himself dealing with many purely political matters that he found highly awkward and distasteful.[98]

One of these occurred in the run-up to the 1944 presidential election. As we have seen, Admiral King had two titles during the war—Commander in Chief, U.S. Fleet, and Chief of Naval Operations (CNO). Of the two titles, King seemed to prefer the former.[99] In King's papers are numerous letters written on letterhead bearing at the top the legend, "United States Fleet: Headquarters of the Commander in Chief." This is a reference to Admiral King, not the president. Shortly before the 1944 election, Admiral Leahy informed Admiral King that the president would be happy if King would refrain from using the title "Commander in Chief." Apparently, FDR was nervous that voters might forget just who had ultimate control over the navy. The prickly King replied that he would accede to Leahy's request only if it were transmitted to him personally by the president. Given FDR's loathing of confrontation, that, of course, never happened, and King used both titles for the remainder of the war.[100] Admiral King did, however, think it was wasteful to have two titles, especially since each office came with its own staff. He was in favor of consolidating the COMINCH and CNO posts, and this was done by executive order in December 1945, when Admiral Nimitz succeeded King as the navy's most senior admiral. It is interesting to note, however, that the title retained for the newly consolidated position and bestowed upon Admiral Nimitz in 1945, and on every subsequent uniformed head of the U.S. Navy, has been that of "Chief of Naval Operations." No other admiral since King has been allowed to call himself "Commander in Chief, U.S. Fleet."[101]

In regard to Admiral Leahy's distaste for the political aspects of his job, Admiral King's biographer Thomas Buell has written that "Leahy was so bewildered by watching Roosevelt during the 1944 presidential elections that the president joked that, when it came to politics, the Admiral belonged in the Middle Ages. Leahy thought that the Dark Ages would have been a more appropriate description."[102] Unlike King, Admiral Leahy was not an aviator and as CNO in the late 1930s had seemed to feel that the navy's future lay with battleships rather than aircraft carriers. The carrier would become the "queen of the fleet" during World War II, but during his tenure as CNO Admiral Leahy had a hand in providing the navy with the six modern battleships of the *North Carolina* and *South Dakota* classes. These ships all gave good service during World War II, and Leahy had seen to it that they were outfitted with 16-inch guns. Doing that was not as easy as it may seem. The *North Carolina* and the *Washington,* construction of which began in 1937, were the first new American battleships to be laid down after the end of the fifteen-year "building holiday" on battleships imposed by the Washington and London Naval Treaties. However, these were still in theory "treaty" battleships, restricted to 35,000 tons displacement each and to guns of no larger than 14-inch caliber. However, the London Naval Treaty of 1936 included an escalator clause stipulating that if any signatory to the naval treaties breached the terms by adding larger guns, the other parties could "up-gun" their own battleships from fourteen to sixteen inch. As rumors began circulating in the late 1930s that Japan was building new battleships with very large main batteries, Admiral Leahy insisted that the new American battleships carry 16-inch guns.[103]

Leahy's wisdom in this regard can be seen in a brief comparison between the battleships he sponsored and the British battleships of the *King George V* class, built at about the same time as the *North Carolina*s and the four *South Dakota*s (i.e., *Massachusetts, Alabama, Indiana,* and *South Dakota*). The British attempted to adhere strictly to treaty limits. Thus, HMS *King George V* and her four sister battleships each carried ten 14-inch guns. Two of this class—*King George V* and *Prince of Wales*—were to participate in the hunt for and destruction of the German battleship *Bismarck* in May 1941. The *King George V* class were certainly good ships, but the new American battleships were better.[104]

During meetings of the Joint and Combined Chiefs of Staff, Leahy often proved an effective mediator of differences of opinion that arose between Marshall and King.[105] Indeed, Leahy's presence in Washington seems to have had a calming influence in general. For instance, the admiral helped to settle a late-1942 dispute over the control of American merchant shipping between Lewis Douglas of the American War Shipping Administration (WSA) and Lieutenant General Brehon Somervell, head of the U.S. Army's Services of Supply (better known as the Army Service Forces).[106]

General of the Army George C. Marshall, U.S. Army Chief of Staff

General Marshall wearing five stars. *U.S. Naval Institute Photo Archive*

American. Born: December 31, 1880, Uniontown, Pennsylvania. Died: October 16, 1959, Washington, D.C. General George C. Marshall was a man who never laughed at the president's jokes and who bristled when the president, or almost anyone else, called him by his first name. Marshall was determined that FDR's considerable charm never sway him from bringing up unpleasant issues that he felt needed presidential attention. These issues included weekly, face-to-face recitations to the president of the latest American casualty figures. This was medicine FDR certainly did not enjoy taking but that Marshall felt was needed to ensure that the president did not become hardened to the human toll of war. Marshall had excelled as a staff officer throughout his career. Words like "cold," and "distant" are often used to describe General Marshall's demeanor during the war.[107] General Ismay has written of him that "it was impossible to imagine his doing anything petty or mean, or shrinking from any duty, however distasteful. He carried himself with great dignity."[108]

Marshall attained the rank of temporary colonel during World War I, but it was not until 1920, eighteen years after he joined the army, that his permanent rank was raised to captain. Marshall was promoted to brigadier general on October 1, 1936. After having waited thirty-four years to attain his first general's star, Marshall made the jump from one-star to four-star rank in one day when on September 1, 1939, he officially became army Chief of Staff (he had been acting Chief of Staff since July 1). President Roosevelt appointed General Marshall over the heads of thirty-four other generals senior to him. Marshall's biographer has added the qualification that most of the generals senior to Marshall were too close to retirement age to be serious contenders for the job and that Marshall was actually fifth on a short list of five candidates.[109] However, with the crisis of impending war it is doubtful if President Roosevelt would have let age be a barrier to appointing the man he wanted, as long as the candidate was physically and mentally fit. Indeed, Admiral King was less than a year from the supposedly mandatory retirement age of sixty-four at the time of his appointment as Commander in Chief, U.S. Fleet. Although the always-ambitious King was distraught over the possibility that he might be retired in the midst of the most interesting and challenging posting of his career, he felt it his duty to remind the president in October 1942 that his sixty-fourth birthday was fast approaching. FDR laughed off any suggestion of retiring Admiral King and kept him on for the duration.[110]

Ismay was right about Marshall's inability to be petty. As Chief of Staff, Marshall was immune from the feeling expressed by some business executives and others in positions of responsibility toward their subordinates—"I went through it, so they have to go through it"—in regard to his own long-delayed promotions. It became a fundamental goal for the new Chief of Staff to do away forever with the arcane system of promoting officers on the basis of seniority. Marshall was determined that in an army he was leading, officers would be promoted upon merit alone.[111]

Despite his reputation for reticence, Marshall's humanity was vibrant and palpable. He had no biological children of his own, but always found time for children who wrote him letters during the war. Indeed, in March 1944 General Marshall wrote a detailed reply to a class of middle-school students in Virginia who had written the Chief of Staff seeking firsthand information on the war from the man in charge. The students were particularly eager to know how General Marshall maintained what the children had heard was a photographic memory.[112] General Marshall corrected this misinterpretation: "Mrs. Marshall tells me that my memory is seriously defective in some respects, frequently to her inconvenience."[113] In April 1943, General Marshall learned that a seven-year-old boy named Mark Reed had waited for him, hoping for an autograph, at an airfield near Asheville, North Carolina, during a visit by the general that had been advertised in the local newspaper. Mark was unable to get close enough for an autograph, and the boy's mother wrote to General Marshall to express her son's disappointment.[114] The general swung into action, dispatching the following letter on April 29:

> My dear Mark: I was very sorry to learn that you were disappointed in your kind effort to greet me at the airport south of Asheville last Sunday afternoon, also that you did not get the autograph you desired. I am sending you a sketch with my best wishes and I hope you will accept this in lieu of the meeting which failed to materialize.[115]

After graduating from the Virginia Military Institute (VMI) in 1901, Marshall married the beautiful Elizabeth (Lily) Carter Coles on February 11, 1902, shortly before he shipped out as a second lieutenant of infantry for a tour of duty in the Philippines. The marriage was a happy one, but Lily suffered from a chronic heart ailment that apparently made the strains of pregnancy and childbirth out of the question for her. The couple remained childless, which was a disappointment since she loved children as much as he did. Marshall served in France during World War I as a staff officer in the U.S. 1st Division under Major General William L. Sibert. During the war, Marshall's diligence and willingness to speak his mind made a good impression on General John J. Pershing, who would become a lifelong friend and mentor. Lily's heart problems grew worse in the 1920s, and she died in September 1927.[116]

Marshall married again in October 1930, a marriage that, like his first, was quite happy. His second wife, Katherine Tupper Brown, was a widow with three children. Marshall greatly enjoyed his role as stepfather to Clifton, Molly, and Allen Brown. Marshall and Allen, the youngest child, were particularly close. When Allen joined the army after Pearl Harbor, both he and Marshall made strenuous efforts to see to it that nobody learned of the connection between them. They were in complete agreement that Allen's success in the army should be measured on the basis of merit alone. Consequently, Allen Brown, stepson of the Chief of Staff, entered the army at the exalted rank of private.[117]

Marshall and Allen were not entirely successful in keeping their relationship—for all intents and purposes that of father and son—secret. Sometimes a well-meaning commander would try to do Allen a favor, thinking General Marshall would approve. When this happened, the officer in question would quickly be disabused of the notion that greasing the skids in any way for the Chief of Staff's stepson was a good idea. For instance, Major General Alvan C. Gillem Jr. wrote to General Marshall in June 1943 asking if the general would be the speaker at the upcoming graduation ceremony at Fort Knox, Kentucky, for officer candidates (in this instance including one Allen Tupper Brown) who had completed a course of instruction in armored warfare and were to be commissioned as second lieutenants.[118] General Marshall was appalled at the idea. In his reply Marshall not only declined the invitation but, no doubt knowing that Allen would be in complete agreement with him, essentially ordered Gillem "to see that [Allen's] graduation bears no comment on his connection with me."[119] Mrs. Marshall's daughter Molly had two children of her own, to whom General Marshall was delighted to be honorary grandfather.[120]

General Marshall's biographer admits that there was something of the "New England Yankee" in General Marshall. This was a reference to his often stiff formality and to Marshall's personal habits, such as that he was always careful to keep his finances in order. Perhaps the only vice Marshall ever had was that he smoked cigarettes until in his fifties, when he quit. His hobbies included horseback riding, gardening, canoeing, and fishing.[121]

As he did for children, General Marshall would sometimes drop formality completely with adults as well. During the war an official car with a Women's Army Corps chauffeur might pull up to a bus stop in the Washington, D.C., area, and a distinguished-looking officer in the back seat would roll down a window and offer a lift to the commuters waiting there on their way to work. Total strangers would suddenly find themselves getting rides to their jobs from the Chief of Staff of the U.S. Army.[122] Such gestures were undoubtedly especially appreciated by the beneficiaries in view of the facts that gasoline was under wartime rationing and that even if they owned cars civilians could not legally purchase items like new tires, the rubber of which was also a closely rationed commodity.

Although General Marshall's strictly merit-based system for promotions and his personality made it useless for acquaintances to petition the Chief of Staff for promotions, Marshall did occasionally do favors.[123] One that shows his humanity quite nicely occurred in June 1944, when Marshall wrote to Lieutenant General Jacob L. Devers, who was then serving in Italy as commander of the U.S. Sixth Army. An Italian-American barber whom Marshall patronized in a shop on the concourse at the Pentagon, Joe Abbate, was terribly worried about his uncle, who was trapped in war-torn Italy. The Chief of Staff offered to intercede, and in a letter that reads partly as a request and partly as an order, Marshall asked Devers to find the uncle, deliver to him a letter (written by the barber's wife) and some cash from Joe Abbate, and to see if he, Devers, could give the old man a paying job.[124] Since Marshall's entire life had been the absolute antithesis of cronyism, he seems to have felt a bit guilty about using his influence in this matter. He confided to Devers, "I don't know how much trouble I am imposing on you but if you have any contact with Messina I should appreciate your helping out in this. Incidentally, Joe had no idea of my taking this action. He was merely telling me the story of his uncle when I offered to get a letter through, and money, if he cared to send it."[125]

Devers duly located the uncle, delivered the money, and got the man a job in the reconstituted, post-Mussolini Italian government. The younger Abbate was known to Devers as well as Marshall, because in addition to his barber shop at the Pentagon, Joe Abbate had been something akin to the official army barber at Fort Myer, Virginia, where General Marshall lived and where Devers had once resided.[126]

Marshal of the Royal Air Force Sir Charles Portal, Chief of the Air Staff

Sir Charles Portal. *U.S. National Archives and Records Administration*

British. Born: May 21, 1893, Hungerford. Died: April 22, 1971, Chichester. Charles Portal became Britain's most distinguished Air Force officer of all time, ending his days as Viscount Portal of Hungerford and a Marshal of the Royal Air Force. The latter title is the equivalent of an American five-star general. His biographer, Denis Richards, speculates that Portal's lifelong love of hawking; i.e., training and using a falcon to hunt smaller birds for him, helped Portal decide to become a military pilot during World War I.[127] Richards notes that directing the Royal Air Force during World War II and hawking both involved Portal in "nature's timeless routines of the pursuer and the pursued, the soaring and the broken wing, combat, blood and death."[128]

Portal married Joan Margaret in 1919. They had two daughters.[129] Portal had joined the COS Committee in October 1940 when he became Chief of the Air Staff.[130] Portal was brilliant and very well liked by the Americans. Always courteous, Portal dealt politely but firmly with explosive personalities like Winston Churchill and Air Chief Marshal Sir Arthur "Bomber" Harris. Indeed, Churchill and Portal got along quite well together.[131]

Like Brooke, Portal was an avid trout fisherman. Indeed, after the first Quebec Conference in August 1943, Portal and Brooke went on a fishing trip to a lake in Quebec Province and landed close to two hundred trout between them. They were apparently superb anglers. As to type of trout caught, it can be surmised that most were (very appropriately) eastern *brook* trout, which are native to those waters and, like the general, are often referred to by the sobriquet "brookie." Portal recorded that they donated their catch to a hospital in Quebec where the "patients probably got a bit tired of a fish diet."[132] Portal, Brooke, and Admiral Cunningham returned to the same area in September 1944 after the second Quebec Conference; Cunningham had to depart early, but Brooke and Portal this time caught over two hundred trout combined.[133] (Most fishermen would consider a hundred trout caught during an entire six-month season of weekend fishing to be an excellent haul.) At the end of this trip, the two men received a telegram from Churchill who had been unable to join the party, but who was keenly interested in its progress. This message shows that not all of Portal's and Brooke's interactions with the prime minister were unpleasant: "Following for CIGS and CAS from Prime Minister. Please let me know how many captives were taken by land and air forces respectively in Battle of Snow Lake."[134] The reply Portal drafted showed that the Chief of the Air Staff was every bit the equal of the prime minister in terms of wit and dry humor: "Casualties inflicted by our land and air forces were approximately equal and totaled about 250 dead including the enemy general who surrendered to Land forces on Tuesday afternoon. In a short rearguard action at Cabane de Montmorency our air forces accounted for the largest submarine yet seen in these waters."[135]

In addition to being a much-needed friend to Brooke, Portal got along well with Admiral Pound, but he felt that Pound was often unable to look beyond strictly naval matters in order to see the big picture in terms of grand strategy.[136] Portal was known for the gentlemanly demeanor with which he treated everyone. However, this did not mean he was a pushover in the councils of the Combined Chiefs of Staff. Because he seems to have avoided overt clashes, Portal's steadfastness shows up best, perhaps, in the context of dealings with the senior commanders who reported to him. He was not afraid to show his subordinates who was boss if he felt they needed reminding. This was true even if the person who needed reminding was someone as powerful as the Air Chief Marshal Sir Arthur Harris, commander in chief of RAF Bomber Command. Harris' command was to become quite large and he himself very influential, enjoying direct access to the prime minister. In addition to driving energy, Harris was also known for his biting sarcasm. This latter quality showed up forcefully in a September 1942 letter to Portal in which Harris complained bitterly after having been ordered by the chief of the Air Staff to send some of his bombers to the Middle East, thus taking them temporarily out of the bombing campaign against Germany. Portal rebuked Harris in no uncertain terms: "I feel bound to tell you frankly that I do not regard it [the letter] as either a credit to your intelligence or a contribution to the winning of the war. . . . I am sure that great benefit would be gained if you could manage to take a rather broader view of the problems and difficulties confronting the Air

Ministry and the other Commands and if this could be reflected in the tone and substance of your letters in future."[137]

The Arnold-Portal airman-to-airman relationship was critically important. They liked each other and worked together quite well, frequently in highly productive one-on-one meetings.[138] Getting on well himself with the Americans, Portal could not help but sense what he called a "political undercurrent" in British dealings with the U.S. Joint Chiefs of Staff. To Portal it seemed that the reason the Americans constantly argued against British plans for operations in the Balkans was a belief that the British were attempting to replace the empire they were losing in the Far East with one in the Balkans.[139] According to the chief of the Air Staff, "At times the British Chiefs of Staff felt that in addition to the defeat of the Axis, the U.S.A. policy was to cripple the British Empire regardless of the consequences."[140]

Portal agreed with Brooke and disagreed with Marshall by supporting Allied landings in Italy to follow the Sicilian campaign. However, Portal differed from Brooke and Churchill in that Portal never intended that Allied troops should slug it out all the way into northern Italy. The air-conscious Portal wanted the airfields around Foggia in southern Italy to be available for use by Allied aircraft. He also favored the seizure of Sardinia.[141] History has since shown that if there had to be an Italian campaign, Portal's idea of confining the operation to seizing the airfields in southern Italy was the way to go.

Admiral of the Fleet Sir Dudley Pound, First Sea Lord and Chief of the Naval Staff

British. Born: August 29, 1877, Isle of Wight. Died: October 21, 1943, London. Admiral Pound may have suffered from narcolepsy, as he appeared to nod off frequently during meetings.[142] Whether it was narcolepsy or some sort of epileptic seizure disorder that was causing Pound's temporary blackouts, the situation enraged General Brooke. A spring 1942 entry in Brooke's diary shows to good advantage Brooke's contempt for the Chief of the Naval Staff: "I went near to losing my temper with old Dudley Pound. I feel it almost impossible to stir him up. . . . [H]e is always lagging about 5 laps behind even when he is not sound asleep."[143] The fact was that Pound had at that time only a little over a year left to live; the possibility that he was seriously ill never seems to have occurred to Brooke.

Pound married Betty Whitehead on October 14, 1908. They had two sons and a daughter. Of Betty Pound's biographer writes, "She was to prove

Admiral Pound, in white, crowded into an elevator with his CCS colleagues, Quebec, August 1943. *Corbis*

the ideal naval wife, devoted to her husband's career and their children, always ready to make a new home and move at a moment's notice."[144] Like Portal and Brooke, Pound was a devoted angler, and he also enjoyed wing shooting. Those who worked for Pound found him somewhat aloof, not unlike General Marshall. However, Pound was capable of spontaneous acts of kindness toward his staff. On one occasion, Pound remembered that one of his junior intelligence officers was interested in naval history and presented him with a book about Admiral Sir George Anson.[145]

Like Brooke, Pound had combat experience, having served as captain of the battleship HMS *Colossus* at Jutland in May 1916. Keeping up with Churchill's hours during World War II and putting up with his outbursts definitely took a toll on Pound. For a man who knew so many people, Winston Churchill seems to have had comparatively few friends. Yet Pound was one of them.[146] With his usual eloquence, Alex Danchev explains how Pound and Churchill were in many ways kindred spirits: "Like Portal, but unlike

Dill or Brooke or Cunningham, [Pound] was congenial to Churchill. The two men used to meet in the early hours of the morning for an insomniac whisky in the Admiralty Map Room. A more propitious circumstance for nurturing a relationship with Churchill can scarcely be imagined."[147] Insomnia indeed lends credence to the possibility that Pound suffered from narcolepsy.

In contrast to the tension between Brooke and Pound, it is clear that Admirals King and Pound had a very high regard for each other.[148] In spite of his reputation for gruff ill humor and occasional downright nastiness, Admiral King regularly wrote letters of condolence to Admiral Pound in regard to the sailors killed when British warships were sunk in action.[149] The surviving correspondence between Pound and King has an invariably friendly tone. Pound prefaced his letters to King with "My Dear Admiral," "My Dear Ernest," or "My Dear Commander in Chief." King's letters to Pound always begin "Dear Dudley."[150]

If, as stated earlier, relations were between Portal and Pound were good, the two men did have some polite disagreements. These often had to do with the best use for long-range bombers. Pound was adamant about the necessity to use long-range land-based bombers to provide air cover for convoys operating in mid-Atlantic, one of the most dangerous areas in terms of U-boat attack. Portal, on the other hand, was reluctant to release long-range aircraft from the bombing campaign against German industrial cities. Pound was desperate to protect the Atlantic sea-lanes, by which troops and supplies were being transported from the United States to England. Similarly, Pound struggled to convince Portal and the Air Staff in 1941 to resume attacks by RAF bombers against German U-boat bases, such as those at Lorient and St. Nazaire, on the French coast.[151]

Admiral Pound's relations with his eventual successor, Admiral Cunningham, were excellent. It was apparently Pound who urged Cunningham to accept the posting as head of the British Admiralty Delegation in Washington in the summer of 1942.[152] While it would probably be inaccurate to say that Pound "handled" Churchill, it does seem that he had more patience when it came to attempting to head off Churchill's wilder ideas than would Cunningham. Like General Brooke, Pound chose his fights with Churchill carefully. Usually, instead of trying to derail a bad Churchillian idea directly, Pound would have his staff make a formal study of whatever pet project Churchill was peddling to the Admiralty and then commission a comprehensive report showing in an evenhanded fashion the logistical and strategic inroads Churchill's idea would make on other, ongoing operations.[153] In the end, according to one of Pound's wartime assistants, Churchill would often say, "Who thought up this damn fool project anyway"?[154]

Pound worked hard at finding common ground with his colleagues on the British Chiefs of Staff Committee. He believed it to be vital that the three British service chiefs cooperate, and he was willing to compromise on occasion to achieve this.[155] Much has been made of the fact that unlike Portal and Brooke, Admiral Pound was an operational commander as well as a staff officer.[156] However, it should be noted that it was not unheard of for Portal or Brooke too to get involved in operational matters once in a while. For instance, Portal's insistence that RAF Bomber Command create the Pathfinders unit was a decision that had important operational results. The American members of the Combined Chiefs of Staff also had operational responsibilities. Admiral King, for instance, kept a close watch on operations in the Pacific theater, and King and Nimitz met face to face remarkably frequently (considering that they were based four thousand miles apart) during the war to discuss them.

As a manager, Pound appears to have had some difficulty in delegating responsibility. Throughout his career, Pound took too much work upon himself. This is one possible explanation for the terrible mistake he made in July 1942 in ignoring the views of on-scene commanders and ordering from London that convoy PQ-17, then off the North Cape on its way to Archangel, scatter to avoid what Pound feared to be an imminent attack by the German battleship *Tirpitz*.[157]

Also-Rans

Lord Louis Mountbatten is a good person with whom to start a list of people who don't quite make the cut as principal members of the Combined Chiefs of Staff. While it is true that Sir John Dill was able to attend the Casablanca Conference only as the guest of General Marshall, not as an official member of the British delegation (although he sat on the British side of the table during the conference), there is evidence that the British members of the Combined Chiefs saw Dill as much more their equal than Mountbatten. As mentioned earlier, Mountbatten attended COS Committee meetings only when combined operations were being discussed.[158] This is quite different from the position of say, Portal, who attended COS Committee meetings even if air operations were not on the agenda. As a vice admiral, Mountbatten lagged at least one grade in rank behind the full British members of the Combined Chiefs of Staff. Mountbatten was a trained naval officer who had had highly eventful combat experience as a destroyer captain early in the war. Upon being named Chief of Combined Operations, Mountbatten was promoted to vice admiral in his home service, the Royal Navy, and also to honorary ranks of lieutenant general and air vice marshal in the British army and the Royal Air Force, respectively.[159]

General Brooke and Admiral Pound resented Mountbatten's presence at COS Committee meetings.[160] Similarly, according to General Marshall's biographer, Mountbatten's youthful good looks "caused many Americans to fear he was better fitted for the role of playboy than that of a serious and hard-working member of Britain's high command."[161] Then there is the matter of Mountbatten's boyish, Churchillian love of wild and bizarre schemes, of which "the Great Quebec Shootout" is undoubtedly the most notorious. At the Quadrant Conference in Quebec in August 1943 Mountbatten fired off a pistol in the room where the Combined Chiefs of Staff were meeting—*while* they were meeting. His purpose was to demonstrate the great strength of a block of ice that had been reinforced with sawdust allowed to melt into its surface. Mountbatten hoped to use such reinforced ice ("pykrete," named in honor of its creator, Geoffrey Pyke, a scientist on the Combined Operations staff) to create "iceberg aircraft carriers." These "Habbakuks," as they were called, could (in theory *only*) help provide air cover against U-boats for convoys in mid-Atlantic and against ground targets in the beachhead area during the cross-channel attack. In the latter campaign, it was hoped, Habbakuks might also do duty as landing craft. As for Mountbatten's shooting spree in Quebec, accounts vary as to who was almost hit when the bullet ricocheted off the impervious pykrete during Mountbatten's reckless demonstration. Mark Stoler says it was Admiral King, Churchill says Air Chief Marshal Portal.[162] Either way, neither King nor Portal was readily replaceable in the Allied war effort, and while many historians find humor in the incident, the entire affair casts serious doubt on Mountbatten's mental stability, to say nothing of his suitability for high command.[163] Even when he was not needlessly endangering lives with such reckless experiments, Mountbatten wasted a great deal of time and money on projects that, like Habbakuk, proved to be dead ends. The more or less permanent monument to the iceberg–aircraft carrier fiasco is the large wooden frame of an experimental Habbakuk that, after its ice finally melted, sank to the bottom of Lake Patricia, northwest of Calgary, Alberta, in western Canada, where it remains to this day.[164]

In a June 1942 memorandum, General Marshall gave explicit instructions to John R. Deane, then a colonel on the Combined Chiefs of Staff Secretariat, regarding the protocol to be followed for an upcoming visit by Marshall, Dill, and Mountbatten to Fort Benning, Georgia (a visit that took place on June 7–8, 1942). Marshall makes it clear that he wanted Dill to ride in his (Marshall's) car and Mountbatten to be driven in a separate car.[165] Marshall's reason left little doubt that he, at least, did not consider Mountbatten to be a full member of the Combined Chiefs of Staff or at all in the same league with Dill: "It will be very important to keep in mind that while this trip is arranged for Lord Mountbatten, who is a Vice Admiral, a Lieutenant General and a Vice Air Marshal, Field Marshal Sir John Dill is very much the senior. It is for this reason that I am taking him with me, in order that Mountbatten can be put in close touch with the officer in charge of the particular demonstration without offending Sir John."[166] Rather than a member, Mountbatten seems to have been more of a hanger-on, reluctantly tolerated by the Combined Chiefs.

Like Mountbatten, General Ismay was also junior in rank to the full British members of the Combined Chiefs of Staff. As Chief of Staff to the Minister of Defence (Churchill), Ismay was more of a liaison to, rather than a member of, the group.[167] This is not to say that General Ismay was expendable. On the contrary, Ismay's services were invaluable, in the sense that he allowed himself to be the target of many of Churchill's temper tantrums. Thus Ismay was a vital safety valve, deflecting some (but not all) of the Churchillian wrath that would otherwise have fallen on the heads of the British Chiefs of Staff Committee members.[168]

General Ismay is somewhat inconsistent in his memoirs in describing his relationship to the Combined Chiefs of Staff and the British Chiefs of Staff Committee. He defines what he saw as his role in this way: "I had three sets of responsibilities. I was Chief of Staff Officer to Mr Churchill; I was a member of the Chiefs of Staff Committee; and I was head of the Office of the Minster of Defence."[169] However, Ismay goes on to say that he never offered advice on either strategy or the suitability of field commanders to Churchill or to the three British service chiefs. Interestingly, Ismay refers to a "triumvirate"— Brooke, Pound, and Portal (or later, Brooke, Cunningham, and Portal)—as making all the big military decisions for the British (subject to Churchill's approval), a trio of which he does not seem to consider himself a part.[170]

His tone is that of an outsider looking in, not that of a full-fledged member of the British Chiefs of Staff Committee. For instance, Ismay writes, "There could be no question of my membership of the [COS] Committee impinging upon the individual and collective responsibility of the three Chiefs of Staff for advising on defence policy as a whole. That triumvirate must remain inviolate, and all military advice tendered to ministerial authority, and all orders and instructions issued to commanders in the field, must continue to bear their signatures, and theirs alone."[171] General Ismay certainly played a critical role in the workings of the Western alliance. In his selflessness and devotion to duty he resembled General Marshall. However, unlike Marshall, nobody either knew or cared to know what Ismay's views on major strategic issues were. For that reason it is difficult to consider General Ismay a full member of the Combined Chiefs of Staff.

After the death of Field Marshal Dill in November 1944, Field Marshal Sir Henry Maitland Wilson was sent to Washington as the new head of the British Joint Staff Mission. Unfortunately, Wilson and General Marshall never became close.[172] Wilson had difficulty in Washington; as Sally Lister Parker has written, "Dill was a tough act to follow."[173] Because he arrived in Washington late in the war and never became close to the U.S. Joint Chiefs of Staff, I have arbitrarily, and perhaps outrageously, excluded Wilson from consideration as a full member of the Combined Chiefs of Staff for the purposes of this study.

Likewise, I have not included American admiral Harold R. Stark as a principal member of the Combined Chiefs of Staff. Stark was seen, quite possibly unfairly, as damaged goods, having been Chief of Naval Operations (CNO) at the time of the Pearl Harbor attack. Almost immediately, President Roosevelt moved to ease Stark out of the decision-making process in regard to grand strategy. Reviving the post of COMINCH, and naming Admiral King to it on December 18, 1941 (one day after FDR had selected Admiral Chester Nimitz to be the new commander of the U.S. Pacific Fleet), was the first step in this process. The second step was to immediately transfer many of Stark's duties to King before going the whole hog and transferring Stark to London as commander of American naval forces in Europe in March 1942 and, as we have seen, giving King the dual titles of COMINCH and CNO.[174] Thus, Admiral Stark was already "on the way out" as CNO by the time the Combined Chiefs of Staff was set up in January 1942.[175]

TWO

Organization, Anatomy of a Summit Conference, and Home Base

The Combined Chiefs of Staff was a corporate-style organization. As such, it was uniquely a product of the industrial age. It represented a "board of directors" style of running a war that relied upon such twentieth-century phenomena as electronic communications equipment, large support staffs both for professional purposes such as planning and for clerical work, and a new type of military officer—one who could work in a bureaucratic setting in which it would be as necessary to communicate effectively with politicians and diplomats as with military peers.[1] This type of command structure is an approach to directing a war that would have been unavailable to any of the combatant nations in the Napoleonic Wars.

Of the two organizations that provided the bulk of the principal members for the Combined Chiefs of Staff, the British Chiefs of Staff (COS) Committee adopted its modern form first, dating back to 1924. Its American counterpart, the Joint Chiefs of Staff (JCS), had its roots in the Joint Army-Navy Board, which had first convened in 1903. The U.S. Joint Chiefs of Staff in its modern form was created in February 1942, as a direct result of the creation of the Combined Chiefs of Staff a month earlier. The JCS was modeled on the British COS Committee and was created because the Americans needed a formal delegation to the Combined Chiefs of Staff. Prior to the Pearl Harbor attack, coordination of army-navy activities in the American military had left much to be desired. The Joint Board had not been nearly as efficient an organization as the Joint Chiefs of Staff came to be.[2]

One reason why the British were ahead of the Americans in recognizing the need to coordinate the activities of their armed forces may have been their earlier recognition of the value of airpower. The Royal Air Force was created as an independent service in 1918. For a long time, what we now call the U.S. Air Force was a part of the U.S. Army. The land-based air organization that fought World War II for the United States was officially known as the U.S. Army Air Forces (USAAF). (The independent air force was to be created in September 1947 under the same legislation that, ironically, while separating the air force from the army, unified the armed forces as a whole by replacing the powerful secretaries of war and navy with one secretary of defense.) The British realized soon after World War I that they were dealing with three services, while for a long time the Americans continued to act as if there were only two. General Henry H. Arnold's seat on the Joint and Combined Chiefs of Staff was therefore a privilege, not a right, granted to him by General Marshall in the latter's role as Army Chief of Staff. Marshall and Arnold worked quite well together, being on excellent terms personally.[3]

For the U.S. Navy the situation was somewhat different. The Chief of the Navy's Bureau of Aeronautics, Rear Admiral John Towers, was a hero to the young aviator officers who believed like Towers that the future of the navy lay with airpower and aircraft carriers. Towers and his followers resented that naval aviators at the beginning of the war were trapped in relatively low ranks. Marc Mitscher for instance, the brilliant officer who as a vice admiral would command the fast carriers of Task Force 58 during the Central Pacific drive, was still a captain at the time of Pearl Harbor despite the fact that he had thirty-one years of naval service and had qualified as a naval aviator as far back as June 1916. (Towers and Mitscher were two of the navy's very first pilots. Mitscher would finally be promoted to rear admiral in July 1942, to vice admiral in March 1944. Admiral Towers was very forceful in pressing his views—a bit too forceful, in fact. The battleship admirals whom Towers regarded as enemies were united in loathing him. Admiral King disliked Towers but was wise enough to see that even a person you don't like can be useful.

King could see both sides of the argument. While he was an aviator who had commanded an aircraft carrier, King had also served in and had a deep affection for battleships. King distrusted Towers enough to prevent him from becoming a member of the Joint and Combined Chiefs of Staff.[4] King therefore spoke for the U.S. Navy on both air and surface matters in the deliberations of the Combined Chiefs of Staff. Washington, D.C., proved not a big enough town for two such strong and unpopular personalities as Ernest J. King and John Towers. King thus solved two of his own problems at one time in October 1942 when he got rid of Towers by sending him out to the Pacific Fleet to serve under Admiral Nimitz as Commander, Air Force, Pacific Fleet. While King was glad that Towers would be four thousand miles away from Washington, he also felt that Admiral Nimitz, a nonaviator, would benefit from having a naval aviation expert stationed at Pearl Harbor. In his new role, Admiral Towers would be responsible for such unglamorous but vital tasks as assigning air groups to new aircraft carriers. The fact that Towers was loathed by the amiable Nimitz, who got along with almost everybody, is probably proof enough that Towers had made even more enemies in the navy than King.[5]

The British Joint Staff Mission in Washington began to operate in January 1941. The JSM was initially attached to the British Purchasing Commission, as a way to hide its real purpose—staff talks—from the American public. This precaution was taken because the United States was still officially a neutral power. Historian Sally Lister Parker dates the real beginning of the British Joint Staff Mission in Washington to June 1941. In that month Air Vice Marshal Sir Arthur Harris and General Sir Colville Wemyss, as well as a British support staff of a hundred persons, arrived in Washington. A few weeks after the Pearl Harbor attack, during the Arcadia Conference in Washington, it was decided that the Joint Staff Mission would represent the British Chiefs of Staff on a day-to-day basis in Washington.[6]

The British Joint Staff Mission in Washington is one example of what makes the Combined Chiefs of Staff a difficult subject to describe, in that it is tangible proof that the Combined Chiefs of Staff organization encompassed much more than eight men sitting around a conference table discussing grand strategy. In its entirety, the Combined Chiefs of Staff was a huge organization. For instance, the British support staff assigned to duty with the British Joint Staff Mission in Washington by late 1942 comprised some three thousand planners, clerks, stenographers, secretaries, couriers, and telephone operators.[7] In addition, much of the initial CCS planning was done by subsidiary organizations, such as the Combined Staff Planners and the Combined Munitions Assignment Board. Many of these combined subsidiaries were, in turn made up of more than one organization. The Combined Staff Planners organization, for instance, was made up of the British

Joint Planning Staff and the U.S. Joint Planning Staff. Similarly, the principals of the Combined Chiefs of Staff came from the U.S. Joint Chiefs of Staff, the British Chiefs of Staff Committee, and (in the case of Dill) the British Joint Staff Mission in Washington. There is also the critically important fact that more than half of the two hundred formal meetings of the Combined Chiefs of Staff took place in Washington, outside of the big Allied meetings like the Yalta Conference, with the British Joint Staff Mission representing the British Chiefs of Staff.[8] The British Joint Staff Mission also exercised considerable influence behind the scenes, and its members were themselves frequently the authors of formal British Combined Chiefs of Staff reports and memoranda. It is therefore essential to incorporate the British Joint Staff Mission in Washington into any discussion of the Combined Chiefs of Staff organization.[9]

The presence of the Combined Chiefs of Staff organization—that is, one supreme military planning agency—in Washington charged with directing the American-British war effort had many benefits. In addition to allowing such activities as planning, munitions distribution, and intelligence gathering to be combined and coordinated, the Combined Chiefs of Staff organization led to greater unity of command in the field. The concept of a theater commander came about during the World War II under Combined Chiefs of Staff auspices. The need for unity in the field as well as at the command center was another lesson that had been learned by the British and the Americans during the World War I. In that conflict, it had not been until April 1918 that Marshal Ferdinand Foch had been given some control over British and American, as well as French, troops on the western front. Even then, Foch's command mandate was limited to controlling when and where to commit the reserve forces of the three nations to battle. As A. J. P. Taylor has written in regard to the situation in the spring of 1918, "Even then there was never a fully coordinated plan of campaign. Three separate armies fought to the end."[10]

In World War II, theater commands proved very efficient, because in each, one commander, regardless of his particular service or nationality, controlled all Allied land, sea, and air forces in his particular theater. For example, in the Southwest Pacific Area, General MacArthur maintained operational control over the Fifth Air Force and the Seventh Fleet. General Eisenhower had large numbers of British troops in his Overlord command. His deputy, as well as his air, ground, and naval commanders (Tedder,

Leigh-Mallory, Montgomery, and Ramsay) were all British.[11] In the Central Pacific, Admiral Nimitz's command included, in addition to the huge Pacific Fleet and six marine divisions, the 27th Infantry Division of the U.S. Army as well as the Seventh Air Force. There were exceptions to the idea of unity. The most significant of these is that late in the war General Arnold refused to relinquish control of the new B-29 bombers that were becoming available in large numbers for bombing the Japanese home islands. Nimitz thus never controlled the B-29 fleets that operated in his theater from air bases in the Mariana Islands.[12]

The mandate of the Combined Chiefs of Staff extended far beyond originating and coordinating the strategies that were to be carried out by their theater commanders. By law, the CCS members had the authority to set production priorities for everything from machine guns to morphine to four-engine bombing aircraft. It was also their responsibility to determine which theater commanders were to get what percentages of finished war materials, supplies, and troops. The American members of the Combined Chiefs of Staff also exercised a great deal of control over the all-important area of shipping.[13] Carrying supplies and troops by sea was far more important to the Allies in World War II than it was for, say, the Gulf War coalition in 1991. While it is true that the United States built more than 20,000 transport aircraft during World War II, these were on the whole much smaller than the C-17 Globemaster IIIs and the C-5A Galaxys that are available today. The excellent Douglas C-54 Skymaster, which entered service in August 1942, was a large, four-engined machine that could lift seven tons of cargo and had the range to carry it across the Atlantic. While not exactly scarce (approximately a thousand being built during the war), there were never enough C-54s to go around. Thus, the bulk of the air transport duty for the Allies in World War II was carried out by the numerous, but much smaller, Douglas C-47 (DC-3) and the Curtiss-Wright C-46 Commando.[14] The Allies in World War II did not have an airplane that could carry a tank. Therefore, what Churchill referred to as the "shipping stranglehold" was a constant worry for the Combined Chiefs of Staff. This was particularly true in 1942, when sinkings due to U-boat activity were quite high.[15] Combined Chiefs of Staff control over American merchant shipping was not absolute, however. The commanding general of the army's Services of Supply (later known as the Army Service Forces), Lieutenant General Brehon Somervell, constantly jockeyed for control of American shipping resources with Lewis

Douglas, the formidable director of day-to-day operations of the American War Shipping Administration, an organization composed of both civilians and military personnel.[16]

In regard to British merchant shipping, the Combined Chiefs of Staff could not give direct orders but rather had to negotiate with a civilian agency, the British Ministry of War Transport, a vast organization that in its New York branch alone employed some two thousand persons in 1944. While British warships were under Admiral Pound's (and later Cunningham's) command, the fact that the civilians at the Ministry of War Transport controlled British cargo shipping can be seen as representing one of the limitations on the command mandate of the Combined Chiefs of Staff.[17] However, the British Ministry of War Transport and its director, Lord Frederick Leathers, had to "play ball" when it came to cooperating with military authorities. For instance, the British Ministry of War Transport made Herculean efforts in support of the North African campaign. That is, the Ministry of War Transport moved troops and supplies to North Africa because that is where the military needed troops and supplies to be sent.[18] Despite their inability to *order* the movement of British merchant ships, the Combined Chiefs often discussed such movements. For instance, the Combined Chiefs of Staff were keenly interested in the world's two greatest ocean liners, the 81,000-ton *Queen Mary* and the 83,000-ton *Queen Elizabeth*. Both ships had been converted into troop transports, in which role they proved quite effective, in that each could make an average speed of thirty knots and was capable of carrying upward of 15,000 troops on a single voyage. Many of the American soldiers who hit the beaches at Normandy had arrived in England on these ships. Combined Chiefs of Staff memoranda regularly included the subject "Movement of the *Queens*" as an agenda item.

Admiral Stark was initially the most senior, and therefore presiding, officer on the U.S. Joint Chiefs of Staff. When in March 1942 Stark left the Joint Chiefs of Staff after his post as Chief of Naval Operations was combined with Admiral King's billet as Commander in Chief, U.S. Fleet, General Marshall briefly became the presiding member of the U.S. Joint Chiefs of Staff. However, when Admiral Leahy arrived in July 1942 as chief of staff to FDR, he automatically became, technically, chair of the Joint Chiefs of Staff. The modern title of "Chairman of the Joint Chiefs of Staff" came about in the 1950s, when the power of that office was, by law, greatly enhanced. The U.S. Joint Chiefs of Staff in World War II did not, in reality, have any such dominant member. In terms of strategic brilliance and organizational ability, Admiral King and General Marshall greatly overshadowed Leahy, the chair. They and Arnold all spoke with authority to the Congress, the president, and the press about their respective fields.

The merger of Stark's duties as CNO with those of King is evidence that the creation of the Combined Chiefs of Staff had a ripple-down effect in which the military command structures of both Britain and the United States became much more streamlined. The creation of the theater commands testifies to this, as does the reorganization of the U.S. War Department and army. On March 9, 1942, General Marshall and Secretary of War Henry Stimson put in place a new and simplified structure for the army in which all of its activities would now fall under just three vast commands. Each would be led by a lieutenant general who was a close and trusted associate of Marshall. There would now be the Army Air Forces (Henry H. Arnold),

Table 2-1. The British Joint Staff Mission in Washington
Membership between December 7, 1941, and August 14, 1945

	Dates of Service in Washington
BAS	
General Colville Wemyss	June 1941–March 1942
Field Marshal Sir John Dill*	January 20, 1942–November 4, 1944
Maj. Gen. Sir Gordon Macready	June 1942–May 1946
Field Marshal Sir Henry M. Wilson*	January 19, 1945–war's end
RAFDEL	
Air Vice-Marshal Sir Arthur Harris	June 1941–February 1942
Air Vice-Marshal Sir D. C. S. Evill	June 1942–March 1943
Air Vice-Marshal Sir W. L. Welsh	May 1943–October 1944
Air Marshal Douglas Colyer	December 1944–war's end
BAD	
Admiral Sir Charles Little	June 1941–May 1942
Adm. of the Fleet Sir Andrew B. Cunningham	June 24, 1942–October 11, 1942
Admiral Sir Percy Noble	December 1942–October 1944
Admiral Sir James Somerville	October 1944–war's end

* Respective heads of the British Joint Staff Mission
Source: Tabulated from Parker, *Attendant Lords*, 42–57, 130–31, 175–94

the Army Ground Forces (Lesley J. McNair), and the Army Service Forces (Brehon B. Somervell). Of Marshall's three deputies, General Arnold was clearly a first among equals—the only one of the three to be a member of the Joint and Combined Chiefs of Staff. General Somervell, however, attended all of the big CCS Conferences as Marshall's logistics planner.[19]

Since the majority of the meetings of the Combined Chiefs of Staff took place in Washington, with Dill and the British Joint Staff Mission representing the interests of the British Chiefs of Staff, it was at these weekly meetings that the real authority of the Combined Chiefs of Staff was built up.[20] The Joint Staff Mission consisted of three elements: British Admiralty Delegation (BAD), Royal Air Force Delegation (RAFDEL), and British Army Staff (BAS). Table 2-1 lists the names of the British officers who headed these sections of the British Joint Staff Mission in Washington during World War II.

Table 2-2. The Combined Planning Staff

Membership in October 1942
British Joint Planning Staff
Captain Charles Lambe, RN
Brigadier Guy Stewart
Air Commodore William Elliot
U.S. Joint Staff Planners
Rear Admiral Charles M. Cooke Jr.
Brig. Gen. Albert C. Wedemeyer
Brig. Gen. O. A. Anderson
Captain R. L. Conolly, USN
Colonel R. T. Maddocks

Source: Tabulated from British Joint Planning Staff, J.P. (43) 265 (Final) July 21, 1943, PREM 3/228/5, U.S. Joint Staff Planners, Minutes of JPS 38th Meeting, October 7, 1942, *Records of the Joint Chiefs of Staff—Meetings,* Microfilm (Frederick, Md.: University Publications of America), reel 5, frames 0207–0210, pp. 1–4, TNA. Accessed at the Lamont Library, Harvard University. See also *Foreign Relations of the United States: The Conferences at Washington, 1941–1942, and Casablanca, 1943* (Washington: U.S. Government Printing Office, 1968): 613, 881, 893

With a few exceptions, the British representatives who served with the Joint Staff Mission in Washington were quite popular with the Americans. Admiral Cunningham's relations with King had become strained during the former's brief stint with the Joint Staff Mission in 1942. Cunningham admired King but felt that the American CNO wasted too much of his energy on interservice and inter-Allied rivalry.[21] According to his biographer, Cunningham found in King "a man of immense capacity and ability, quite ruthless in his methods, . . . not an easy person to work with."[22] The working relationship between the two men seems to have improved later on. Their strategic visions began to come together in regard to the Pacific theater when Cunningham became a full member of the Combined Chiefs of Staff in October 1943 following Pound's resignation. By war's end, King was ready to offer praise for Cunningham's efforts.[23] Admiral Noble's relations with King were courteous but not friendly. Sally Parker sees this as a pattern with the members of the British Joint Staff Mission in Washington—they always liked Marshall but sometimes disliked King.[24] In addition to his brusque manner, the British found offensive King's determination to repudiate the "Germany first" strategy agreed upon at Arcadia in favor of all-out action against Japan. Even Dill, who was on excellent terms with all the American members of the CCS, remarked to Churchill in the summer of 1942 with some chagrin that "King's war is against the Japanese."[25] Admirals Little and Somerville got along exceptionally well with King, while General Macready was a big hit with everybody in Washington. Well liked by Dill and the Americans, Macready sat on the Combined Munitions Assignment Board as a procurement expert.[26]

In the Parker's apt phrasing, the members of the Joint Staff Mission were "attendant lords" who were not supposed to initiate strategic ideas on their own. However, the Joint Staff Mission was able to clarify very effectively what the principals had decided, both on a day-to-day basis and after the big wartime conferences, such as Trident (May 1943).[27] To do this they relied heavily upon accurate, comprehensive, and up-to-date information relayed to them by cipher telegram or cable from their masters in London. Unfortunately, this information was not always quickly forthcoming. In a November 1942 Joint Staff Mission telegram to Brigadier L. C. Hollis, an aide to the British Chiefs of Staff, Dill pleaded with the COS Committee to keep the JSM within the loop of current information:

> You realise we have had little or no guidance on London policy over [Admiral François] Darlan and [General Charles] de Gaulle. If we have to do idiot boy every time, U.S. Chiefs of Staff will tend more and more

to take control and you will always be a day behind. I realize period of gestation in Whitehall is usually much longer than here where U.S. Chiefs of Staff short-circuit civil departments entirely. But it is very hard to stall when we do not know at all how matter is being processed at home. . . . For us here no news is definitely bad news. Should be most grateful for most immediate reply however brief in such cases or telephone call.[28]

There were other aspects of the CCS organization besides the relationship between the Joint Staff Mission and the British chiefs where improved communications were needed. The Combined Staff Planning staffs had been surprised to find that the Combined Chiefs of Staff principals had arrived in Washington for the May 1943 Trident Conference with strategic ideas that were new to each other. Therefore, in the first few CCS meetings at Trident the two sides had to take the time to bring each other up to date on their respective viewpoints.[29] This is surprising, in that Marshall and Dill were in the habit of working out points of conflict before CCS meetings or conferences.[30] This system, however, seems to have broken down in the weeks leading up to Trident.

As a solution, the Combined Staff Planners (see Table 2-2) suggested that it would be beneficial if CCS members had a better understanding of each other's views before arriving at big conferences. This could be accomplished, the planners felt, if the British and American Joint Planning Staffs each did a better job of exchanging their proposals and papers on a continuous basis in between the big conferences. As a means of accomplishing this, the Combined Staff Planners proposed that American planning officers go to London to serve temporarily with the British Joint Planning Staff and that the British release staff officers for similar duty in Washington. The planners also felt that the respective heads of the American and British Joint Planning Staffs should meet face to face on a regular basis.[31] It seems that the Combined Staff Planners could readily perceive the great benefits that accrued to the Combined Chiefs of Staff by having the Joint Staff Mission in Washington work with the Americans on a day-to-day basis. They wanted the same type of arrangement for the planning section of the CCS organization.

Details of all of the major Allied wartime conferences have been presented by numerous historians.[32] There are several reasons why simply retracing the course of the big wartime conferences is not the best way to understand the Combined Chiefs of Staff, although looking at one of them here will be useful. First, more than half of the formal meetings of the Combined Chiefs of Staff took place on Friday afternoons in the Public Health Building in Washington, D.C., not at the big conferences such as Casablanca or Yalta. In those weekly (by late 1944, sometimes less frequent) Washington meetings Sir John Dill and the British Joint Staff Mission, deputized to represent the three London-based British principal CCS members, would confer with the U.S. Joint Chiefs of Staff.[33] Second, the principal members of the Combined Chiefs, as well as the planners, constantly sent reports and memoranda back and forth to each other across the Atlantic between the big conferences. But perhaps the most important reason why the formal conferences with all of the principals present do not provide a complete picture of the way the Combined Chiefs of Staff operated is the critical link that was provided by Sir John Dill and his informal interactions with the U.S. Joint Chiefs of Staff, particularly with General Marshall.[34] Of Dill and Marshall, Alex Danchev writes that "they exchanged an unprecedented amount of information."[35] Indeed they did. The two men kept each other well informed. This two-way conduit of information meant that the U.S. Joint Chiefs were often made aware of information from Churchill that the prime minister thought was being seen only by the British Chiefs of Staff. This information sometimes included important decisions that FDR had communicated to Churchill but of which he had neglected to inform his own Joint Chiefs of Staff. Being unaware of what their head of state was thinking and doing was a problem for the U.S. Joint Chiefs of Staff, because there was no set schedule by which the Joint Chiefs of Staff met with the president during the war. Sometimes they would not see FDR for several weeks. The British Chiefs of Staff, on the other hand, met with Churchill almost every day during the war. Informal communication with Marshall also meant that Dill was able to keep his British colleagues well informed of conversations Marshall had had with Admiral King, FDR, and others.[36] While the amount of sensitive data that Dill was able to transmit to London enraged some Americans, such as the Anglophobic isolationist General Wedemeyer, Alex Danchev is undoubtedly correct in stating that without the Marshall-Dill friendship the Combined Chiefs of Staff system simply would not have worked.[37]

General Marshall and General Dill, standing, center right behind the president and the prime minister on the afterdeck of the battleship HMS *Prince of Wales* during the Atlantic Charter meetings, August 1941. It was at these meetings that the friendship between Marshall and Dill, a friendship that was to become the cornerstone of the Combined Chiefs of Staff organization, began. *U.S. Naval Institute Photo Archive*

The Casablanca Summit

Contrary to what some high school history textbooks indicate, the Casablanca Conference in January 1943 was not convened in order that President Roosevelt could proclaim the doctrine of unconditional surrender. Casablanca was a military conference, dominated by meetings of the Combined Chiefs of Staff. The Allies were already fighting a total war at the time of Casablanca. There was no need to define the parameters of the struggle. The stakes were already all too apparent. Russian troops who during the Casablanca Conference were fighting the closing stages of what would be their great victory over the German Sixth Army in the battle of Stalingrad had only to survey the complete destruction of their city and count their dead to know that they were in a fight to the finish. The president's announcement at the end of the Casablanca Conference that the Allies would accept only the unconditional surrender of the Axis powers was more of a statement of his confidence in Allied victory than a manifestation of any change in policy.

General Marshall's biographer speculates that the president was indeed motivated to make the unconditional-surrender pledge at least in part by a desire to give hope to the hard-pressed Russians.[38] Also, it is quite likely that the president felt it necessary to say something that sounded significant to the press about the Casablanca Conference, but he could not tell the assembled reporters what had really happened at Casablanca, because that would have meant disclosing to the enemy classified information about upcoming military operations. Consummate politician that he was, FDR made his announcement at Casablanca as a clever way of tossing to the press a bone that would intrigue reporters enough that, he hoped, they would not pester the Combined Chiefs of Staff for details about the specific plans that had been discussed and approved at the conference. Thus, the Casablanca Conference was convened so that the principals of the Combined Chiefs of Staff could make military plans and hash out disagreements over strategy, and FDR grabbed all media attention with "unconditional surrender" to allow the Combined Chiefs to remain in the background—which is exactly where the Combined Chiefs liked to be in regard to the media.

The Combined Chiefs of Staff, and some aides, at the conference table during the Casablanca Conference. Left to Right; Rear Admiral Charles M. Cooke, Admiral Ernest J. King, General George C. Marshall, Lieutenant General Henry H. Arnold (hidden), Brigadier Vivian Dykes, Brigadier General Albert C. Wedemeyer, Major General Sir Hastings Ismay, Vice Admiral Lord Louis Mountbatten, Admiral of the Fleet Sir Dudley Pound, General Sir Alan Brooke (wearing eyeglasses), Air Chief Marshal Sir Charles Portal (hidden), Field Marshal Sir John Dill. *U.S. National Archives and Records Administration*

Some detail about what happened at the Casablanca Conference is useful, if only to show that Casablanca was *not* all, or even mostly, about unconditional surrender. During the conference, the Combined Chiefs of Staff typically met twice daily to discuss strategic plans. Sometimes the second, or afternoon, meeting consisted of the CCS delivering a progress report personally to FDR and Churchill. Typically, CCS meetings during the Casablanca Conference were fairly small. While traveling to the conference with the president, Admiral Leahy had become ill and had been forced to remain in Trinidad for treatment. The American practice at Combined Chiefs of Staff meetings in Washington was often to have a dozen or more staff officers on hand as advisers, assistants, and observers. Meetings of the U.S. Joint Chiefs were even more crowded, often with as many as three dozen staff officers present.[39] In contrast, at Casablanca, Marshall, King, and Arnold had only a few staff officers actually in the conference room with them while meeting with their British counterparts. The British contingent was much larger. Brooke, Pound, Portal, Mountbatten, and Ismay were all in attendance, as was Field Marshal Dill (who had come as Marshall's guest).[40] The American staff officers present included Rear Admiral Charles M. Cooke, a vociferous advocate of expanded operations in the Pacific, who as King's top planner served on the Joint and Combined Planning Staffs. General Marshall was accompanied by Lieutenant General Somervell. Somervell, who sat on the Combined Munitions Assignment Board, was an extremely energetic individual who exerted a great deal of influence over the production and distribution of munitions and supplies. Also on hand to assist Generals Marshall and Arnold was the aforementioned planner Brigadier General Albert C. Wedemeyer. The British staff officers present at CCS Casablanca meetings included Air Vice Marshal Sir John Slessor of Portal's staff and Captain Charles Lambe, Royal Navy (RN), director of plans at the Admiralty and Admiral Cooke's colleague on the Combined Planning Staff. The Combined Secretariat for these meetings consisted of two officers, the American brigadier general John R. Deane and a British brigadier, Vivian Dykes.[41]

The Americans would live to regret that they took to Casablanca so small a delegation. Historians have noted that the Americans arrived at Casablanca in a state of unpreparedness that is surprising in view of the fact that the American Combined Chiefs principals had already seen, at the Arcadia Conference just after Pearl Harbor, how well prepared the British were for conferences. One reason for American unreadiness at Casablanca is that the U.S. Joint Chiefs of Staff, being a fairly new organization, had not yet settled down into a smoothly running machine. The much older British Chiefs of Staff Committee system gave the British a great advantage at this stage of the war when it came to interservice planning.[42]

The range of topics discussed by the Combined Chiefs of Staff at Casablanca was quite broad. The topic that required the most immediate attention was the heavy loss of Allied merchant shipping in the Atlantic to German submarine attacks. Everyone agreed at Casablanca that it was imperative to defeat the U-boat menace. Samuel Eliot Morison claims that this meant a greatly accelerated program for building submarine-hunting ships, such as destroyer escorts (a smaller, less sophisticated type of destroyer) and small aircraft carriers that could be used to provide air cover to convoys in mid-Atlantic. This, says Morison, resulted in "placing landing and beaching craft in a lower category. That is why a worldwide shortage of such craft occurred in 1944."[43]

General Marshall backed Admiral King's desire to see the proportion of Allied resources devoted to the war in the Pacific increased from 15 percent to 30 percent. The Americans secured British concurrence for continued operations against the Japanese in the southwest Pacific and the opening up of a drive across the Central Pacific. Admiral King had every reason to be pleased with these results. He had even received the green light for Allied operations against the Japanese in Burma.[44] King must have been especially gratified, because he and Cooke had not had time to prepare adequately for the Casablanca conference, having had many serious crises to deal with in late 1942, such as the tough fighting on Guadalcanal. This is not to say, however, that the lives of the other members of the Combined Chiefs of Staff had been at all uneventful in the weeks leading up to the conference.[45]

General Marshall had much less reason to be pleased with the results of the Casablanca conference. The "Germany first" principle was reaffirmed at Casablanca, with the Americans slated to continue the daylight bombing campaign against German cities that was just beginning at the time of Casablanca. The British would continue their by-then-extensive nighttime bombing campaign. However, instead of his desired 1943 cross-channel attack, Marshall had to swallow an Allied invasion of Sicily that was scheduled to begin after the North African campaign ended. As Marshall had feared, Torch was leading to what seemed to be an open-ended Allied commitment to Mediterranean operations. There was also talk of trying to get Turkey to join the Allied war effort.[46] His biographer admits that at Casablanca "Marshall got much less than he had wanted. However, he had been fairly certain before he came to Casablanca that he must accept a campaign against Sardinia or Sicily."[47] General Wedemeyer, who was never fond of Britons, put it more bluntly in his much-quoted aside of the Americans at Casablanca, "We came, we listened, and we were conquered."[48]

In addition to being better prepared for the conference, Britain "won" at Casablanca (in that they kept the war effort against Japan limited for the time being without being forced to set a date for a cross-channel invasion in Europe) because in January 1943 the British had more troops in the war against Germany than did the Americans. An important qualification needed here is that calling the North African campaign that was in progress at the time of the Casablanca conference "the war against Germany" is a bit of a misnomer. In the North African campaign, the British and the Americans fought against French forces loyal to Vichy, the Italians, and the Germans. It was also stretching a point considerably to consider North Africa to be part of the European Theater of Operations. Also, and perhaps most importantly, the decisions made and not made at Casablanca prove that despite the fact that the United States would eventually raise a much larger army than Britain and that American industrial capacity was very much greater than that of Britain, the British stubbornly refused to admit the fact of their complete dependence on their American ally. According to Kevin Smith, a scholar of the diplomacy of logistics, at the time of Casablanca the British Chiefs of Staff and the prime minister were still "determined to maintain strategic dominance" in the Western alliance.[49] This attitude infuriated the Americans. In time, the staggering weight of troops, tanks, ships, aircraft, and numerous other types of supplies and weapons produced by America would tip the balance in favor of the United States in regard to setting the strategic agenda for the Western alliance in Europe, but Casablanca was not that time.[50]

The often-contentious strategy planning meetings of the Combined Chiefs of Staff at Casablanca took place without the president and the prime minister, who were on-site but met for the most part separately from their military planners. After they had reached agreement on particular issues, the Combined Chiefs would meet with FDR and Churchill to present their findings for approval. The politicians actually had little to do with the plans that were made at the Casablanca Conference.

The Combined Chiefs of Staff (minus Admiral Leahy and Field Marshal Dill) at Casablanca with their civilian superiors and with two uniformed aides. Standing, left to right, Lieutenant General Brehon Somervell, Lieutenant General Henry H. "Hap" Arnold, Admiral Ernest J. King, General George C. Marshall, Admiral of the Fleet Sir Dudley Pound, General Sir Alan Brooke, Air Chief Marshal Sir Charles Portal, Vice Admiral Lord Louis Mountbatten. *U.S. National Archives and Records Administration*

Where They Worked

The Combined Chiefs of Staff met weekly, beginning on January 23, 1942.[51] In Washington, the British Joint Staff Mission had its headquarters, from February 1942 onward, in the Public Health Building, which was located at the corner of 19th Street and Constitution Avenue, directly opposite the War and Navy Department Buildings.[52] The latter two were "temporary" structures that had been built during World War I but survived to see service in the second war (and for decades thereafter). The Public Health Building was also where regular meetings of the Joint and Combined Chiefs of Staff were held.

The Public Health Building was a sort of neutral ground for the American military. As we have seen, the existence of the Combined Chiefs of Staff allowed for greater unity of command, both interservice and international. This unity was more or less imposed upon the branches of the American military, which had not previously been inclined to cooperate.[53] Until the Department of Defense was created under the National Security Act of 1947, the War and Navy Departments were separate entities. General

Marshall and Secretary Stimson had moved into the brand-new (in fact, it was unfinished at that time) Pentagon building on November 15, 1942. Their previous offices had been located across the Potomac in the War Department building, also known as the Munitions Building, on Constitution Avenue. Admiral King and Navy Secretary Frank Knox, however, remained in the Navy Department building, next door to the Munitions Building. Admiral Leahy's office was in the White House. Therefore, while after the creation of the Department of Defense in 1947 all Joint Chiefs of Staff meetings would take place in the Pentagon, those meetings required some logistical planning during World War II. The Public Health Building held, in terms of a meeting place for the Joint and Combined Chiefs of Staff, the further advantage of being close to the White House, to which the Joint Chiefs went for their meetings with the president.[54] During the war, the Public Health Building was often referred to in memoranda as "the Combined Chiefs of Staff Building."[55]

In addition to their headquarters in the Public Health Building, the British Joint Staff Mission used office space in several other buildings in the District of Columbia. These included the Grafton Hotel and an edifice known as Bastedo House, the latter located at 3055 Whitehaven Street, adjacent to the British embassy.[56] An undated Joint Staff Mission document probably written in late 1941 or early 1942 includes a brief note about housekeeping at Bastedo House that reinforces the fact that African-American civilians were not sharing in the wartime boom as much as the white workers, who were enjoying high-paying, unionized jobs in aircraft factories and other munitions plants. The document states that "house cleaning, which presumably will be done by coloured women, is being arranged through the British Purchasing Commission."[57] Some of the members of the administrative staff of the British Joint Staff Mission had their living quarters in an apartment building at 1424 Sixteenth Street.[58]

As an organization, the British Joint Staff Mission grew rapidly. By the end of 1942, its Washington support staff numbered some three thousand members. That figure alone gives a glimpse of how vast an organization the Combined Chiefs of Staff actually was. The British were constantly looking for extra office space—something hard to come by in wartime Washington, D.C.[59] For example, in June 1943 General Deane was informed by one of his colleagues on the Combined Secretariat, British Brigadier H. Redman, that the Joint Staff Mission hoped to get a new wing added to the third floor of the Public Health Building, which would provide the British ten new offices.[60]

For their off-site conferences, a few examples will show that the Combined Chiefs of Staff were able to work in some very comfortable and efficient surroundings. The Anfa Hotel served as Allied headquarters for the Casablanca Conference. This plush, medium-sized resort had been transformed by the U.S. Army, along with its fourteen adjoining villas, into an Allied conference headquarters under heavy security. No expense was spared in providing a secure facility within which the Combined Chiefs of Staff, the president, and the prime minister could work. Having been one of the Allied objectives in the Torch campaign, Casablanca was still technically a war zone. Army units had set up around the hotel area a perimeter that included barbed wire and artillery emplacements, as well as a sizable detachment of troops. Allied aircraft provided constant air cover.[61]

At the Trident Conference in Washington, D.C., in May 1943, Combined Chiefs of Staff Meetings were held in the Governor's Room of the Federal Reserve Building. At Trident there were, as at Casablanca, usually two CCS meetings per day, or at least one meeting to discuss strategy and a second (afternoon) session at the White House to bring the president and the prime minister up to date on the progress of the discussions.[62]

The setting for the Quadrant Conference at Quebec in August 1943 was quite beautiful. The Combined Chiefs of Staff were housed (for both Quebec conferences) in the elegant Château Frontenac, a first-class resort hotel operated by the Canadian Pacific Railroad and situated on a bluff overlooking Quebec City and the St. Lawrence River.[63] CCS meetings were held there as well, in room 2208. The American staff was larger in Quebec than it had been at Casablanca. In addition, Admiral Noble, General Macready, and Air Vice Marshal Welsh of the British Joint Staff Mission attended the Quadrant Conference as part of the British delegation. This shows how important the British Joint Staff Mission had become to the Combined Chiefs of Staff organization. While the Combined Chiefs were meeting at the Château Frontenac, Churchill and Roosevelt held their meetings at the nearby Citadel, to which the Combined Chiefs went to give their progress reports.

On six of the eleven days of the Quadrant Conference, the CCS had only one meeting instead of the usual two. This was due, in part, to the fact that the war was going better and some of the larger issues had been settled.

There was, therefore, a decreased level of urgency. The job of distributing memoranda and keeping the minutes was made easier at Quadrant for the Combined Secretariat by the fact that its staff consisted of four or five officers per CCS meeting, instead of the two that had sufficed at Casablanca.[64]

Churchill and, especially, President Roosevelt traveled a long way to meet with Stalin at the Teheran Conference in late November 1943 and at the Yalta Conference in the Crimea in February 1945. At Yalta, the Livadia Palace and nearby villas provided perhaps the most interesting locale of any of the Allied wartime conferences. The Red Army had only recently ejected the Wehrmacht from the Crimea, and the region bore plainly the scars of the brutality of the Great Patriotic War. After arriving by air at Saki, the British and American delegates proceeded by automobile the ninety miles to the palace. During the drive, the members of the Combined Chiefs of Staff could see firsthand why the Russians had pressed so hard for an early second front. Marshall's biographer Forrest Pogue records that "although the Crimea had been cleared of the enemy, the rolling, snow-

Figure 2-1. The Combined Chiefs of Staff Organization in July 1942

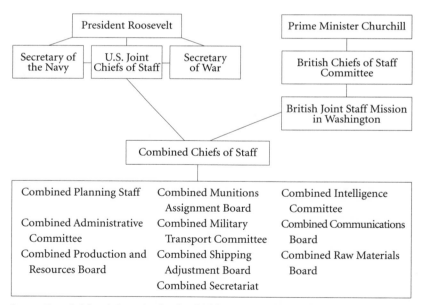

Source: Compiled from information listed in the following: Parker, *Attendant Lords*, 1–11; Combined Chiefs of Staff, CCS 9/1, "War Collaboration between United Nations," February 10, 1942, LC, King Papers, box 22/ "Joint Chiefs of Staff Charter"/1–2.

covered countryside was still strewn with shells of burnt-out buildings, wrecked tanks, and smashed railroad equipment."[65]

The Livadia Palace itself had been looted by the Germans of its interior furnishings but was still structurally sound. The Russians, despite the supposedly classless society of the Soviet Union, were great respecters of rank. They went all out to make the Livadia Palace as comfortable as possible for the conference delegates. The palace had been built as a vacation resort for Czar Nicholas II and his family. That the stern and strict Admiral King was lodged in what had been the czarina's boudoir was an irony greatly appreciated by everyone but King.[66] The CCS principals, the president, and the prime minister each had fairly spacious quarters in and around Yalta. Lower-ranking officers were crowded into shared bedrooms. Everyone was attacked by bedbugs; there were not enough bathrooms, and the fixtures in the bathrooms apparently did not work very well. Indeed czarist ideas about what passed for indoor plumbing were a lively topic of conversation.[67] General Arnold was recovering from a heart attack and thus missed the Yalta Conference. His replacement at Yalta, Army Air Forces lieutenant general Laurence Kuter, noted that "excepting only the war ... the bathrooms were the most generally discussed subject at the Crimean Conference."[68]

THREE

The Combined Chiefs of Staff and the War in the Pacific

The Allied war effort in the Pacific was carried out by predominantly American forces. By mid-1944, the American Pacific Fleet had developed into a vast and powerful striking force capable of operating for months at a time in the western Pacific without returning to a fixed shore base such as Pearl Harbor. It was a fleet that repeatedly proved itself fully capable of protecting American marines and infantry from air or surface attack during the amphibious landings of the Central Pacific drive. While that campaign was under way, the land-based U.S. Army Air Forces were attacking Japanese shipping, harbors, and shore installations throughout the Central, South, and southwest Pacific areas with great success. This was an American theater of operations. Consequently, the Combined Chiefs of Staff delegated the control of day-to-day events there to the U.S. Joint Chiefs of Staff. The instructions of the Joint Chiefs were, in turn, carried out by the two theater commanders in the Pacific—Admiral Chester W. Nimitz, Commander in Chief, U.S. Pacific Fleet and Pacific Ocean Areas, and General Douglas MacArthur, Supreme Allied Commander, Southwest Pacific Area.[1]

This is not to imply that the Combined Chiefs of Staff as a whole were out of the picture as far as the Pacific War was concerned. Large strategic issues, such as whether and when to begin a campaign in the Central Pacific, were debated at Combined Chiefs of Staff meetings. Indeed, at the same time that the Combined Chiefs of Staff was being set up at the Arcadia Conference in Washington, in late December 1941 and early January 1942, its members set the initial tone for the Pacific. It was during the Arcadia discussions that the British received a pledge from the Americans to put the war against Germany first in order of priority, an idea that had already been accepted in principle by the Americans even before Pearl Harbor, in the "ABC-1" report, which had been ratified during British-American military discussions held in Washington between January 29 and March 27, 1941.[2] The Combined Chiefs had the right of approval over what in the way of supplies, munitions, and troops would be sent to the Pacific theater. This was similar to the manner in which, in August 1943, the British Chiefs of Staff were given direct control over operations in the newly created Southeast Asia Command, while the Combined Chiefs of Staff as a whole were to allocate supplies and decide on overall strategic objectives there.[3]

Admiral Nimitz, who took command of the U.S. Pacific Fleet on December 31, 1941, was perhaps the most capable of the theater commanders with whom the Combined Chiefs of Staff interacted during the war. The gentle demeanor and gracious good humor that Nimitz projected belied the strategic genius and gifts of command that lay beneath. Nimitz had all of the interpersonal skills of Eisenhower, coupled with real ability as a strategist.[4] Samuel Eliot Morison has paid eloquent tribute to the calming influence Admiral Nimitz immediately began to have upon the personnel of the Pacific Fleet when he arrived at Pearl Harbor a few weeks after the devastating Japanese attack of December 7, 1941:

> Chester Nimitz was one of those rare men who grow as their responsibilities increase. . . . Ever calm and gentle in demeanor and courteous in speech, he had tow-colored hair turning white, blue eyes and a pink complexion that gave him somewhat the look of a friendly small boy, so that war correspondents, who expected admirals to pound the table and bellow as in the movies, were apt to wonder "Is this the man?" He was the man. No more fortunate appointment to this vital command could have been made.[5]

The example of Nimitz shows that not every success that accrued to the Western Allies during the war can be credited to the Combined Chiefs of Staff. Admiral Nimitz was selected for the Pacific Fleet command by President Roosevelt, in consultation with Secretary of the Navy Frank Knox, on December 17, 1941—before the Combined Chiefs of Staff had even been set up. In May 1942, it was Nimitz who retained Rear Admiral Frank Jack Fletcher in command of Task Force 17 (the carrier *Yorktown* and its escorts) despite doubts harbored by Admiral King regarding Fletcher's abilities after what King considered to have been Fletcher's lackluster performance in the battle of the Coral Sea. It was Nimitz who accepted Vice Admiral William F. Halsey's recommendation that Rear Admiral Raymond Spruance be named as Halsey's replacement as commander of Task Force 16 (carriers *Enterprise* and *Hornet* and their escorts) when Halsey had to be hospitalized for a serious skin ailment just prior to the battle of Midway. The wisdom of Nimitz was shown when Fletcher and Spruance proved to be an excellent team indeed at Midway in June 1942. It was also Nimitz who was quick to understand the significance of the information being provided to him by code breakers who, prior to Midway, had succeeded in cracking part of the Japanese military code and thereby determining that Midway was indeed the Japanese target. Indeed, Nimitz was ahead of Admiral King in correctly interpreting the intelligence data as indicating that the next Japanese attack would occur in the Central Pacific (specifically, at Midway), as opposed to the South Pacific. In a move that would greatly aid the American effort at Midway, it was again Nimitz who determined that the carrier *Yorktown*, which had been badly damaged in the Coral Sea, could be patched up and made ready for action in seventy-two hours instead of the three months predicted by the repair specialists at the Pearl Harbor navy yard.[6]

Later in the war, during the Central Pacific drive, Admiral Nimitz made skillful use of Ultra code-breaking intelligence when planning the invasion of the Japanese-held Marshall Islands that began on January 31, 1944. Nimitz correctly interpreted the intelligence indications that the Japanese defenses in the center of the Marshalls chain were unexpectedly weak. Therefore, he surprised Admiral Spruance, by now the commander of the U.S. Fifth Fleet, by ordering him to bypass the eastern Marshalls and invade Kwajelein Atoll, the largest atoll in the world and the heart of the Marshalls chain. The Marshalls campaign was highly successful, and Admiral Nimitz deserves much of the credit for that.[7]

Therefore, in highlighting the crucial role of the Combined Chiefs of Staff in the success of the Western alliance, it is not my intention to in any way downplay the significance of the contributions to victory of talented field commanders like Admiral Nimitz or the undeniable sagacity shown by FDR in appointing such gifted men.

If American public opinion was galvanized by the Pearl Harbor attack into fully supporting war against Japan, opinion in England was equally outraged by humiliating British defeats at the hands of the Japanese, such as the fall of Singapore. However, in the deliberations of the Combined Chiefs in 1942 it was the Americans, in particular Admiral King, who pressed for immediate expansion of the war effort against Japan. This idea made the British extremely nervous in 1942, as did the fact that by December 1942 there were already 346,000 American troops in the Pacific theater, the equivalent of more than seventeen divisions of infantry and marines, while only 170,000 American soldiers had arrived in England by that time.[8] It is interesting to note that "Germany first" notwithstanding, it was at Guadalcanal, in the Solomon Islands of the South Pacific, on August 7, 1942, that American ground forces were first committed to battle in World War II.

The British could do little during 1942 to resist the American desire to carry out offensive, and not merely defensive, operations against Japan. This was due to a profound transformation in the character of the Alliance that took place that year. In short, during 1942 the Americans proved that they would be overwhelmingly the more powerful of the two Western Allies. American military strength grew very rapidly in 1942. By January 1943 the strength of the U.S. Army stood at seventy-three divisions, while the British army comprised fewer than thirty. At this time, Britain was getting a whopping three-fourths of its destroyers, destroyer escorts, and corvette-type submarine-hunting ships from the United States. The Americans were also supplying Britain with vast quantities of light bombers, such as the excellent Douglas A-20. Further evidence of this power shift became apparent in March 1942, when the president and the prime minister divided the globe into three areas of strategic responsibility. All of the Pacific became an American zone; the two nations were to share responsibility for the Atlantic Ocean and Western Europe, while the Mediterranean, the Middle East, and India would be Britain's responsibility. Under this arrangement, the United States became responsible for the defense of the self-governing British dominions of Australia and New Zealand. This, incidentally, gave the U.S. Joint Chiefs of Staff leverage against the British when planning operations in the Solomon Islands and in New Guinea. The Americans could simply claim that they had to protect the lines of communication between the United States and Australia. Even from Singapore westward, the British were forced to ask for American equipment and supplies to such an extent that it really became an inter-Allied, rather than a strictly British, zone.[9]

The British members of the Combined Chiefs of Staff have been characterized as constantly opposed to devoting resources to the war against Japan. According to this school of thought, the British chiefs wanted the Americans simply to conduct a holding action against Japan until after the Allies had vanquished Germany.[10] Only then would it be acceptable to conduct full-scale war against Japan.

This certainly was the British attitude at the outset of the British-American alliance. There is evidence that in 1942 the British chiefs fought hard against the American "pull toward the Pacific." British resistance, however, began to weaken in 1943. There are several reasons for this. The British were certainly up against a great deal of American public, as well as military, opinion that favored all-out war against Japan to avenge Pearl Harbor. However, there is more to it than that. The British chiefs had by the end of 1943 come to believe that full-fledged operations against Japan would not be an undue drain upon resources for the war against Germany and that such operations represented a militarily sound course of action. This sentiment, which the British chiefs began to display in the spring of 1943, received a boost when Admiral Cunningham became a member of the Combined Chiefs of Staff in October. From that time onward, the British chiefs not only looked with more sympathetic interest at ambitious American plans for the Pacific theater but began to desire an active part for Britain in those plans as well.

In short, Cunningham persuaded the British Chiefs of Staff of the viability of the Pacific strategy—a plan to send British forces, particularly naval forces, to the Pacific to operate with the Americans. This brought the British chiefs into conflict with Churchill, who wanted the British to concentrate their naval forces for the war against Japan in the Indian Ocean. The evidence shows that it was the British Chiefs of Staff, and not Churchill, who were instrumental in getting a British battle fleet into the Pacific in December 1944, and it also shows that this was the correct strategy. The fact that the British chiefs could clearly see the value of the Central Pacific drive may have made it easier for the American Joint Chiefs to quietly give precedence to that campaign in early 1944, at the expense of MacArthur's southwest Pacific advance.[11]

Christopher Thorne examines closely in his pioneering work, *Allies of a Kind: The United States, Britain and the War against Japan,* the grave differences that existed between British and American war aims in Asia. Thorne points out very effectively that the Americans were constantly pressing for action to retake Burma from the Japanese as a way to reopen land communications with China, while the British gravitated away from Burma and toward Singapore. This certainly describes the attitudes of such British politicians as Churchill and Foreign Secretary Anthony Eden, as well as that of Vice Admiral Mountbatten and the British military personnel serving under him in the Southeast Asia Command. However, it would seem that at the time that SEAC was created, in August 1943, the outlook of the British members of the Combined Chiefs of Staff as they turned away from Burma was geared more toward the Pacific, as opposed to Singapore and Malaya.

The trend on the part of the Americans of substantially increasing the resources committed to the war in the Pacific continued on a much larger scale during 1943.[12] The Americans could claim sole title to Guadalcanal from February 1943, having driven the last Japanese forces from the island. Meanwhile, MacArthur's forces in the southwest Pacific had taken the eastern half of New Guinea from the Japanese. In addition, on November 20, 1943, the Central Pacific drive got under way when American marines and infantry landed at Tarawa and Makin in the Gilbert Islands. Both had been British possessions before being taken by the Japanese a few days after the Pearl Harbor attack. The Gilberts campaign, known as operation Galvanic, was a furious three-day battle. At Tarawa a thousand American marines and approximately 4,500 Japanese naval infantry and Korean laborers were killed.

At the end of 1943, with Galvanic a costly success and Nimitz's forces poised to move from the Gilberts to the Marshalls, there were 1,878,152 American service personnel—navy, army, and air combined—involved in the war against Japan. This is slightly more than the 1,810,367 Americans who were deployed against Germany at that time.[13]

At the Casablanca Conference, in January 1943, the long-simmering differences between the Allies over the war in the Pacific broke into the open. The Combined Chiefs of Staff were thus forced to hammer out a compromise agreement. Clearly, at the time of the Casablanca Conference the British chiefs were still firmly wedded to the idea of maintaining a strictly defensive posture against Japan while focusing almost everything on the defeat of Germany.[14] Their dismay at the unwillingness of the Americans to accept any delay in offensive actions against the Japanese was evident when the British Joint Planning Staff reported in December 1942 that in the "U.S. Navy's opinion 'There is no such thing as strategic defensive in the Pacific.'"[15]

The American Joint Chiefs of Staff clearly had two strategies in the Pacific War, one for dealing with the Japanese and one for dealing with opposition from their British colleagues. From mid-1942 onward, the Americans operated under a liberal interpretation of the instructions that had been periodically set out for them in Combined Chiefs of Staff memoranda. These instructions were that the Allies must "maintain and extend unremitting pressure against Japan with the purpose of continually reducing her military power and attaining positions from which her ultimate surrender can be forced."[16] Through mid-1943, the British interpreted this to imply limited offensives, only to prevent consolidation of Japanese positions. The Americans interpreted these instructions as a blank check.

Admiral King reported at Casablanca to his colleagues on the Combined Chiefs that only 15 percent of Allied resources were currently being used against Japan and that this was not enough to prevent the Japanese from consolidating the gains they had made in the wake of the Pearl Harbor attack. As a solution, General Marshall suggested a split in Allied resources of 70 percent for Europe, 30 percent for the Pacific.[17]

The Combined Chiefs of Staff discussions at the Casablanca Conference were one of many occasions on which General Marshall outlined his strategic views. At Casablanca, Marshall made clear that in his heart he believed Germany to be the principal enemy and that it had to be beaten first. Nevertheless, he backed King at Casablanca by urging immediate offensive action in the Pacific. The reason for this seeming incongruity is that Marshall dreaded a sudden American reverse in the Pacific that would necessitate American abandonment of all commitments in Europe until the Pacific situation could be put right.[18] Marshall had already had some scares. For example, in the autumn of 1942 the crisis in the South Pacific, particularly the agonizingly drawn-out American effort to seize Guadalcanal, had been so tense that the Americans had seriously considered, but thankfully ultimately rejected, the idea of withdrawing the sizeable American contingent of troops, aircraft, and ships that had been earmarked for the joint Anglo-American Torch landings in North Africa, scheduled to begin in November. The Guadalcanal operation had been planned hurriedly and carried out on a shoestring; Marshall urged that more U.S. troops and equipment be sent to the Pacific because he felt that the Guadalcanal-style "hand-to-mouth policy" was dangerous for the Allies.[19] General Marshall told his colleagues on the Combined Chiefs of Staff at Casablanca "that the United States could not stand for another Bataan"—a reference to the way in which American forces had been run out of the Philippines by the Japanese in the spring of

1942.[20] Therefore, while Marshall was most interested in the war in Europe, he knew that planning for operations in Western Europe could not go forward unless it was accompanied by Allied success against Japan.

As stated previously, British military opinion underwent a dramatic transformation during the course of 1943 in regard to the war against Japan. At the beginning of the year, General Brooke vehemently opposed the American pull toward the Pacific.[21] This is interesting in light of the way in which the British chiefs later came to support the idea of the American Central Pacific drive and even wanted to participate in it. Never one to compromise easily, Brooke in early 1943 wanted to use all Allied resources against Germany alone;[22] he was alarmed at Casablanca to see Marshall backing King and the Pacific so heavily. From the time of Casablanca onward, Generals Brooke and Marshall would often find themselves at odds. They seemed to personify British-American differences of strategic viewpoint.[23]

During the course of the Casablanca Conference, Field Marshal Dill and Air Chief Marshal Portal were sympathetic to the American viewpoint. Dill and Air Vice Marshal Sir John C. Slessor (an aide to Portal) brokered an agreement on the Pacific that Brooke and the Americans could accept. It involved taking the fortified Japanese South Pacific air and naval base at Rabaul in New Britain, as well as bases in the Marshall and Caroline Islands. This plan was adopted with the proviso that these operations must not slow down the pace of the war against Germany. The spirit of compromise exhibited by Portal, Slessor, and Dill at Casablanca was reassuring to the Americans and may have helped to pave the way for the more in-depth agreements over Pacific strategy at which the Combined Chiefs of Staff would arrive later in the year.[24]

The Americans saw justification for the adoption of full-scale operations in the Pacific at an early date in plans outlined in July 1942 by the Combined Chiefs of Staff in one of their better-known papers, referred to as "CCS 94." The Americans interpreted this document to be something of a green light for the Pacific. CCS 94 all but committed the Western Allies to a descent upon the coast of northwest Africa (Torch) that autumn, precluding an invasion across the English Channel until after 1943. Added perhaps as a palliative to the American Joint Chiefs of Staff, who were adamantly opposed to the whole idea of what they regarded as a wasteful diversion to North Africa, was a provision that fifteen groups of American aircraft that had been destined for the buildup in England were to be diverted to the Pacific theater instead. Included were seven groups of

bombers, four of transport planes, and two each of fighters and observation planes.[25] The arrangement outlined in CCS 94 was confirmed in September 1942. The Americans therefore concluded that if the British were
not serious about the cross-channel invasion, it was time to reverse the
Arcadia decisions and concentrate on the war against Japan. (Incidentally,
the decision for Torch—one of questionable validity in terms of overall
strategy—was a rare instance of a major military campaign being framed
more by the president and the prime minister rather than by the Combined Chiefs of Staff. Opposition came mostly from the American chiefs,
while Brooke, Pound, and Portal gave their cautious support to the Torch
plan, although General Brooke was slower in warming to the idea than
were Pound and Portal.)[26]

Part of the reluctance of the British to commit Allied forces to the
Pacific theater during 1942 was their conception of the vast naval forces that
would be required to defeat Japan and what that would mean to the Battle of
the Atlantic. The British Chiefs of Staff felt that an aggressive Allied strategy
in the Pacific would so strip the Atlantic of naval forces that the security of
the British Isles and the Atlantic shipping lanes would be in grave danger.
The American warships most needed by the British in the Atlantic were the
small ships that excelled in submarine hunting, such as destroyers and escort
carriers.[27] In the summer of 1942, Dill wrote to Brooke in reference to the
war against Japan that "it is only by building the authority of the Combined
Chiefs of Staff that we can do anything to curb the tendency of the U.S.
Chiefs of Staff to take unilateral action without consultation."[28]

The defeat of the U-boats in the Atlantic by the summer of 1943 and the
American successes at Midway and on Guadalcanal seem to have had considerable effect upon the views of the British members of the Combined Chiefs
of Staff in regard to the war in the Pacific. This new attitude became apparent at the Trident Conference, in Washington in May 1943. There the British
chiefs agreed to an American plan that involved the following objectives:

1. Conduct of air operations in and from China
2. Ejection of the Japanese from the Aleutians
3. Seizure of the Marshall and Caroline Islands
4. Seizure of the Solomons, the Bismarck Archipelago, and Japanese-held
   New Guinea
5. Intensification of operations against enemy lines of communication.[29]

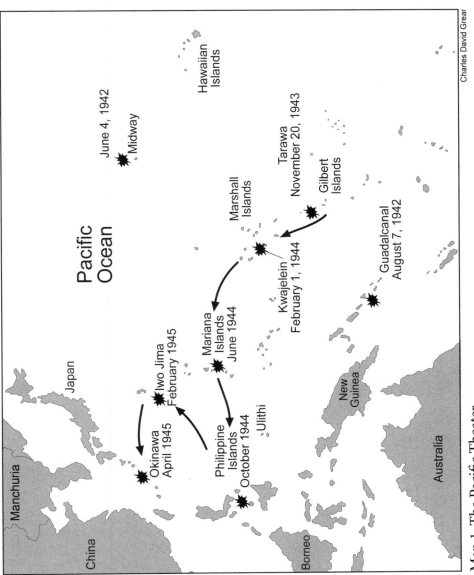

Map 1. The Pacific Theater

Charles David Grear

In addition to ongoing success against the U-boats, the British chiefs at Trident were in a generous mood in regard to the ambitious American plans for the Pacific theater because, according to Sir Michael Howard, by the spring of 1943 the availability of Allied resources, such as shipping, aircraft, and munitions, had caught up with Allied strategic planning.[30] This point is, however, in need of qualification. Specifically, the British Chiefs of Staff were now aware that simultaneous American offensives in the Central and South Pacific areas would not interfere with limited Allied operations in the Mediterranean, such as the exploitation of Torch. However, Allied resources in spring 1943 would, in the view of the British Chiefs of Staff, still not be sufficient to allow for a 1943 Overlord. The knowledge that the warships of the Royal Navy were more than adequate to deal with any surface action that the German navy might offer prevented the British chiefs from becoming unduly alarmed that new American heavy warships, such as the *Essex*-class large aircraft carriers, were being sent to the Pacific.[31] Also, whereas the primary fear of the British Chiefs of Staff in regard to Overlord was that the Allied armies would not prove large or powerful enough to defeat the German forces stationed in France, the early phases of the Central Pacific drive did not require large numbers of troops. It is true that as the islands Nimitz attacked became larger (e.g., Saipan, Okinawa), he used more and more infantry of the U.S. Army. However, Nimitz also accomplished a great deal with a modest number of marines, of which he never had more than six divisions' worth. Most of the fighting by American forces on Guadalcanal was carried out by the 1st Marine Division. Similarly, in the Gilberts, Tarawa was seized by the 2nd Marine Division, while the 27th Infantry Division took Makin. Clearly resources, in the form of numbers of troops, went further in the Pacific than they did in Europe.[32]

The U.S. Joint Chiefs of Staff were to get even greater concessions from the British in regard to strategy in the Pacific. At the Quadrant Conference, at Quebec in August 1943, the Americans received British sanction for "the seizure of the Eastern Carolines as far west as Woleai and the establishment of a fleet base at Truk[, and] . . . [t]he capture of the Palaus, including Yap[, as well as] the seizure of Guam and the Japanese Marianas."[33]

This British support for operations in the Pacific is in marked contrast to the concerns of the British members of the Combined Chiefs of Staff while the North African campaign was being planned. A few weeks before the Torch landings Dill had written to Brooke about American concerns in the Pacific in a much more conservative vein: "Americans very anxious about Guadalcanal. . . . If things go badly at Guadalcanal, as well they may, I fear a still greater drain on resources for Pacific, though call of Pacific strategically may wane as difficulty of doing the job without our full assistance becomes apparent."[34]

The call of the Pacific never waned for the Americans. By the beginning of 1944, the Americans were on the offensive everywhere in the Pacific theater. The preparations for the February 1944 assault on the Marshalls indicate the vast naval and amphibious power upon which the Americans were able to draw by that time. To seize three atolls in the Marshalls—Kwajelein, Majuro, and Eniwetok—Admiral Raymond Spruance's Fifth Fleet had at its disposal twelve aircraft carriers, eight battleships, six cruisers, thirty-six destroyers, 85,000 troops, and more than a thousand combat aircraft (both carrier- and shore-based). As in the Gilbert Islands, the fast new American aircraft carriers were crucial to the success of these operations. American carrier-based aircraft destroyed every Japanese airplane in the Marshall Islands on the first full day of the assault (February 1, 1944).[35]

For Admiral King, the path through the Central Pacific seemed obvious. It had figured prominently in discussions and war games at the Naval War College, in Newport, Rhode Island, in the 1920s and 1930s. The results had led to the formulation of a series of what were known as "Orange" plans (Japan having been referred to as "Orange" in the games). By the mid-1920s, it was clear to American naval planners that in the case of war against Japan the first order of business for the United States would be to build up an overwhelming superiority of naval strength in the western Pacific. Also inherent in these interwar American plans was the idea that the island bases that had been mandated to Japan after World War I, such as the Marshalls and the Carolines, would have to become advanced bases for American forces.[36] King referred to these twenty-year-old plans when he began stressing the need to advance through the Central Pacific. As early as July 1942 King began telling Nimitz that following the successful conclusion of American operations in the South and southwest Pacific, he should prepare to seize the Japanese fleet base at Truk in the central Carolines, as well as Guam and Saipan in the Japanese-held Marianas. King was determined in the wake of the Casablanca Conference to maintain the initiative in the Pacific, believing it crucial to keep the Japanese off balance.[37]

At Trident, King fought for and got, with the help of Admiral Pound, a draft statement allowing "a vigorous prosecution of the Pacific war."[38]

King liked the idea of a Central Pacific drive, which, he felt, would interfere with Japanese communications, allow the United States to come to grips with the Japanese fleet, and possibly "provide bases from which to bomb the Japanese home islands."[39] His insistence on the Central Pacific drive at a time when American forces were already advancing through the Solomons and in New Guinea shows King's mastery as a strategist. When the Guadalcanal campaign ended in February 1943, Admirals Nimitz and Halsey were both opposed to the idea of operations in the Central Pacific. They believed it would be better to press on in the Solomon Islands.[40] This seems to have been one of the rare occasions when the brilliant Nimitz needed to be nudged in the right direction by Admiral King. According to Grace Person Hayes, in her official history of the war against Japan, "To Admiral King the Pacific commanders seemed to be missing the point. It was quite necessary, he thought, to attack in the Central Pacific as well as in the Southwest Pacific in sufficient strength and at such a time that the two areas could support each other. At least an attempt should be made [as King put it] 'to whipsaw enemy rather than enable him to concentrate in Solomons or attack on Jaluit–Gilbert–Samoa line or on Midway–Pearl Line.'"[41]

The firm backing by the Chief of Naval Operations for the Central Pacific drive also demonstrated his appreciation of practical realities. King believed it was essential to get the United States heavily committed to the Central Pacific as a way to put an end to British complaints about the transfer of American naval vessels from the Atlantic.[42] This ability of the British members of the Combined Chiefs of Staff to influence the amount of supplies flowing to the Pacific theater sometimes had a hand in determining strategy there. Nimitz risked bad tides at Tarawa because King wanted to get the Central Pacific drive under way before the British could go back on their Quadrant pledge to devote more Allied resources to the war in the Pacific. Consequently, American casualties at Tarawa's Betio Island were heavier than they might have been, as many marines were forced to wade ashore under fire in chest-deep water because their landing craft were unable to float over the coral reef surrounding the island. In late December the tide would have been higher in the Gilberts.[43]

The way was made easier for King in dealing with the British over the Pacific issue in that, as Thorne writes, while the Central Pacific drive was getting under way, "little or no progress was being made on the ground during this period either in China or Southeast Asia."[44] From September 1942 to February 1943 British and Indian forces under Field Marshal Sir Archibald Wavell had conducted an offensive against the Japanese in the Arakan, but with disappointing results. Wavell's forces ended up back where they started. At that point, the Allies seem to have given up on traditional military operations in Southeast Asia for a time, turning instead to Brigadier Orde Wingate's "Chindit" operations. The first of Wingate's guerrilla campaigns took place from February to April 1943.[45]

MacArthur's advance in the southwest Pacific was steady but slower than what the wide-open spaces of the Central Pacific promised. The situation facing MacArthur was complicated. In addition to the strategic necessity of defeating Japanese forces on New Guinea, MacArthur had been instructed by the Joint Chiefs of Staff in July 1942 to take the key Japanese naval and air bases at Rabaul and Kavieng, in the Bismarck Archipelago. Consequently, MacArthur and his staff devised the Elkton plan of April 1943, a two-pronged advance to surround both Japanese bases. MacArthur's own forces were to move along the north coast of New Guinea and onto nearby islands, such as Woodlark and Trobriand. Meanwhile, the right arm of the pincer, consisting of Admiral Halsey's South Pacific forces, were to move north through the Solomon Islands from Guadalcanal. Halsey was under the command of Admiral Nimitz. However, since many of his operations, such as those against the Green Islands in February and March 1944, took place in the Southwest Pacific Area, Halsey cooperated closely with MacArthur. This unusual arrangement worked out well, because Halsey turned out to be one of the few naval officers MacArthur was able to get along with. In the end, it was possible to bypass rather than invade Rabaul and Kavieng. Halsey took Emirau, in the St. Mathias group, in March 1944 in an unopposed landing. By that time, MacArthur's forces had gone ashore on Manus, in the Admiralty Islands. These two operations provided the Americans with adequate substitutes for Rabaul and Kavieng, thus obviating the need to invade the Japanese strongpoints.[46]

By the summer of 1944, the overall plan being articulated by the U.S. Joint Chiefs of Staff for defeating Japan called for air and sea blockade, bombing, and destruction of the Japanese air force and navy, to be followed by invasion.[47] Clearly, the scale of the war against Japan had by then increased dramatically, such that the American Joint Chiefs felt it necessary to reassure the British chiefs that the Pacific campaign would not lessen the American commitment to Overlord (cross-channel) and Anvil (southern France) as the paramount operations for 1944.[48] There is a certain irony here, for at Trident and Quadrant it had been the JCS (especially Marshall, with his frustration at the British penchant for operations in the Mediterranean) who had pressed the British chiefs to give "overriding priority" to Overlord as the principal Allied campaign for 1944.[49] There was, however, a great deal of difference between the American views of operations in the Pacific and in the Mediterranean. As we shall see in chapter 5, Marshall and the U.S. Joint Chiefs of Staff felt that Allied operations in the Mediterranean were contributing very little (and at great Allied cost) to the defeat of Germany. The American successes in the Central Pacific, on the other hand, were clearly contributing a great deal to the defeat of Japan.

The British Chiefs of Staff were firmly against Culverin, Churchill's pet plan for an attack against the Japanese in Sumatra. Instead, the British chiefs were by February 1944 strong supporters of operations in the Pacific, particularly the Central Pacific drive. The British chiefs felt that the Central Pacific would provide greater benefits than the southwest Pacific. They saw the latter as difficult terrain and allowing only slower advances, although they conceded that the southwest Pacific drive would require smaller naval forces than would the Central Pacific campaign.[50] This British preference for the Central Pacific may have helped Admiral King to bring Marshall, Leahy, and Arnold around to his view of its paramount importance.

Clearly, the absence of British objections to American plans for the Pacific theater after mid-1943 was due not to a surrender by the British to American pressure, as is sometimes claimed, but rather to a dawning realization that those plans were sound and feasible. Another incorrect but prevalent view is that the British, once behind the idea of offensive operations against Japan concurrent with the war in Europe, were only interested in operating British forces in the South and southwest Pacific. While it is true that the British intended to establish a naval base, or bases, in Australia, where space for docking and repair facilities was much more plentiful than in the Central Pacific, where only limited land area was available, it appeared to the British Chiefs of Staff superfluous to continue slugging it out in the southwest Pacific when there was the opportunity to advance by leaps and bounds in the Central Pacific.[51] By early 1944, all the members of the Combined Chiefs of Staff seem to have been united as to how the Pacific War should be run, namely, by using both lines of advance in the Pacific, preeminently the Central Pacific route. Growing Allied power had made it clear that, in contrast to the strategy laid out earlier at the Arcadia Conference, full-scale operations against Japan in the Pacific need not await the defeat of Germany.

The creation in spring 1942 of two separate theater commands in the Pacific had certainly been due, at least in part, to interservice rivalry and the need to handle Douglas MacArthur delicately rather than to strategic vision. Neither the Joint Chiefs of Staff nor the president were willing to inform MacArthur (with his monumental ego and his seniority) that his command should be a part of the vast Pacific Ocean Areas command of Admiral Nimitz. Intensely jealous of the proportion of American resources, such as ships and aircraft, being sent to Nimitz, MacArthur fought even the slightest hint that the U.S. Joint Chiefs of Staff might be trying to place his advance into a supporting role with respect to that of Nimitz.[52] This is part of the explanation as to why MacArthur was allowed to conduct offensive, rather than strictly defensive, activities. According to Hayes, in April 1942, when MacArthur's Southwest Pacific Command was set up, the U.S. Joint Chiefs "did not contemplate large-scale offensives under General MacArthur's command or, indeed, in the Southwest Pacific Area. Moreover, the demands of other theaters precluded allocating to that area equipment or forces sufficient for an extensive program."[53]

While the existence of two theater commands in the Pacific may not have been the most efficient type of command structure, the system provided some unexpected benefits to the Allies. One of these was additional protection for Australia and New Zealand, which, as we have seen, was an American responsibility. Also, with two lines of advance in the Pacific, MacArthur's and Nimitz's forces were able to protect each other's flanks and made it necessary for the Japanese to disperse their own forces.[54]

The attitude of the Combined Chiefs as a whole in regard to the value of the Central Pacific drive had come around to King's way of thinking by the late summer of 1943. The decisions made by the Combined Chiefs of Staff at the first Quebec Conference (Quadrant) were heavily weighted toward the Central Pacific, as opposed to MacArthur's southwest Pacific advance.[55] This represented a significant change in the views of the Combined Chiefs of Staff. King—according to his biographer, Thomas B. Buell—in pressing the Central Pacific drive after Trident "was alone in supporting Nimitz over MacArthur."[56] In view of the great rewards that the Central Pacific strategy was to bring, it seems clear that Admiral King was easily the most gifted strategist among the Joint Chiefs of Staff, and probably of the Combined Chiefs of Staff as well.

The Central Pacific drive really picked up steam during the first eight months of 1944. Through the adroit use of the fast carriers, Nimitz's forces under Admiral Spruance were able to bypass strong points, such as Truk, in the Caroline Islands, and jump straight to the Marianas after the Marshalls campaign. This was an advance of a thousand miles westward in less than four months. MacArthur's forces in the southwest Pacific could not match the spectacular pace of the Central Pacific drive. In April 1944 MacArthur was still on the northern coast of New Guinea. He had been moving westward along that coast since January 1943.[57]

By spring 1944, the British Chiefs of Staff were discussing with Churchill three different strategies for the war against Japan. The first was the prime minister's Bay of Bengal strategy, aimed at restoring British prestige by moving against Japanese-occupied portions of the empire, such as Malaya and Singapore, using northern Sumatra as a jump-off point.[58] The second option was the Pacific strategy, which the British Chiefs of Staff preferred. This would involve, as stated by the British chiefs, "The concentration of all available British naval, amphibious, land and air forces to strengthen the main drive in the Pacific."[59] The third option, referred to as the "middle strategy," envisaged a British and Dominion campaign that would use Australia as a base for an advance on Borneo. The next step in this plan was flexible; it could be a British move north into the Pacific to assist the Americans or, depending upon the situation, operations against Malaya or Singapore. The British chiefs were lukewarm about the middle strategy, proposing it because (as we shall see) they were desperate to get Churchill away from the Bay of Bengal strategy.[60]

The desire of the British members of the Combined Chiefs of Staff to put a British battle fleet into the Pacific, as opposed to the Indian, Ocean brought them into conflict with both Admiral King and their own prime minister. King wanted the Royal Navy to leave the Pacific to the Americans and fight the Japanese in the Indian Ocean only. It seemed clear to the British that King perceived the potential of a British fleet in the Pacific as a threat to his ability to control day-to-day operations there.[61] According to Admiral Cunningham, Churchill's desire to put the fleet in the Indian Ocean was based on his desire to reoccupy lost parts of the British Empire, as well as the need to help Mountbatten, whose Southeast Asia Command had not initially been given enough troops and equipment to carry out large-scale offensives.[62] European imperialism was never a popular subject in the United States during the war.[63] Therefore, such an emphasis upon politics and recovering parts of the empire lost to Japan led to the derisive comment in the American military that SEAC really stood for "Save England's Asian Colonies."[64]

It was in the autumn of 1943, shortly after Admiral Cunningham had taken Pound's place with the Combined Chiefs of Staff, that the idea of putting a British fleet into the Pacific really took hold among the British chiefs. There was a precedent for this. Early March 1943 had found the British aircraft carrier HMS *Victorious* riding at anchor in Pearl Harbor, having been temporarily loaned to the Americans for operations in conjunction with the U.S. Pacific Fleet.[65] The idea for a powerful, all-British battle fleet to operate against Japan in the Central or South Pacific, or both, had originated with Admiral Cunningham. He correctly realized that it was in the Pacific that the war against Japan was being decided, not on the ground in China or Burma, and not in the Indian Ocean. It was in the Pacific, therefore, that the British could make their greatest contribution to victory in the war against Japan. It would also be much easier for Britain to provide logistical support for a fleet in the Pacific, rather than in the Indian Ocean. In addition to contributing materially to Allied victory over Japan, Cunningham knew that the Pacific strategy would give Great Britain leverage in any peace talks and in the postwar world. Brooke and Portal supported Cunningham's views fully in regard to a British Pacific fleet.[66]

Churchill's opposition was vigorous. Cunningham would recall in a postwar interview that Churchill's objections were so stubborn that "when at the Quebec Conference in September 1944 Mr. Churchill offered Mr. Roosevelt the British fleet for use in the Pacific (under American command) it came as a great surprise to the British Chiefs of Staff."[67] The offer was accepted by the president, a decision about which King was not happy. From the way Churchill had talked leading up to the conference, the British chiefs had no idea that they had finally succeeded in convincing him.[68] Cunningham claimed that "it was mainly due to Lord Portal's eloquence in debate that . . . Mr. Churchill finally agreed to the Pacific Strategy."[69] In fact, although both Churchill and Ismay soft-pedal the issue in their respective memoirs, there was apparently a real threat that the British chiefs, and perhaps Ismay as well, would have resigned if Churchill had persisted in his Bay of Bengal strategy.[70]

At the height of this crisis—in the summer of 1944, when the British chiefs were thoroughly at odds with the prime minister as to where the British fleet should fight Japan—Cunningham made a revealing entry in his diary explaining why he found Churchill's Bay of Bengal strategy so outrageous. He wrote that at a meeting with Churchill, Eden, Attlee, and Oliver Lyttelton (minister of production) the British Chiefs of Staff "had hoped to get some decision on Far Eastern strategy but we were treated to the same old monologue of how much better it was to take the tip of Sumatra & then the Malay Peninsula & finally Singapore then it was to join with the Americans & fight Japan close [to] home in the Pacific. The attitude of mind of the politicians about this question is astonishing. . . . They will not lift a finger to get a force into the Pacific. They prefer to hang about the outside and recapture our own rubber trees."[71]

In the same entry, Cunningham notes that Churchill's obsession with recovering lost parts of the empire seemed due to a desire not only to repair British prestige in the Far East but also to forestall the Americans. Cunningham felt that Churchill was overly concerned that the anticolonial Americans might declare immediate independence for Malaya and Singapore if Japan should surrender before Britain could reoccupy its prewar Asian territories.[72] Here is a parallel to Churchill's Balkan strategy in Europe. As with the Balkans, vis-à-vis the Russians, Churchill wanted to be on the ground in Asia with British forces for positioning purposes when the war ended. In this way he could outmaneuver a former ally (the Americans) who, like Russian forces in the Balkans, might have different ideas about the postwar fate of the territories concerned. As Thorne has pointed out, the heightened sense of anticolonial feeling that had become apparent in the United States during the war was a highly divisive issue between Churchill and Roosevelt and between the British and American elements of the Combined Chiefs of Staff.[73]

What Cunningham, Brooke, and Portal found so exasperating about Churchill's plans in the Far East is that those plans had no basis in strategic reality. The British Chiefs of Staff also felt that Churchill failed to perceive that the correct strategic option for Britain—the Pacific strategy—would quite likely bring political benefits to England as a by-product. Under this line of thinking, it seemed to the British chiefs, especially Cunningham, that the Americans would be far more likely to accede to postwar British wishes for Asia if Britain had provided concrete assistance in the final campaigns against Japan. The best way to provide such concrete assistance was to get a British fleet into the Central Pacific at the earliest opportunity.[74]

Not surprisingly, it seems that Admiral Cunningham came to despise the prime minister while serving on the Combined Chiefs of Staff.[75] This sentiment shows up repeatedly in Cunningham's diary, often in relation to the debates over the Pacific strategy. For instance, in regard to a report written by the British Chiefs of Staff for the Americans, just before the second Quebec Conference, in regard to the Pacific strategy, Cunningham's contempt for Churchill's abilities as a strategist is readily apparent: "Message to USCOS drafted this morning came back after dinner as amended by the P.M. As usual full of inaccuracies, hot air & political points. Not the sort of business like message we should send to our opposite numbers."[76]

The First Sea Lord suspected duplicity even when Churchill was brought around to the viewpoint of the British members of the Combined Chiefs of Staff. There is evidence that Churchill's offer to the Americans at the Octagon Conference of a British Pacific fleet did not indicate an actual change of heart on the part of the prime minister. The Chief of the Naval Staff recorded in his diary that at Quebec there was "one good political point he [Churchill] wishes to make. He wants to be able to have on record that the US refused the assistance of the British Fleet in the Pacific. He will be bitterly disappointed if they don't refuse!!!"[77] Churchill's hopes were dashed when President Roosevelt showed that he agreed with the British Chiefs of Staff by accepting the idea of a British fleet for operations in the Pacific. Had FDR refused the offer, Churchill could conceivably have gained leverage to coerce the British chiefs into approving the Culverin operation against Sumatra.[78]

According to Sir David Fraser in his biography of Brooke, with American acceptance at the second Quebec conference of a British fleet for operations against Japan, "the 'Pacific Strategy' quietly died."[79] He is apparently referring to the facts that the British Pacific fleet would operate under American control and that there would be no British land-based air or amphibious (infantry) components involved.[80] However, as far as the British Chiefs of Staff were concerned, the fact that a British battle fleet, including two battleships and four aircraft carriers, took up station with the American Pacific Fleet in December 1944 meant that the Pacific strategy was very much alive.

The British Chiefs of Staff had hopes that their fleet would operate in the Central Pacific. At Okinawa, it did.[81]

In pressing so hard for a British fleet in the Pacific, the British Chiefs of Staff were motivated by an urgency that grew out of American accusations that the British were following a "go-slow" policy in the war against Japan. Portal, Cunningham, and Brooke were eager to convince their American colleagues on the Combined Chiefs of Staff that this was not the case at all. As we have seen, American successes in the Pacific had caused the British members of the CCS to feel more optimistic about the potential for full-scale operations there. According to Grace Person Hayes, the situation among the Allied high command at the close of the Quadrant Conference in August 1943 was such that "there was no longer talk of [merely] holding a line in the Pacific until Germany should be defeated."[82]

Some of these accusations were reported to Cunningham by his staff. As director of plans at the Admiralty, Captain Charles Lambe, RN (a future Admiral of the Fleet and First Sea Lord), served as presiding member of the British Joint Planning Staff. He was thus very much a part of the Combined Chiefs of Staff Organization, and a close adviser to Admiral Cunningham.[83] Like Sir John Dill, Captain Lambe was sympathetic to the American viewpoint in regard to the war against Japan. Lambe kept Cunningham informed about American doubts as to Britain's resolve in that theater. Such information underlay Cunningham's motivation to press so vehemently for a British Pacific fleet. In a searching two-page analysis to Cunningham entitled "Anglo-American Relations," Lambe reported in February 1944 several areas where the Americans were extremely upset with British actions or lack of action. He felt that the Americans had good reason to be upset with British conduct of the war against Japan to date:[84]

> Seen from their angle, [the Americans] have during 1943:
> 1. Watched U.S. built Escort Carriers handed over to us and not used *anywhere* for months (modifications, etc.).
> 2. Heard at Trident, Field Marshal Wavell make long defeatist monologue about India and Burma. The impression given was disastrous.
> 3. Seen the only offensive carrier borne air operations of 1943 undertaken in the whole Atlantic carried out by [USS] *Ranger* while she was on loan. . . .
> 4. Heard us pressing for our Fleet Carriers to go to the Pacific but asking in the same breath for the Americans to give us 100% maintenance service in the area.[85]

Lambe further suggested that as a desperate remedy to dispel this negative image in the eyes of the Americans "C in C [Commander in Chief] Eastern Fleet should be ordered to carry out an operation with F.A.A. [Fleet Air Arm] aircraft *regardless of its importance* during the next six weeks."[86] Lambe clearly saw the need for quick action. He advised Cunningham that to do nothing would be to play into the hands of Churchill, with his bad ideas about how to fight the Japanese (e.g., Culverin). Lambe also urged Cunningham to meet face to face with Admiral King—privately, away from the formality of a Combined Chiefs of Staff meeting—in order to resolve this issue.[87]

Captain Lambe made a good impression on Admiral Cunningham, who decided that Lambe was the right man to help energize the British war effort against Japan. In mid-1944, Lambe was put in command of the aircraft carrier HMS *Illustrious,* which, after striking Japanese-held targets in the Dutch East Indies, moved into the Pacific. There the *Illustrious* and three other British carriers operated alongside American carriers during the Okinawa campaign as part of the newly constituted British Pacific Fleet, which became a subsidiary of the massive U.S. Fifth Fleet.[88]

Cunningham was getting similar advice from the British Admiralty Delegation of the Joint Staff Mission in Washington. From Washington Admiral Noble informed the First Sea Lord that Admiral King was very unhappy about the results of the Sextant (Cairo/Teheran) Conference of November–December 1943. King apparently blamed the lack of enthusiasm he felt the British chiefs exhibited in regard to Allied operations in the Far East for the cancelation of Operation Buccaneer, a proposed Allied assault to oust the Japanese from the Andaman Islands in the Bay of Bengal. The Americans had seen this operation as a prerequisite for a campaign to drive the Japanese out of Burma and thus reopen overland communication with China.[89] The serious conflicts that erupted between the British and the Americans over strategic planning for operations against Japan on the Asian mainland have already been described elsewhere by historians in eloquent detail;[90] there is no need to repeat them here. However, it is interesting to note that the cancelation at Cairo of the Andamans campaign served not only to infuriate the U.S. Joint Chiefs of Staff but also, as Christopher Thorne points out, to "put the weight of the Allied attack against Japan into the two Pacific spearheads."[91] This may have been a factor in the increasing support the British members of the Combined Chiefs of Staff displayed during 1943 in regard to expanded American operations in the Pacific. For them, such a course of action may have provided a welcome alternative to an extensive land campaign in Burma.[92]

Noble also forwarded to Cunningham the views of British and American staff officers in Washington in regard to American accusations of the British "going slow" against Japan. A member of Noble's staff at the British Admiralty Delegation of the Joint Staff Mission in Washington, Commander Richard Smeeton, RN, wrote after serving as an observer aboard the new American aircraft carrier *Essex* during Galvanic, "As a personal note I must confess that the recent Galvanic operations left a slightly bitter taste in my mouth; while our own carriers were apparently inactive, I did not enjoy seeing our Ally employing nineteen aircraft carriers in a hard fought battle for the Gilberts, where incidentally we promptly installed a British administrator!"[93]

An American friend of Smeeton's in Washington, Captain Artie Doyle, USN, expressed similar views from the American side. Doyle was a naval aviator who would go on to command the *Essex*-class carrier USS *Hornet* during the final year of the war in the Pacific.[94] While attending the Sextant Conference as a member of King's staff, Doyle was alarmed by the extremely pessimistic attitude shown by some members of the British delegation in regard to operations against Japan. Doyle felt the British were far too cautious, even defeatist. Doyle wrote Smeeton that it had been his impression at the Sextant Conference that the admirals of the Royal Navy's Fleet Air Arm high command had been sadly lacking in any kind of initiative, due to excessive war weariness.[95] Perhaps he was struck by the contrast between those officers and the American "aviator admirals," such as Marc Mitscher, Frederick C. "Ted" Sherman, J. J. Clark, and Arthur Radford, who were always very aggressive and eager to show what their aircraft carriers could do. Doyle informed Smeeton that, due to his frustration over British pessimism during the Cairo/Teheran sessions, he "finally challenged a statement that 150 CV based VF [carrier-based fighter-plane squadrons] weren't enough to cover an amphibious landing. How the hell could Halsey and MacArthur have got anywhere with that attitude?"[96] (In naval parlance, VF refers to a fighter *squadron*. However, it is possible that Doyle was referring here to 150 fighter *aircraft*, total.)

The British Chiefs of Staff apparently took such criticisms to heart. It is very interesting that, apparently under Cunningham's tutelage, the British chiefs ultimately eschewed peripheral strategies and opted for a plan "to strike at the centre and, if necessary, to invade Japan."[97] It is interesting that the British chiefs were here acting the way the U.S. Joint Chiefs did with Overlord. That is, the British chiefs used the Pacific strategy to battle Churchill's colonial and peripheral Bay of Bengal idea just as Marshall and the U.S. Joint Chiefs of Staff argued forcefully against British ideas for peripheral, diversionary campaigns in the Mediterranean and the Balkans because such sideshows would have endangered the primacy of Overlord in Allied planning.[98] This seems to indicate that by the spring of 1944 Cunningham's influence with his British Chiefs of Staff Committee colleagues had grown considerably. In view of the dislike of peripheral strategies that he demonstrated during the debate over the Pacific strategy, it is interesting to speculate whether the British Chiefs of Staff would have come out at Casablanca for an early Overlord had Cunningham been with them then.

FOUR

Related Advantages

Working with Allies and Mobilizing Fully

On February 6, 1945, a rather unusual event occurred. On that day a German submarine, *U-862*, torpedoed and sank an American troopship that had been in transit between Australia and Ceylon. Sinkings due to submarines in wartime are not in and of themselves unusual. The novel aspects of this particular attack were, first, that the Indian Ocean was not the normal stalking ground for German submarines, and second, that such activity there represented a type of combined operation between Germany and Japan, something that was exceedingly rare in World War II. The German fleet commander, Admiral Karl Doenitz, had dispatched a number of German U-boats to the Indian Ocean beginning in June 1943. The disastrous defeat his submarines had suffered at the hands of the Allies in the Battle of the Atlantic had forced him to find a new locale for operations. Doenitz chose the Indian Ocean as a less dangerous hunting ground; he knew that Allied antisubmarine defenses there would be nowhere near as formidable as the gauntlet of Allied submarine-hunting ships and aircraft that, by the summer of 1943, had become highly specialized in the art of tracking down and destroying any U-boat that dared to threaten the Atlantic sea-lanes.[1]

Admiral Doenitz got some assistance from his Japanese ally during his Indian Ocean venture. The Japanese built a naval base for German use on the island of Penang in the Strait of Malacca. In addition, Japanese submarines sometimes operated in tandem with German U-boats in the hunt for Allied merchant ships in Indian Ocean waters. While German U-boats operating there succeeded in sinking fifty-seven Allied ships, for a combined total of 365,807 tons, the German loss rate quickly became as catastrophic as it had been in the Atlantic. Twenty-two of the U-boats sent to the Indian Ocean were sunk by Allied air and surface attack.[2]

It may never have occurred to the crews of these German submarines that they were engaging in just about the only form of cooperation the German-Japanese alliance would ever know. Such a situation contrasts sharply with the large-scale combined operations that the Allies were able to carry out during the war. On large, strategic issues of crucial importance, Germany, Japan, and Italy each operated in an almost entirely unilateral manner. Such independent behavior was, of course, motivated by self-interest. However, the nearly complete lack of thought the Axis nations gave to trying to determine what were the best interests of their alliance as a whole (and how to act on those interests as a coalition) worked greatly against the best interests of each of the three nations individually. Admittedly, it might have been difficult for the Axis nations to find any common ground, even if they had tried. For example, Japan's goals in Southeast Asia were geared largely toward acquiring natural resources. Germany, on the other hand, was fighting an ideological war of annihilation against Russia, a war in which German strategic objectives were at best of secondary importance. The military campaigns of the Axis nations did have some common aspects, but not of the types that were conducive to the forging of an effective coalition. For example, in contrast to its forays into Southeast Asia, Japan's war against China was just as lacking in strategic objectives as was Hitler's war against the Soviet Union. Also, all three of the Axis nations felt they could win their respective military objectives quickly.

Their failure to work effectively as a coalition was especially damaging to the Axis nations in World War II because they and their satellites (such as Bulgaria, Hungary, Romania, and Thailand) were opposed by an alliance that, though comprising twenty-six nations, was able to operate with more efficiency and greater cohesion than had any previous alliance. To be sure, the Big Three nations—the United States, Great Britain, and the Soviet Union—had far more influence in setting the Allied agenda than did less powerful members of the alliance, such as Brazil and New Zealand. Nevertheless, the Allies fought as a true coalition right from the beginning, although, like all coalitions, they had their problems. The difference was that inter-Allied friction never reached ruinous proportions.

On January 1, 1942, a mere three weeks after the Pearl Harbor attack, the Allies signed the "Declaration of the United Nations," in which the importance of full cooperation between nations was spelled out explicitly. This agreement stated that full-scale war against the Axis was necessary and identified "complete victory" as the goal.[3] (This, incidentally, proves that the unconditional surrender of the Axis nations was an Allied war aim long before the Casablanca Conference convened.) In striving toward that objective, the declaration stated, "Each government pledges itself to co-operate with the governments signatory hereto and not to make a separate armistice or peace with the enemies."[4]

The collective memory among Combined Chiefs of Staff members, all of whom had been in uniform during World War I, of how badly the alliance that finally muddled through to victory in World War I had been mismanaged created a desire to cooperate more effectively in order to achieve better results the second time around.[5] Indeed, the lack of cooperation and planning that had been characteristic of the alliances on both sides during World War I provided an important lesson for the future. It was to be demonstrated during World War II that the British and the Americans, and to some extent the Russians, learned these lessons far better than did the Germans and the Japanese. Franklin Roosevelt and the Joint Chiefs of Staff were fully aware that maintaining an aloofness from one's allies could be very costly. By joining the allied side in World War I as an "associated" instead of an "allied" power, the United States had greatly handicapped the peace process at Versailles in 1919.[6] At that time, President Woodrow Wilson had an entirely different agenda for peace from his British and French cobelligerents. In World War II, the Americans made more of an effort to find common and consistent war aims in all the decisive theaters. However, they were not always successful in this attempt.

A consistent set of war aims was something the Axis nations clearly lacked. Japan's war with China was already in a holding pattern by the time Hitler attacked Poland on September 1, 1939, having ground to a virtual halt largely for lack of any specific objectives. In the Pacific, Japanese war aims consisted of little more than digging in to fortify Japan's newly captured island empire and hoping that its navy could serve as enough of a deterrent to keep the Americans away while Japan used its newly acquired resources to strengthen its domestic economy and its military machine.[7] German General Staff officers such as General Franz Halder were greatly dismayed to find in the spring of 1941, while planning Barbarossa, that in the forthcoming invasion of the Soviet Union Germany had *no* strategic objectives. It was difficult for the German generals to develop a coherent plan or timetable for a campaign in Russia that was to be an ideological war of annihilation against what Hitler and Nazi propaganda described as "Asiatic-Jewish Bolshevism."[8]

The disastrous Nivelle offensive of April 1917 showed how dangerous had been the World War I practice of allowing a major military campaign to be dictated by the vanity of a supreme commander in the field. General Robert Nivelle sent the French army into a futile frontal assault against a heavily defended and prepared German position, despite the fact that high-ranking civilian and military French officials, such as Paul Painlevé and Philippe Petain, had urged him not to undertake a campaign that was destined to fail even before it began. The terrible slaughter that resulted was a direct cause of the mutinies in the French ranks that occurred in May 1917.[9] Similar mismanagement was apparent on the Allied southern front in World War I. In one of the most dramatic allied setbacks of World War I, Austrian and German troops broke through the Italian lines at Caporetto on the Austro-Italian border on October 24, 1917. The Italians were forced into an eighty-mile retreat in which they suffered 80,000 casualties. Eleven infantry divisions from the western front had to be rushed to Italy to help restore the situation.[10] The defeat at Caporetto was very significant for allied strategy in World War I; according to Leon Wolff, "if nothing else, Caporetto had proved that the Allies could not go on much longer without coordinating their war efforts."[11] This change in outlook quickly became apparent. While noting that British and French troops had begun to arrive in Italy, the November 5, 1917, edition of the *New York Times* quoted the U.S. secretary of war as stating that "the western front today stretches from the North Sea to the Adriatic. The Venetian Plain has become part of the western battle front."[12]

It was precisely to avoid such disjointed and belated strategic planning that the Combined Chiefs of Staff was created in January 1942. It was clear to the Allies in World War II that it was much better to allow grand strategy to be planned by a command staff that was removed from any one particular front and thus able to take into account the war situation as a whole. In that way, offensive operations could be planned and resources allocated in the most efficient manner possible.[13]

The war against the German U-boats makes a good starting point for discussing British-American cooperation during World War II. The German defeat in the Battle of the Atlantic became apparent in April and May 1943. It was characterized both by the ability of Allied shipyards to produce new merchant ships faster than German U-boats could sink them and by the fact that new antisubmarine equipment and tactics, such as escort carriers organized into "hunter-killer" groups and short-wave, ten-centimeter radar carried by patrol aircraft, were enabling the Allies to track down and destroy U-boats at sea in greatly increasing numbers. The Battle of the Atlantic is an example of a combined operation in which the British and the Americans achieved success because they worked together. The two nations shared the duty of providing warships to escort convoys of merchant vessels in the North Atlantic shipping lanes, and Allied aircraft from the decks of aircraft carriers hunted submarines with great success. British and American crews also operated long-range patrol aircraft from both sides of the Atlantic to provide constant air cover for convoys. The two allies also exchanged technical information about innovative antisubmarine weaponry, such as the Hedgehog-type depth charge.[14]

From July 1942 onward, with the exception of the month of December 1942, Allied shipping construction outpaced sinkings due to U-boats. However, it was the sharply rising curve of German submarine losses in the spring of 1943 that was the most important aspect of the Allied victory in the Atlantic. The losses inflicted upon Admiral Doenitz's submarine fleet were accompanied by greatly reduced Allied merchant tonnage sunk. In March 1943, German submarines sank 514,744 tons of Allied merchant shipping in the Atlantic, while only eleven U-boats were destroyed by the Allies. Two months later, in May, Allied shipping losses were well under half the March rate, while the number of U-boats destroyed shot upward. U-boat losses during May 1943 are a matter of some debate, but everyone agrees that they were catastrophically heavy—more than a German submarine per day was sunk. At least thirty-seven, and as many as forty-seven, German submarines were lost due to Allied air and sea action that month. The latter figure represented fully half of Doenitz's total force. Admiral Pound's biographer puts the figure at forty-one U-boats destroyed during May.[15] These figures tell the tale. As Churchill wrote, "By June 1943 the shipping losses fell to the lowest figure since the United States had entered the war. The convoys came through intact, and the Atlantic supply line was safe."[16]

After the Pearl Harbor attack, the Axis powers made some half-hearted attempts at outlining a joint plan for the conduct of the war. Germany, Japan, and Italy supplemented the Tripartite Pact of September 27, 1940, by signing further diplomatic and military agreements in January 1942. This was little more than window dressing, however. The Allied camp, by way of contrast, constituted a real alliance. From the Pearl Harbor attack through the surrender of Japan, the Allies fought together as a true coalition, while the Germans and the Japanese hurt each other greatly through their inability, or unwillingness, to coordinate their war efforts in any meaningful way.[17]

There are many examples of the consistent failure to cooperate among the Axis. As the war turned against Germany, Hitler and his General Staff desperately wanted to see Japan open an offensive against the Russians in maritime Siberia.[18] This would have greatly eased the German situation in the war against Russia. Instead, Japan and Russia maintained a shaky, suspicion-laden truce until Soviet forces moved into Manchuria on August 7, 1945, three months after the defeat of Germany and only one week before Japan itself surrendered to the Allies. From the time it began on June 22, 1941, the German-Russian war was a diplomatic disaster for Japan, because it made it almost inevitable that Britain, the United States, and the Soviet Union would become full military allies. Japan's prime minister, Konoe Fumimaro, was fully aware in the summer of 1941 that engaging in hostilities against the Russians and the Americans simultaneously was out of the question for Japan. It was the fervent desire of the Konoe government to drive those two powers apart. What the Germans did by invading the Soviet Union was to bring them together. It is true that FDR and Winston Churchill had hoped that Russia would enter the war against Japan at an earlier date. However, the Russians clearly did much more to help the Allied effort as a whole by concentrating all of their military and industrial energies upon defeating Nazi Germany.[19]

The amount of important information the Axis nations kept from each other boggles the mind. In spite of the Tripartite Pact, Germany, Japan, and Italy repeatedly kept each other in the dark in regard to issues of vital strategic significance. A prime example is that no official advance notice was given to Germany by Mussolini before Italian forces moved into Greece from Albania on October 28, 1940.[20] Mussolini deeply resented not being privy to the details of previous German moves. Now was his chance to cash in. In his own words, Mussolini complained that "Hitler always faces me with faits accomplis. This time I am going to pay him back in his own coin. He will find out from the papers that I have occupied Greece."[21]

The Germans hid their intentions from the Japanese, as well as from the Italians. On the eve of Barbarossa, Hitler did not even bother to inform his Japanese allies that he had decided to invade the Soviet Union. Other actions toward Japan seem to display very little in the way of careful consideration on the part of Hitler. Historians such as Jeremy Noakes and Geoffrey Pridham have noted that Hitler's impulsive decision to declare war upon the United States after Pearl Harbor remains something of an enigma. It was not mandated by the Tripartite Pact, since Japan itself had not been attacked. Even if it had been mandated by the pact, violating treaties had never caused Hitler to lose sleep. It is also odd that Hitler made his declaration of war against the United States on December 11, 1941, in a speech to the Reichstag in Berlin. That was out of character for him—sudden, surprise attack was much more Hitler's style. Also, the prospect of keeping the United States neutral, or at least out of Europe, was one reason that Germany had signed the Tripartite Pact in the first place. The Germans had hoped that as Japan targeted Britain's Asian possessions, the Americans could be frightened by the prospect of a two-front war into remaining on the sidelines. There had been no discussion between Tokyo and Berlin as to what the appropriate German response should be if Japan were to make a surprise attack against the United States.[22]

None of the Allied nations were prepared, in terms of military strength and munitions production, for a major war when it came. Yet one of the greatest assets of Great Britain, the United States, and the USSR was that each realized from the outset how desperate was the struggle in which they were all engaged. An interesting fact in regard to the Allied nations in World War II is that each did everything it could to avoid going to war but once involved did not hesitate to impose very strict emergency measures that, designed to win the war, resulted in harsh restrictions upon the everyday lives of their citizens.[23]

The British had waited until they were two years into World War I before instituting conscription. There was no such hesitation in World War II. Similarly, the Americans instituted their first-ever peacetime draft in 1940. This was part of an American mobilization of resources that had really began in 1939, although American entry into the war was delayed for two years. Important spurs for early mobilization of the U.S. economy were the munitions orders placed by the British and the French after war broke out in Europe, but before Pearl Harbor. In March 1940, the British and French governments sought and obtained permission from President Roosevelt and General Arnold to purchase the latest combat types of American aircraft.[24]

The Americans therefore put the 1939–41 period to good use in terms of industrial mobilization. By the end of 1940, for example, federal government money flowing from a new U.S. government agency known as the Defense Plant Corporation was beginning to be used to finance the construction of new aircraft factories in the United States. Indeed, the impressive photographs taken in 1942 or 1943 of the bustling interiors of cavernous American aircraft factories during World War II are usually not of plants that had been idle during the Great Depression; they instead show factories that had not even *existed* in 1935. One of the most amazing aspects of the American wartime economy was that before all those weapons and supplies could be produced, a great many brand new factories had to be built. Direct government financing of the construction of new munitions plants, or favorable government loans to private companies that wished to build or expand their own factories, would become standard practice during the war.[25] Aircraft manufacturers took advantage of loans that were available. However, according to the official historians of the Army Air Forces, when it came down to loans versus direct government financing to build new aircraft factories, "More commonly, the government simply built the plant at its own cost, usually acting through the Defense Plant Corporation, and then leased it to a private concern for operation. . . . By February 1941 federal financing of new plant facilities had reached a figure almost ten times the sum invested by private agencies."[26]

A good example of this procedure in operation is that during 1941, as American entry into the war began to look more and more like a certainty, it became apparent that the Boeing factory in Seattle would not be able to produce by itself all the B-17 bombers that would be needed. Consequently, by order of the Army Air Forces (that is, General Arnold) and the Office of Production Management (OPM), two other manufacturers, Douglas and Vega (the latter an affiliate of Lockheed), were recruited to build B-17s under license. Boeing and Douglas were bitter rivals, and it must have been with considerable distaste that the directors at Boeing, forced by Arnold and OPM, handed over the blueprints for their best-selling aircraft, the B-17, to Douglas engineers. This meant that by order of two federal government agencies, B-17s (some 12,000 in all) would be built by Boeing in Seattle, by Vega in Burbank, California, and by Douglas in a brand-new factory in Long Beach, California. The construction of the Douglas–Long Beach facility was apparently initially to have been financed by a government loan under highly favorable repayment terms, with Douglas being the building's owner of record. However, unfavorable tax laws in California that would have greatly increased the cost for Douglas resulted in a decision to make Douglas–Long Beach a factory owned lock, stock, and barrel by the federal government.[27] That is, the federal government purchased the land, paid the construction costs, and owned the finished factory as well as every single machine tool inside the plant. All Donald Douglas had to do was operate the plant—at a booming profit. There is a name for this kind of government planning and ownership of the means of production—socialism. For the three years and nine months that the United States was involved in World War II, the American economy, self-proclaimed bastion of free enterprise and laissez-faire economics, achieved miracles of production never seen before or since under this most un-American form of government.

The success of Allied economic mobilization is indicated by the production figures. In 1942, its first full year as a combatant, the United States was able to produce 47,836 aircraft. This was three times as many aircraft as Germany was able to manufacture in the same period and almost double what Germany and Japan together were able to turn out that year. In 1943, the number of American aircraft produced for the year shot up to over 85,000, comfortably maintaining a three-to-one margin over German aircraft production. The Russians had to move entire munitions factories, piece by piece, from European Russia over the Ural Mountains so that full wartime weapons production could take place, unhindered, outside the path of the German advance. Despite these difficulties, Russian aircraft production was up to almost 35,000 for the year 1943, while German production lagged behind at 24,807 aircraft for 1943. In the United States, a ruling of the War Production Board that became effective on February 1, 1942, halted the production and sale of civilian passenger automobiles in the United States. Henceforth, the resources of the American automobile industry would be used solely to manufacture military vehicles, aircraft, and other assorted munitions for the duration of the war.[28]

Douglas builds B-17s at Long Beach. Every inanimate object you see in this photograph was owned by the federal government. The factory itself was built at taxpayer expense, and the federal government owned the building and all of the machine tools inside it. Boeing was forced to turn over the B-17 blueprints to its hated rival, Douglas. *Library of Congress, Prints & Photographs Division, FSA/OWI Collection*

For a variety of reasons, Germany did not even begin to institute a true wartime economy until the beginning of 1942 at the earliest. Hitler felt the war would be short. Indeed, his Blitzkreig strategy depended upon it. The Nazis were consistently opposed to allowing German women to work in munitions factories. This in itself served to severely limit the production of war materiel in Germany, because labor was always in short supply.[29] Also, as Richard Overy has noted, German industrial workers and factory managers were strangely resistant to the idea of true mass production and its corollary, the standardization of designs, preferring to build relatively modest numbers of a wide variety of weapons exhibiting the highest degree of craftsmanship rather than huge numbers of just a few types of weapons that were "good enough."[30] However, the most important reason behind the failure of Germany to adopt an effective war economy at an early date had to do with morale. According to Gordon Craig, "Hitler was convinced that it was the home front's collapse that had defeated the German army in 1918, and he was resolved to prevent a repetition of that."[31]

This, by the way, is interesting evidence that deep down, Hitler knew the "stab in the back theory" to be what it truly was—pure propaganda. Germany had been militarily defeated in 1918, and Hitler knew it. Accordingly, trying to prevent the German people at home from becoming depressed because of the new war was an important wartime goal of the Nazis. This task was difficult for Joseph Goebbels and his propaganda apparatus right from the start, because German public opinion was never enthusiastic about World War II, even during the victories of the early days. With this in mind, Hitler's government remained unwilling to ask the German people to reduce their use of consumer goods in any appreciable way during the war. This meant that until early 1942 the German economy was mobilized only to the extent that it had been in 1936—when the Four Year Plan had been set in motion.[32] During this entire period, according to Gordon Craig, "the production of armaments did not increase significantly, nor did that of consumer goods decline."[33] Overy has pointed out that unlike Russian and American military and civilian leaders, who believed that the winner in the war would be the side that outproduced the other in terms of munitions and supplies, Hitler "did not consider economics as central to the war effort. Rather, he stuck to the view that racial character—willpower, resolve, endurance—was the prime mover; weapons mattered only to the extent that they could be married to the moral qualities of the fighting man."[34]

Consequently, and also as a result of the fact that Britain lost no time in mobilizing fully during World War II, as early as 1940 British aircraft production pulled ahead of that of Germany. In fact, weapons production programs in general in Germany exhibited no special urgency until 1942. For the initial phase of Barbarossa the Germans were able to field 3,648 tanks. However, the vast majority of these were antiquated machines. Fewer than five hundred were Panzer IVs, which were in 1941 the only German tanks that had any chance at all against the Russian T-34s and KV-1s. In June 1941 the Russians had 15,000 tanks available, of which 1,861 were of the T-34 or KV-1 type.

It was not until the spring of 1942 that German munitions factories began to be kept open at night to operate second, and perhaps third, shifts. This is quite surprising, since by that time Germany had been at war for two and a half years. American, British, and Russian munitions makers showed no such hesitation in instituting night work in weapons factories. German aircraft production lagged badly early in the war, comprising less than 12,000 units in 1941—a year in which the United States produced more than 26,000 aircraft, even though until the very end of that year it was not yet a formal combatant.[35] The Russians would go on to produce T-34s, the war's finest tank, on a grand scale in terms of numbers. Even when the German Tiger and Panther tanks entered service in late 1942 and early 1943, the Russians still held the tank advantage. The new German tanks were responsible for the Russian decision to up-gun the T-34 from a 76.2-mm gun at the outset of the war to an 85-mm cannon later. However, although the Tiger in particular has attained almost mythical status among tank enthusiasts, it was always "not" many things that the T-34 "was." The Tiger was *not* fast, it was *not* mechanically reliable, it was *not* easy to repair, it did *not* turn quickly, and it was *not* easy to produce.[36]

Behind this German lack of preparation for war lies the origins of the Blitzkrieg strategy. Violent attacks of short duration utilizing sophisticated technological weapons (such as tanks and aircraft) were designed to lead to quick victories. Blitzkrieg was supposed to keep German casualties to a minimum and the German people from getting war weary. The industries of each conquered nation could be added to the German war economy, thus dispensing with the need to expand German production at home. The ability of the Russians to regroup and defeat the Germans outside Moscow in December 1941 meant that the war in Russia would be long and would require a belated and extensive mobilization of German resources. The German defeat in the battle of Moscow proved that Blitzkrieg had failed utterly.[37]

Like Germany, Japan was completely unprepared for a long war. At the time of America's entry into the war, Japan had a vast and powerful navy. Among the most important parts of that navy were the elite highly trained carrier-based air squadrons, such as those that had carried out the Pearl Harbor attack on December 7, 1941. There was, however, no real plan to replace Japanese ships that might be sunk or combat pilots who might be killed. Japan expected the war with the United States to be short, victorious, and virtually free of Japanese casualties. Defeat in the battle of Midway (June 3–6, 1942) was disastrous for Japan in many ways. Four irreplaceable Japanese aircraft carriers were sunk, and Japan's navy would never again hold the strategic initiative in the war. It is interesting to note that equally

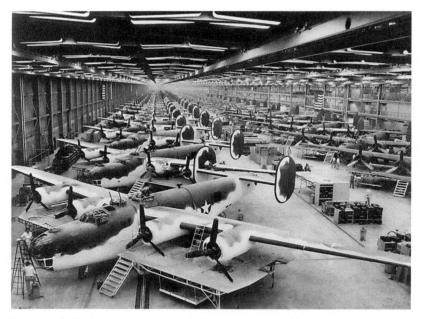

B-24Ds on the line in another government-built, government-owned factory—the Consolidated-Vultee plant in Fort Worth, Texas, shown here in late 1942 or early 1943. Supervisors rode bicycles to get around inside this massive facility. *U.S. Air Force Historical Research Agency and General Dynamics, Inc., respectively*

as irreplaceable as the four aircraft carriers were the hundred experienced Japanese pilots who were killed at Midway. As with the ships, there was no way for Japan to make good these losses. In the period from December 7, 1941, until August 14, 1945, Japan added only three full-sized aircraft carriers to its battle fleet from new construction (and lost in action by the end of 1944 all six of those that it had possessed at the outset of the war). Largely as a result of the Two-Ocean Navy Act of July 1940, enacted while the United States was still at peace, the Americans placed eighteen large, fleet-type, aircraft carriers into commission during the same time period. (In addition, the Americans already had six large carriers in service at the time of the Pearl Harbor attack.) The British completed six large aircraft carriers of their own between 1940 and 1945. The disparity in output is even more dramatic if small aircraft carriers are included. The Americans built 119 of these during the war, while Japan started the war with six small carriers and created a dozen others during the war, mostly by converting ships initially built for different purposes. The Japanese also had no large-scale training program for new pilots during the war, while the Americans went all out for pilot training. As the war continued, the flying skills of Japanese aviators deteriorated markedly due to losses and lack of adequate training for replacements, while American pilots got better and better and became available in ever growing numbers.[38]

Clearly, in terms of both cooperation and mobilization, the Allies were way ahead of the Axis nations throughout the war. Indeed, cooperation was simply one form of their all-out mobilization for war. The Allied nations understood fully that they were in for a long war. This is why Britain, the United States, and the Soviet Union mobilized fully right from the outset (or even before the outset) of hostilities. Allied cooperation reached truly unprecedented levels in many areas, such as the aforementioned mobilization. For example, the Americans and the British regarded the munitions they each produced as collectively constituting a (more or less) common pool from which both nations could draw as needed.[39] Clearly, the Allies, particularly the Americans and the British, understood that a long war would require close international cooperation to ensure victory. As the common "munitions pool" indicates, this inter-Allied cooperation was so extensive that it sometimes approached a type of joint sovereignty between the United States and Great Britain.

There were degrees of cooperation among the Allies. As noted earlier, the most powerful members of the alliance, The United States, the Soviet Union, and Great Britain, exercised much greater control over the war effort than did the other members of the Grand Alliance. Even within the Big Three nations there was the important variation that the Americans and the British cooperated very closely while both endured strained and difficult relations with the Soviet Union. For instance, the headline for the May 8, 1945, edition of the *New York World Telegram* announced much more than the end of the war in Europe when it proclaimed, "Nazis Give Up: Surrender to Allies and Russia Announced."[40] On the surface, such a headline may not seem surprising, in view of the fact that the German surrender to Eisenhower, which was signed at Reims on May 7, 1945, was followed two days later by a second ceremony in Berlin, where the remnants of the German army had recently suffered their final defeat at the hands of the Russians. However, referring to the "Allies and Russia"—that is, as two different things—has a deeper significance. There were often serious disagreements between the Americans and the British in regard to strategy. This however, did not prevent the military efforts of both nations from functioning as one, highly cohesive whole. The Russians, on the other hand, with no permanent representative on the Combined Chiefs of Staff, were left to conduct their military efforts in isolation, at least until the Cairo/Teheran Sextant Conference.[41] There were some in the Combined Chiefs of Staff organization who felt that the Russians wanted it this way. Major General John R. Deane, in his capacity as head of the U.S. Military Mission in Moscow, fit into this category. Deane felt that, even after the Overlord campaign had opened a second front in Western Europe, "the Soviets have a natural desire to remain operationally unhampered by Allies."[42] Indeed, it seemed that the Grand Alliance had two distinct components, the Russian and the British-American. Despite this mistrust between Moscow and its Western Allies, the level of Russian interallied cooperation was much higher than that for the German-Japanese alliance.

General Deane had arrived in Moscow in October 1943 as part of a shake-up of American political and military representatives that, it was hoped, would lead to improved relations between Washington and Moscow. Deane seemed particularly well suited to his new assignment. He knew about plans, and he had high-level contacts from his days on the Secretariat of the Joint and Combined Chiefs of Staff.[43] Deane brought with him a small but talented staff that included a Lend-Lease expert, Brigadier General Sidney Spalding, who had participated in the negotiations over the Third Russian Protocol. As part of this shake-up, Averell Harriman replaced Admiral William Standley as U.S. ambassador to Moscow. Standley thought the Russians did not appreciate the Lend-Lease aid they were receiving from the British and the Americans and had been quite vocal in expressing this view while he was in Moscow. Clearly this kind of attitude wouldn't do, and Standley had to go.[44]

Whether or not Deane's view was accurate that the Russians did not want to work within a coalition format, it is interesting to speculate as to what would have happened had the Combined Chiefs of Staff organization included a Russian delegation. Would Russian membership have created among the Combined Chiefs irresistible pressure for a cross-channel invasion in 1943? If Overlord had been moved up by a year, would that have decreased tension within the alliance to a degree that would have allowed, as FDR wished, Moscow, Washington, and London to work together as a team after the war? The most obvious reason for the lack of a Russian representative on the Combined Chiefs of Staff is that Russian forces were fighting an independent campaign. Russian CCS representation would have been essential if large numbers of British and American troops had been fighting side by side with the Russians on the Eastern Front. The many combined operations in which the British and the Americans collaborated directly necessitated a CCS-type organization for them. As Maurice Matloff has indicated, "down to the fall of 1943 close collaboration with the USSR was, perhaps, not immediately necessary."[45]

That was a situation that clearly needed to change as the date for Overlord approached. As far as the Russians were concerned, that date was not soon enough. It was at the Trident Conference in Washington, D.C., in May 1943 that the American Joint Chiefs of Staff were finally able to get their British counterparts to allow a date (May 1, 1944) to be set for the Overlord landings in northwestern France. While the Americans were relieved to be able to pin the British down to an actual date, the Russians were appalled that Overlord, after so much delay already, was still an entire year in the future. The prospect of being forced to carry nearly the entire burden of the war against Germany for so long before they could expect their allies to open a real second front in Europe was a crushing disappointment for the Russians. It is therefore not surprising that in the wake of the Trident Conference the Russians briefly withdrew their ambassadors from Washington and London. Their anger that Trident did not provide for a 1943 Overlord may have led the Russians even to toy with the idea of a separate peace with Germany.[46] The postponement of Overlord, specifically that Trident did not provide for a 1943 Overlord, probably represented the greatest rift between the Soviet Union and its Western Allies during World War II.[47]

It is well known that this delay in crossing the channel sparked intense debate between the British and American members of the Combined Chiefs of Staff. Like the Russians, General Marshall was acutely disappointed that Overlord was not going to take place in 1943. General Brooke, on the other hand, was greatly relieved that the invasion would not take precedence over Allied operations in the Mediterranean for some time yet. The reason that such serious disagreements did not ruin the British-American alliance is that the Combined Chiefs of Staff organization provided a framework within which arguments resulting from differences of opinion could be part of a healthy working relationship and not become irretrievably divisive forces.

General Deane's position in Moscow gave him a unique opportunity to view firsthand, and over a sustained period of time, the deep level of mistrust existing between the Western Allies and the Russians. In both the United States and England, Joint Staff planners were constantly discussing and refining the strategic ideas of the CCS principals; Deane found that planning was done very differently in the Russian command hierarchy. In a report to the U.S. Joint Chiefs of Staff, under the heading "Subordinate Officials Cannot Discuss," Deane related how he had been forced to give up trying to discuss anything relating to strategy with his Russian counterparts. Every idea mentioned to the Russians by the U.S. Military Mission in Moscow received immediate negative criticism, after which the Americans would be informed by the Russian officials that higher authority would have to be consulted. Consequently, Deane adopted the approach of simply submitting his ideas and asking that they be forwarded for approval, "without endeavoring to enter into discussion."[48]

Even normal day-to-day discussion was difficult for the American mission in Moscow. Deane complained to his superiors in Washington that

> We do not have a telephone directory nor are we allowed to learn individuals' telephone numbers. We are not permitted to visit the offices of Soviet officials without a previous appointment. All such appointments must be made through one officer who has been designated as a foreign liaison officer. When officials are not ready to discuss questions the usual replies to requests for appointments are that the person we desire to see is ill, at the front, or otherwise engaged. There are absolutely no telephone conversations.[49]

This is a stark contrast to the informal discussions in Washington between members of the British Joint Staff Mission and the U.S. Joint Chiefs of Staff that went on every day.

The lack of cooperation between the Western Allies and the Russians had serious consequences, not only in broad strategic issues but also in immediate tactical events. One of these occurred on November 7, 1944, when, due to mistaken identity, a column of Russian vehicles and their protecting fighter planes in Yugoslavia were attacked by a large group of American Lockheed P-38 Lightnings. When it was over, it was apparent that Russian losses had been heavy. Six Russians lay dead on the ground amid the wreckage of twenty vehicles. In addition, three Soviet aircraft had been shot down and two Russian pilots killed. Among the Russian dead in the column was a lieutenant general.[50]

Casualties due to "friendly fire" are certainly not unheard of in any battle situation. However, this particular incident had been easily preventable and was a source of very bitter feeling (understandably) on the part of the Russians. They correctly perceived that this unfortunate incident bore testimony to the lack of detailed planning between the Western Allies and the Russians. There had been an agreement as far back as July 1944 between General Deane and the Russian General Staff upon a line of demarcation between areas in which Allied aircraft operating from bases in southern Italy would attack Balkan targets and those that would be bombed exclusively by Russian aircraft. However, this bomb line was out of date by the time of this tragic encounter between Russian and American forces; it only covered Hungary and Romania.[51]

In an attempt to rectify the situation, the Combined Chiefs of Staff directed the American and British military missions in Moscow to work with the Russians to draw a new bomb line in Yugoslavia that, it was hoped, would avert any more such incidents "pending the establishment of effective liaison."[52] (November 1944 seems rather late in the war for the CCS finally to be establishing operational liaison with the Russians.) At that time, General Aleksei Antonov of the General Staff of the Red Army represented to Deane in Moscow that he agreed that operational liaison machinery should be set up at once (first in Moscow and later among commanders in the field) to coordinate the air activities of all Allied air forces operating in Yugoslavia.[53]

There were other areas, besides tactical operations, where relations between Russia and its allies were far more cumbersome and suspicion-laden than they needed to be. For example, the crews of British and American merchant ships felt like prisoners during their turnaround times in port at Murmansk and Archangel.[54] Such ill treatment was also accorded to the so-called No. 30 Mission, which seems to have been a subset of the British Military Mission in Russia. No. 30 Mission consisted of British technicians and radio communications people posted in the Soviet Union to assist the Russians in assembling and using their Lend-Lease tanks and aircraft and to handle matters related to the routing and scheduling of the Anglo-American northern convoys of merchant ships to Russia. In July 1943 there were approximately four hundred British personnel in the Soviet

Union, serving either in north Russia or with the British Military Mission in Moscow. The vast majority of these Britons (more than three hundred) were stationed near the north Russian ports. No. 30 Mission personnel did not exactly receive a warm welcome upon their arrival in January 1942. In fact, they were initially left stranded at Archangel, despite being eager to get to their bases and start work.[55] In a rambling and somewhat contradictory account, the leader of No. 30 Mission (and of the entire British Military Mission in Russia), Lieutenant General Giffard Le Q. Martel, listed some of the difficulties under which the British personnel under his command were forced to operate.

According to Martel, things ran fairly smoothly until July 1942. At that time the Russians began to demand that British military personnel bound for duty in north Russia obtain Russian visas before they arrived. The most pressing problem with this demand, aside from the insult, was the delay (often considerable) before the Russians would grant visas.[56] A few months later, in September 1942, the Russians began to censor the mail of No. 30 Mission personnel. As with the visas, the insult to the British was twofold. First, there was the implication that the British commanders on the spot could not be trusted to ensure that military secrets did not circulate in the mail of the personnel under their command. Second, Russian censorship involved lengthy delays that were infuriating to British soldiers, who were eagerly awaiting mail from home.[57]

In addition to imposing seemingly arbitrary restrictions upon British personnel, the Russians seemed very unwilling to make use of the technical expertise those personnel were prepared to offer. General Mason McFarlane of the British Military Mission in Moscow provided to the War Office a lively account of the difficulties of keeping the Russians in spare parts for their Lend-Lease equipment. McFarlane reported, "Russian methods are not our methods. Their principle is the continental one of running a machine until it blows up and then replacing it with a new one. . . . I cannot convince the Russians that our assistance on the stores and spare parts side would be invaluable."[58]

One on occasion, a group of British technicians from No. 30 Mission was given the task of assembling American Bell P-39 Airacobra fighter aircraft that had been shipped to the USSR in crates. This did not work out so well. Shunning the assistance of this group, which had set up its workshop in the inland city of Kineshma, some two hundred miles northeast of Moscow, the

Russians preferred to assemble the P-39s on their own at Ivanovo, fifty miles from Kineshma. The British technicians at Kineshma were left with virtually nothing to do.[59]

No. 30 Mission also experienced great difficulty in caring for its own sick and wounded in the Soviet Union. Upon arrival in north Russia, the British intended to set up hospital accommodation for their personnel at Vaenga and Archangel. The Vaenga hospital was set up.[60] However, when the equipment and materials for the Archangel medical unit arrived, on a British ship, the Russians would not allow any of it to be unloaded. In fact, the doctors, nurses, and technicians for this hospital all returned to England without ever setting foot on Russian soil. This was particularly galling for the British serving with No. 30 Mission, as Martel indicated to the COS Committee:

> At that time, there were a considerable number of British casualties needing urgent medical attention in Archangel [where] there was a Russian hospital, and the Russians were most anxious to help in every way, but they were unable to compete with the influx of survivors from the convoy P.Q. 17. Many of these men died or had limbs amputated unnecessarily. . . . There can surely never have been a previous case in history in which one nation has treated the casualties of an allied nation in such a callous manner.[61]

In other areas, however, the Russians were quite helpful to Martel and No. 30 Mission. The British found that they were eventually able to reduce the number of their people stationed in north Russia because of the willingness of the Russians to make the facilities of the ports available to the British. This included the use of heavy equipment to repair ships that had been damaged by enemy action or the elements in transit.[62]

The Russians were also quite open with certain types of information. They provided Martel everything he wanted to know about how Russian equipment and tactics stood up under the test of battle and about German strengths and weaknesses. In regard to plans for their own forthcoming offensives, however, the Russians tried not to tell Martel anything at all. They were similarly secretive about intelligence reports, Russian troop strengths in various sectors of the front, and the overall supply situation in regard to such things as weapons and food.[63]

It seems Martel was trying to say that in some ways the Russians were helpful, in some ways not. Maybe "unpredictable" is a better word to describe Russia's behavior toward the Western Allies, rather than "bad" or "good."

At approximately the same time, a British embassy report from Kuibyshev gets to the crux of the matter as to why Britain had not been welcomed with open arms as an ally by Russia. Among the conclusions listed is this very prescient and succinct observation:

> The root of the trouble is no doubt political. . . . Soviet Government are only interested in us as allies to the extent to which they think our activities will assist:
> (a) their own victory in the war.
> (b) their own security after the war. . . .
>
> As regards (a) they are disappointed we have not been able to send forces to the Eastern Front or achieve success elsewhere. Our material aid is important but not decisive. They accept the explanations politely, but they are not interested in the reasons or motives. We move up and down their chart by results alone and at present we are not very high.[64]

Lend-Lease aid was certainly vital to the Russian war effort.[65] However, the food, medicine, communications equipment, and clothing that arrived via Lend-Lease was more important than the weaponry. It is true that the Western Allies sent forty convoys of ships to the northern Russian ports. Many of these convoys, such as the aforementioned PQ 17, suffered heavy losses en route due to attacks from German aircraft and submarines. Carried on these voyages were vast quantities of equipment of various types—for example, medicine, communications equipment, several thousand American light trucks and Sherman tanks, and five thousand British tanks.[66] This certainly represents a significant form of cooperation between the allies. However, more important to Russian victory were the high-quality weapons produced in their own munitions factories. British and American aid certainly eased the Russian shortage of mechanized transport and provided extra aircraft and tanks. However, the Russians themselves produced 11,000 of the up-gunned version of their own vastly superior T-34/85 tanks and a total of 29,000 tanks in the year 1944 alone.[67] In addition to the T-34 variant with the 85-mm gun, Russian 1944 tank production included the KV-1 and

Stalin heavy models, as well as, presumably, the earlier-model T-34 with the original 76.2-mm gun. All of these Russian tanks were qualitatively superior to anything in the German arsenal—and to anything the Americans or the British could give the Russians.[68] What the Russians really needed more than Lend-Lease aid was an early second front in northwestern Europe to force Germany to divide its forces between two widely separated enemies.

The primary reason for not including the Russians within the machinery of the Combined Chiefs of Staff, as noted, was that the Western Allies did not have to plan combined operations with the Russians on an everyday basis. The Americans and the Russians were, however, able to work together to plan Operation Frantic, a campaign that was dear to the heart of General Arnold. These were the shuttle-bombing missions conducted by American heavy bombers that took off from Fifteenth Air Force bases in southern Italy, bombed Germany and German-controlled areas in Eastern Europe, and then landed in the Ukraine. After refueling and replenishing on Russian soil, the aircraft would take off again to drop more bombs on German industrial targets during the return trip to their home bases. The eighteen shuttle-bombing missions of the Frantic campaign (which began on June 2, 1944) have been well documented elsewhere.[69] These missions indicate that although the Western Allies and the Russians were deeply suspicious of each other, they were able to work together.

The Allies had a procedure that, although somewhat complicated, allowed the British and the Americans to exchange with the Russians closely guarded technical information describing new weapons and equipment. Under this system, the Combined Intelligence Committee (part of the CCS) was directed to prepare monthly reports containing technical information that was deemed appropriate for release to the Russians. These reports were then sent to the Combined Chiefs for approval. If approved, the monthly reports were sent to the American and British missions in Moscow for transmittal to the Russians.[70] Examples of the types of information provided under this system to the Russians by Britain include details of ASDIC (sonar), Hedgehog depth charges, the Churchill and Cromwell tank designs, rockets and hollow-charge projectiles, muzzle brakes for artillery and tank guns, jet propulsion for aircraft, H2S ground-mapping radar, aluminized explosives, plastic armor, flashless cordites, and armor-piercing ammunition.[71] While reasonably effective, this method of exchanging technical data was considerably more cumbersome than the manner in which the Americans and the British shared information. The Western Allies basically told each other everything in regard to weaponry. This included, from June 1942 onward, all information about the highly sensitive Manhattan Project. Such a level of trust is certainly a testimony to the intimacy of the alliance between Britain and the United States.[72]

General Deane elaborates on the tone of the relationships between the Allies when describing his first impressions upon arriving in the Soviet Union to attend the Moscow foreign ministers' conference in October 1943. Deane attended the first meeting of the three foreign ministers—Cordell Hull, Anthony Eden, and Vyacheslav Molotov—with their assorted staffs and interpreters on October 18, the very day he arrived in Moscow.[73] According to Deane, after all the parties had assembled in Molotov's outer office,

> We went through a handshaking procedure that was typical of all British-American-Soviet relations. The British and Americans paid no attention to each other beyond a casual nod or "Howdjdo," but both Anglo-Saxon delegations shook hands with every Russian in the room. This process was repeated every time we met or departed from a group of Russians. It was indicative of the casual and informal relationship we had with our British ally as contrasted with the formality and reserve which attended our relations with the Russians.[74]

Clearly, the reserve that Deane mentions was evident in Allied discussions and debates to which the USSR was a party. However, while the British and the Americans did a much better job at working with each other than either did in working with the Soviet Union, the cooperation of the three nations together was not all that bad, considering the vast amount of territory over which their forces were arrayed. Indeed, the instances in which the Allied nations worked at cross-purposes were far fewer than those of the Axis nations, which consistently conducted their respective war efforts in isolation and to each other's detriment.

In that regard, it should be mentioned that the aforementioned Moscow foreign minister's conference had some very positive aspects, despite its awkward moments. Out of it came the "Four-Power Declaration," a signed pledge by the USSR, Britain, the United States, and China to continue to cooperate after the peace had been secured. Lasting peace was the aim. This declaration was the basis for the foundation of the United Nations.[75]

Maurice Matloff has described the significance of the occasion: "Marking the first time since the outbreak of war that British and U.S. staff officers had met face to face with Soviet military representatives and discussed strategic plans, the conference was a landmark in the development of closer collaboration among the Allied Powers in World War II." [76]

FIVE

The Combined Chiefs of Staff and Overlord

Everything about the planning for the Overlord cross-channel invasion was agonizing, even the process of choosing its commanding officer. The classic cross-channel versus Mediterranean controversy among the Allies can be summed up by saying that General Marshall wanted the Allies to invade across the English channel in late 1942 but that the British, particularly General Brooke, would not hear of this and pressed instead for Allied operations in the Mediterranean. The first large-scale result of this impasse was the Torch campaign in North Africa, which commenced on November 8, 1942. Torch caused the cross-channel invasion to be delayed until June 6, 1944. Historians have long debated whether or not Torch and other Allied Mediterranean operations were necessary and whether a 1942 or 1943 Overlord could have taken place had Torch not been undertaken. It is generally considered that a 1942 cross-channel attack by the Western Allies would have been a disaster and thus that Brooke was undoubtedly correct in believing that the Allies were simply not ready at that time.[1] However, 1943 was another matter altogether.

Nobody ever would have heard of Dwight D. Eisenhower had it not been for General George C. Marshall. Indeed, many people are surprised to learn that there was an American general who outranked Eisenhower during the war. Actually, early in the war several generals outranked Eisenhower. In fact, Eisenhower did not even have his first general's star at the time George C. Marshall attained four-star rank in September 1939. It was Marshall's system as army Chief of Staff of promoting officers based on merit rather than seniority that allowed Eisenhower to jump from absolutely unknown colo-nel in the summer of 1941 to five-star general and national hero three and a half years later. Then, in the most dishonorable act of his life, Eisenhower repaid his mentor and former boss by acceding to Senator Joseph McCarthy's request that he, Eisenhower, remove supportive references to General Mar-shall (who was the witch-hunting McCarthy's target du jour at the time) from a speech that Eisenhower was preparing to deliver in Wisconsin during the 1952 presidential election campaign.[2]

General Eisenhower was by no means the first choice for the command that made him a legend—that of Supreme Commander, Allied Expedition-ary Force.[3] Generals Marshall and Brooke, Field Marshall Dill, and Lieuten-ant General Frank Andrews (who had taken over command of American forces in Western Europe while Eisenhower was serving in the Mediter-ranean) were all considered by the president, the prime minister, and the Combined Chiefs of Staff for the command of the cross-channel assault.

General Marshall had seemed like the most logical choice for this com-mand. The Allied invasion of northwestern Europe had been his idea more than anyone else's. He was widely respected by the British and American staff officers who would be involved in the detailed planning for Overlord. In addition, Marshall wanted the job badly and was supported in his quest for it by Secretary of War Henry Stimson. In the summer of 1943, the sec-retary of war had become convinced that only with General Marshall as its commander could British objections to Overlord be overcome. There were also those in Washington, such as FDR and Stimson, who were worried that Marshall's contribution to Allied victory in the war would be forgotten if he remained in Washington instead of taking on the Overlord command. They, and others, felt that it was imperative that General Marshall not share the fate of the U.S. Army Chief of Staff during World War I, General Peyton C. March, whose name had quickly been forgotten by the public while every-one remembered the name of General Pershing because of the latter's role as commander of the American Expeditionary Force in Europe in 1917–18.[4]

There were also, however, strong pressures to keep Marshall in Washing-ton. The strongest such pressure came from General Marshall's colleagues on the Joint Chiefs of Staff, who helped to convince the president that Mar-shall's work as a member of the Combined Chiefs of Staff was so important that it could not be done by anyone else. General Arnold and Admirals King and Leahy urged the president to find another commander for Overlord and thus retain Marshall as army Chief of Staff. On this the president was somewhat torn. He needed Marshall in Washington as his preeminent military adviser, while realizing that Marshall was fully entitled to what was certainly the war's most prestigious field command for an American army officer. In the end, FDR was forced to concede that General Marshall was irreplaceable as a member of the Combined Chiefs of Staff.[5] The president broke the news to General Marshall in December 1943, in a manner that showed how vitally important the Combined Chiefs of Staff had become to the Allied war effort: he used the oft-quoted expression, "I feel I could not sleep at night with you out of the country."[6] It has been suggested that what this interchange really signified was that Marshall himself, not the Combined Chiefs of Staff, had become indispensable.[7] Without meaning to detract in any way from General Marshall's greatness as an individual, I believe that the existence of the Combined Chiefs of Staff organization gave General Marshall a forum in which his talents could shine at least a little bit more brightly than they would have had the CCS never been set up.

Initially hoping to reward General Brooke for his efforts as CIGS by giving the cross-channel command to him, Winston Churchill had changed his mind by late summer 1943. At the Quadrant (Quebec) Conference in August 1943, the prime minister informed President Roosevelt that since American ground troops would greatly outnumber British in the cross-channel campaign, its commander should be an American. At that point Churchill fully expected that the American named would be none other than General Marshall.[8] Thus, at Quadrant, Brooke was informed by Churchill that he would not be getting the Overlord command. General Brooke was greatly disappointed to learn that a command that Churchill had frequently promised him had slipped from his grasp. The official reason, that because the Americans would provide a far greater number of the troops for Overlord than the British it seemed only fair that the commander be an American, is certainly a valid one.[9] In retrospect, however, it seems odd that Brooke should have been at all surprised at having been rejected for command of an operation that he had tried time and again to kick into the tall grass. Indeed, it seems surprising that Brooke had even wanted the Overlord command, in view of his consistently morose outlook on the whole idea of a cross-channel attack. The Americans were appalled at the prospect of the Overlord command going to Brooke, whose views about the operation had never seemed enthusiastic and often downright obstructionist.[10] Secretary Stimson was undoubtedly referring to Brooke when he bluntly summed up the American view just prior to Quadrant in a memorandum to FDR: "We cannot now rationally hope to be able to cross the Channel and come to grips with our German enemy under a British commander."[11] The hypothetical scenario of Brooke commanding Overlord and supervising American generals like Patton and Bradley, who undoubtedly knew that Brooke had no stomach for the operation, is a frightening one.

While both Marshall and Brooke were disappointed that they did not receive the Overlord command, and Brooke's considerable baggage aside, the fact is that by late 1943 the Combined Chiefs of Staff had become essential for global Allied strategic planning. Accepting a field command would have been a demotion of sorts for any of its members. Taking up the Overlord command would have required Marshall or Brooke to exchange the global outlook they had acquired in strategic thinking in order to become, in the words of General Arnold "just another Theater Commander."[12]

General Andrews, a U.S. Army Air Forces officer, was highly regarded by General Marshall. The fact that Andrews had earned the trust of the Chief of Staff, coupled with the fact that he had already proven—in the Caribbean Defense Command and as the commander of the European Theater of Operations of the United States Army (ETOUSA)—that he could handle a theater command, made Andrews a serious contender for the Overlord appointment. Tragically, however, in May 1943 a plane in which General Andrews was returning to the United States crashed while attempting to land in Iceland, killing Andrews and all but one of the other passengers and crew.[13]

It is vital to keep in mind that by the time Overlord took place in June 1944, the Russians had already won their war. The great Russian victories at Moscow, Stalingrad, and Kursk had set the stage for Operation Bagration, the all-out Russian offensive against German Army Group Center in the summer of 1944. Army Group Center was the only German army group in Russia that could still claim to be a cohesive fighting force in early summer 1944. This Russian offensive, which began a few weeks after the Normandy landings, resulted in the complete destruction of Army Group Center, which had been Hitler's strongest force in the East. During the Russian summer 1944 offensive, German casualties in Russia were averaging 200,000 men per month.[14]

Thus, while the planning and launching of the Overlord D-Day landings of June 6, 1944, are considered by many historians to constitute the
crowning achievement of the Combined Chiefs of Staff, it needs to be put
into perspective. The war in Russia makes clear that Hitler's armies were
already beaten (although still possessed of a nasty sting) by the summer of
1944.[15] What Overlord did, perhaps, rather than defeating Germany, was to
help define the magnitude of Germany's defeat. Without a cross-channel
invasion, would the Russians have been content to expel Hitler's armies
from Russian soil, gain control of Poland as a buffer state, and then negotiate a peace that left a greatly weakened Nazi regime in power in Germany
and perhaps still in possession of occupied France? Was it Overlord that
made the difference between a German defeat on the above lines and what
actually occurred, that is, the complete destruction of the Nazi regime, the
liberation of France and the Low Countries, and the military occupation of
Germany by Allied troops? These are hypothetical questions that cannot be
definitively answered. The role of the Combined Chiefs of Staff in planning
Overlord can, however, be explored.

Part of the opposition of Brooke and Churchill to an Allied cross-
channel invasion may have been simply that it was not a British idea. General Marshall was the primary sponsor of the cross-channel strategy, but the
British wished to utilize American resources without ceding to the Americans
the right to dictate strategy.[16] If true, perhaps this feeling (the Americans
would call it stubbornness) arose from British resentment that the Americans were relative latecomers when it came to active belligerency in both
world wars. Why should these Johnny-come-latelies get to run the show?
Indeed, Churchill and Foreign Secretary Anthony Eden found highly insulting a 1942 suggestion by FDR that perhaps the best way for the Allies to
approach Stalin would be through personal diplomacy on the part of the
American president. The implied exclusion of the British from these proposed inter-Allied negotiations enraged Eden, because, as Warren Kimball
writes, "To the foreign secretary, Europe was Britain's business since the
Americans could not be trusted to abandon isolationism and make a permanent political commitment to the region."[17] The feeling that the Americans
needed to be tutored by their British allies shows up in a comment made in
April 1945 by Churchill's great friend, and South Africa's premier, field marshal Jan Smuts, that, as Churchill's private secretary Jock Colville recorded
in his diary, "the Americans were certainly very powerful, but immature and

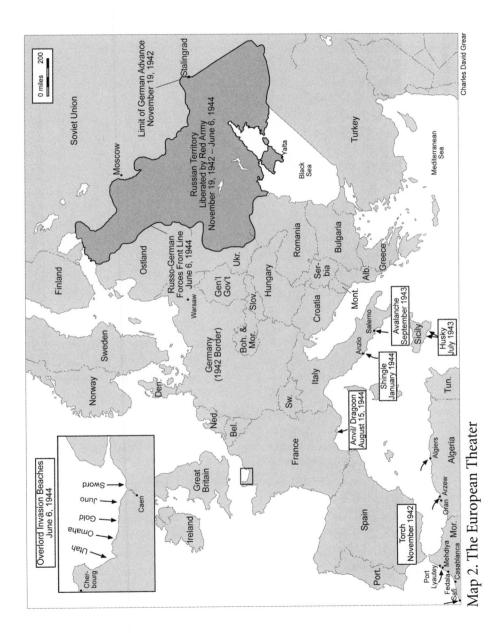

Map 2. The European Theater

Charles David Grear

often crude."[18] Future prime minister Harold Macmillan expressed similar sentiments about the Americans during the war.[19] If anything, the sentiment felt by Churchill and his military and civilian advisers that "Britain knew best" increased as victory drew nearer. From at least the time of the Teheran Conference onward, Churchill was alarmed about Russian postwar plans for Eastern Europe and about Britain's declining strength vis-à-vis the two emerging superpowers, the United States and Russia.[20]

Also undoubtedly on Brooke's mind were the lingering feelings of inferiority among the British high command, mentioned in chapter 1, regarding the quality of the British army as opposed to that of the German army. In this regard, Alex Danchev has noted that "not until the end of 1942 was it possible convincingly to refute Neville Chamberlain's laconic aside to Anthony Eden, then secretary of state for war, in the dark days of 1940—'I'm sorry Anthony, that all your generals seem to be such bad generals.'"[21] Portal on at least one occasion said that Winston Churchill shared Brooke's doubts about the fighting quality of the British army in World War II.[22]

Then there was the issue of airpower. Marshall seems to have had a better understanding than Brooke of how overwhelming Allied airpower could do much to prevent a recurrence of the trench warfare that Brooke remembered from World War I.[23] For instance, General Marshall had been informed by the U.S. Joint Staff planners in May 1943 that in the May 1944 cross-channel assault he envisioned, the Allies would enjoy air superiority of eight to one over the Germans in the vicinity of the invasion area. Indeed, tactical air strikes during the Normandy invasion by Allied fighter-bombers such as the Hawker Typhoon and Lockheed Lightning used in the role of flying artillery disrupted German transportation and supply operations in frontline areas on a massive scale and in a manner that would have been impossible in World War I.[24]

The most fundamental issue dividing the Western Allies on Overlord was that Brooke believed that it could succeed only after aerial bombing from the West, Allied victories in the Mediterranean, and Russian victories in the East had destroyed the ability of Germany to conduct coordinated military operations.[25] He seemed to feel that the war might end in a manner reminiscent of World War I—that is, with a sudden, unexpected German collapse. Brooke saw Overlord as a way to take advantage of such a collapse. Marshall and the U.S. Joint Chiefs of Staff did not believe that the German armed forces were going to collapse. They felt that Overlord, as an adjunct to the great victories being achieved by the Russians, was essential to ensure the defeat of Germany.[26] This feeling among the American members of the CCS was backed up by the U.S. Joint Intelligence Committee, which advised the Joint Chiefs of Staff in October 1943 that the prospect of a sudden German collapse was highly unlikely and that British reports to the contrary were painting an overly optimistic picture.[27]

Brooke's attitude was very frustrating to Marshall, because, as Brooke's biographer points out, for Brooke "the invasion of Western Europe must not take place before those preconditions had been met which would ensure its success."[28] Brooke later spelled out what he felt some of those preconditions had been when he replied to questions posed by J. R. M. Butler and Sir Michael Howard in regard to sections of the *Grand Strategy* series that he had reviewed. Brooke believed that the Western Allies should use their powerful navies to pursue a maritime strategy.[29] This would have meant a return to Britain's strategy in the Napoleonic Wars, that of maintaining control of the seas, limiting Britain's commitment of troops on the continent, and outlasting the opponent. This older British strategy may have appealed to Brooke because he had seen in World War I the way British casualties could increase exponentially when Britain enlarged upon its historic maritime strategy in order to become a major European land power—and Britain had been a major land power in World War I. Indeed, by the end of World War I, the British Empire had placed more than 9,000,000 men under arms.[30] The majority of these were British-controlled troops on the western front. Brooke further stated to the *Grand Strategy* authors that a cross-channel invasion in World War II could take place only after "we . . . clear North Africa, open the Mediterranean and regain 1,000 tons of shipping, eliminate Italy, bring in Turkey."[31] (Brooke probably meant to say a million tons here. That was the figure he usually used when discussing the shipping deficit that needed to be made good.)

For General Marshall, such a proliferation of conditions that had to be satisfied before Brooke would consent to a cross-channel assault had a strong air of unreality. It certainly did not seem to represent the outlook of a man who really believed in the operation. It seemed that Brooke wanted to wait until Germany was completely exhausted by its war against the Soviet Union and only then finally undertake Overlord, merely as a means to move an occupation force across the channel to take up garrison duty in an already defeated Germany. It must have seemed to the Americans that

Brooke's strategy would make the war in Europe last until 1948 or 1949.[32] Marshall seemed to be more keenly aware than Brooke that in war, you do not always get to choose *when* you want to fight. The Russians had counter-attacked against the invading Germans outside Moscow (only twelve miles from Red Square) in December 1941 not because they had been ready or eager to do so but because they had had to. The Russians had not had the luxury of waiting until they were completely ready before undertaking the Moscow counteroffensive.

The Russian victory at Kursk in July 1943 seemed to vindicate the American line of thinking that a 1943 cross-channel operation would have been quite feasible. Kursk presented the Western Allies with a golden opportunity (but one that Torch and Sicily prevented them from taking advantage of) to open a second front successfully in Normandy in 1943. Admittedly, Allied casualties in a 1943 invasion of Western Europe would have been heavy. This is especially evident in light of the fact that although the June 1944 Overlord landings took place after the strength of the German air force had been broken, the campaign in Normandy was still a bloody and difficult fight.

British intransigence about Overlord was intensely irritating for both Marshall and King. During the Arcadia Conference in Washington in December 1941 and January 1942, the British had extracted a renewal of the American pledge to concentrate first on the defeat of Germany. That much was perfectly in keeping with General Marshall's own views. However, after formalizing the "Germany first" pledge, the British rejected Marshall's plan for a 1942 cross-channel attack and seemed less than sanguine about an attack in 1943, yet insisted that during all of this inaction in Western Europe the United States must keep the war against Japan on the "back burner," to the disgust of Admiral King.[33]

Certainly, one of General Brooke's greatest contributions to the Allied war effort was his ability to neutralize the ill-conceived schemes of the prime minister, such as Churchill's abortive Jupiter plan to launch an offensive against German forces in Norway in 1943. In such cases, Brooke's cautious approach to warfare was an important asset to the Allies. To Marshall, King, Arnold, and Leahy, however, Brooke's desire to agree only to those operations that seemed guaranteed of success beforehand appeared inconsistent with qualities demanded of officers entrusted with strategic decision making for war on a global scale. Admiral Cunningham, Brooke's colleague on the British Chiefs of Staff Committee, understood that American entry into the war meant that the resources available to the Allies would increase exponentially. Perhaps Brooke was not as successful as was Cunningham in making the transition from thinking in terms of Britain fighting alone to thinking about Britain as part of a coalition with tremendous resources at its disposal. Brooke seemed preoccupied with not losing the war. Marshall was obsessed with winning it.[34]

Despite the conflict it aroused during CCS meetings, Overlord would never have been possible without the Combined Chiefs of Staff. At the instigation of General Marshall, the War Department in Washington had by the spring of 1942 prepared plans for both the Roundup operation (as the proposed large-scale cross-channel attack was then designated) and the requisite process of building up large American forces in England (known as Bolero).[35] From that time on, Marshall pressed relentlessly for the cross-channel invasion to be given top priority. In this effort, the Chief of Staff was backed by his colleagues on the Joint Chiefs of Staff, Arnold being particularly vigorous in his support for Overlord. In-depth planning for the operation began in April 1943 under Combined Chiefs of Staff auspices when a British officer, Lieutenant General Frederick E. Morgan, was appointed by the Combined Chiefs of Staff to serve as chief of staff to the Supreme Allied Commander of the Allied invasion of Western Europe (who, in a perfect example of the complicated and difficult nature of Overlord planning, had not yet been named). The organization Morgan thus set up, commonly referred to as COSSAC, was charged by the Combined Chiefs with responsibility for carrying out the detailed advance planning for a May 1944 cross-channel assault.[36]

Morgan and his COSSAC staff did much to make Overlord a reality. In addition to Morgan's ability to solve some of the most difficult planning questions for the operation, the very presence of a British officer working in London to prepare the Overlord plan did a great deal to get the British Chiefs of Staff and their prime minister finally to show some enthusiasm for the undertaking.[37] Morgan himself certainly believed in the soundness of Overlord as a strategic concept. His appointment took on greater significance after the Trident Conference of May 1943, at which the U.S. Joint Chiefs received formal British approval for a May 1944 Overlord.[38] The positive influence that General Morgan had upon the British members of the Combined Chiefs of Staff goes to show that the subordinate committees, staffs, and organizations of the CCS organization were so important that without them the principals never would have been able to carry out successful coalition warfare on a global scale.

At Trident, the Combined Chiefs decided that Morgan could plan on having twenty-six Allied infantry and three airborne divisions for the assault and set a target date of May 1, 1944. Morgan was also told that after the initial assault phase was complete, a minimum of three divisions per month would be added to the Allied force in France. The Combined Chiefs wanted to see COSSAC's outline plan by August 1, 1943.[39]

Morgan made his deadline, completing his plan in July. It was Morgan and his COSSAC staff, keeping in mind the resources that had been allocated by the Combined Chiefs of Staff at Trident, who chose the Caen region in Normandy as the assault area.[40] According to Maurice Matloff, Morgan selected the stretch of the Normandy coast running from the River Orne to the Cotentin Peninsula "partly . . . on the grounds that the sector was weakly held, the defenses were relatively light, and the beaches were of good capacity and sheltered from the prevailing winds."[41]

While it is true that General Eisenhower and his staff worked out many of the details of the actual landings and directed the operations of Allied forces once they were ashore in France, it is important to note that when Overlord received the CCS stamp of approval in May 1943, Eisenhower was involved in a completely different campaign—the command of Allied forces in North Africa. By December 1943, when Eisenhower was appointed to command Overlord, planning for the operation had been under way by Morgan's COSSAC staff for seven months. Thus, the Combined Chiefs of Staff had already settled almost all of the largest issues of the operation. They told Eisenhower exactly what forces would be at his disposal, as well as when and where his troops would land on the French coast. Eisenhower did make one critical contribution to the overall plan, which was to insist that the landings take place on a wider front than the three-beach/three-division front envisioned by General Morgan and the COSSAC planners. Eisenhower's idea, which may have originated with General Montgomery, was to land on five beaches, which would mean at least five divisions landed by sea on the first day.[42]

One reason for Brooke's lack of enthusiasm for the cross-channel attack was his sense that the Americans did not understand how vast an operation Roundup/Overlord would have to be. Marshall's desire to undertake the operation, at least in limited fashion, in 1942 seemed to Brooke the height of fantasy. Brooke noted during Marshall's April 1942 visit to London that Marshall had urged that the Western Allies put troops ashore on the coast of France in September 1942. Marshall promised that American forces would be available for such a campaign. However, Brooke was astounded to learn that the Americans would be able to make available only two and a half of their own divisions for a September 1942, assault.[43] Brooke concluded justifiably that this would be "no very great contribution. . . . Furthermore they had not begun to realize what all the implications of their proposed plan were!"[44] It should be noted, however, that the pace of the Bolero transfer of American forces to England in preparation for operations on the continent was expected to increase dramatically in late 1942 and early 1943. The Combined Staff planners stated in May 1942 (before the planning for the North African invasion, Torch, threw such plans into disarray) their opinion that there would be 51,000 American troops in England by July 1942 and that these troops could be ready to participate in a campaign in France in September. By September 1, 1942, available shipping would allow 105,000 American troops to be transported to England, and at least 794,000 American troops would have arrived by April 1, 1943.[45]

With the aforementioned doubts on his mind, it is therefore strange that a few days after he had complained about Marshall's two and a half divisions, Brooke and his colleagues on the British Chiefs of Staff Committee would, in what Brooke referred to as a "momentous meeting," agree to Marshall's plans for a cross-channel invasion in 1943 at the latest, perhaps even a limited campaign in 1942.[46] The proposed limited operation to seize a foothold in France in 1942 was known as Operation Sledgehammer. Marshall therefore returned home thinking that he had secured British agreement to, at the very least, an April 1943 cross-channel assault involving roughly forty-eight American and British divisions. Brooke's biographer admits that this was an odd promise for the CIGS to give, in that Brooke was by no means convinced at that time that a 1943 Overlord was the correct strategy for the Allies to follow. Such a strategy entailed large risks, a situation Brooke found intolerable.[47]

Part of this ambiguity may have been due to the fact that while their common language was invaluable in forging the close alliance between Britain and the United States, differences in the way they expressed themselves caused problems between the British and American members of the Combined Chiefs of Staff. According to Sir David Fraser, "When the British, having considered the American proposals at the level of prime minister and Chiefs of Staff, returned their final answer they gave an impression of more harmony than really existed. It is a British characteristic to find a formula of agreement in order to preserve some sort of unity in an organization, while postponing a crunch of opinion until real decisions on action have to be taken. It is an American characteristic to take at literal value the written word."[48]

Brooke apparently hoped to postpone the "crunch of opinion" for a very long time. After the war he reiterated that he had never had any intention of allowing British troops to participate in a cross-channel attack in either 1942 or 1943, unless Germany were to undergo a sudden collapse beforehand. Brooke found it frustrating that Marshall regarded Allied operations in North Africa and Italy not as stepping-stones toward a coup de grâce against Germany but rather as separate campaigns, undertaken seemingly to mark time. The CIGS felt that Marshall did not appreciate the benefits that might accrue to the Allies from a maritime, Mediterranean strategy.[49] Indeed, at the Quadrant Conference General Brooke pressed for Allied troops to advance into northern Italy, which was farther north than Marshall and his American CCS colleagues wanted to go in the Italian campaign. The British themselves were not united on the northern Italy idea. Sir Charles Portal favored confining Allied operations to seizing the airfields in southern Italy and invading Sardinia. Brooke was perplexed and disappointed that General Marshall did not share his own view that the Italian campaign would be complementary to Overlord, by way of pulling German troops into Italy, troops that the Germans would then be unable to use to repel the cross-channel invasion.[50] Perhaps Marshall's view that the Italian campaign was a distraction from, rather than a benefit to, Overlord would have been more clear to the CIGS had Brooke taken a moment to ponder an irony of his view of the supposedly related nature of Italy and Overlord—the fact that, as Mark Stoler has written in regard to a critical stipulation demanded by the British, the Overlord commander's brief would extend only to controlling Allied forces in "northwest Europe, as the British insisted the Mediterranean remain a separate theatre and be under British command."[51]

Indeed, it was the American attempt to obtain a unified command in Western Europe and the Mediterranean that caused Sir John Dill's name to be put forward in regard to the command of Overlord in November 1943 by the U.S. Joint Chiefs of Staff. The Americans reasoned that the British Chiefs of Staff could have no objection to giving their colleague Dill such a truly unified supreme command. For their part, the Americans felt that Dill was the one British officer whom they would have no hesitation whatsoever in accepting as an overall commander for Overlord.[52] In pointing out his capabilities for such a command, the Joint Chiefs of Staff praised Dill to the president in a memorandum authored by Admiral Leahy, saying that "Sir John Dill is well known to our officials and to the American public. He has worked on an intimate personal basis with the U.S. Chiefs of Staff since our entry into the war. We have the highest opinion of his integrity of character and singleness of purpose. He understands our organization, our characteristics, our viewpoint on many subjects, and our way of doing business."[53]

The suggestion of Dill by the Americans as commander of operations that would include the cross-channel attack was also undoubtedly a manifestation of the fact that he was infinitely more palatable to the Americans than Brooke. Everything about General Brooke seemed to bother the Americans, not just his foot-dragging in regard to the cross-channel attack. Andrew Roberts has noted that the French-born Brooke had always been bilingual. His manner of speaking immediately put Americans on guard when they first made his acquaintance. In regard to French and English, Roberts notes, Brooke "spoke both languages very fast, something that some Americans were to come to dislike and mistrust." Then, as now, fast talkers make people nervous.[54]

Putting Dill forward as a possible super-commander in Europe coordinating Overlord and Mediterranean operations was also undoubtedly a bribe on the part of the Americans, an attempt to stop British backsliding in the form of the continuing post-Trident and post-Quadrant doubts expressed by Churchill and the British Chiefs of Staff about the cross-channel attack. Marshall's biographer Forrest C. Pogue and General Ismay in his memoirs both say that British refusal to combine the Mediterranean and Overlord commands was a major reason why General Marshall did not get the Overlord command. President Roosevelt apparently feared that the American press and public might think a general of Marshall's seniority and stature was being unfairly punished if he were to have his responsibilities restricted to one part of the European theater—even though Marshall himself dearly wanted the appointment.[55]

General Marshall clearly did not see North Africa and Italy as part of any comprehensive strategy. For him, they were wasteful diversions. Why then during the Trident Conference in Washington in May 1943 did Marshall concur in a Combined Chiefs of Staff decision that seemed to make an Allied campaign in Italy inevitable—or perhaps more appropriately, unavoidable? In a directive prepared by the Combined Staff Planners at the end of Trident, General Eisenhower, then commanding the Allied forces in North Africa, was "instructed, as a matter of urgency, to plan such operations in exploitation of HUSKY [Sicily] as are best calculated to eliminate ITALY from the war and to contain the maximum number of German forces."[56] The directive went on to say that Eisenhower's plans to detach Italy from the Axis camp had to be made with the understanding that they were secondary to, and in support of, a major Allied campaign to land twenty-nine Allied divisions in northwestern France on May 1, 1944. The Combined Chiefs wanted to see Eisenhower's plans by July 1, 1943.[57]

Andrew Roberts speculates that at a CCS "closed session" meeting during the Trident conference the Americans engaged in some horse trading: the British got approval for an Allied campaign in Italy, while the Americans forced the British to put in writing that the cross-channel attack was not only "on" for spring 1944 but would be the paramount Allied campaign in the European theater that year. Trident marked the first occasion on which the Combined Chiefs employed a closed session—no witnesses present or minutes taken. The practice would become more common at future Allied summit conferences as debates between British and American Combined Chiefs of Staff members became more bitter.[58]

Much of Marshall's bitterness over the decision to undertake Torch, which had received final approval by FDR and Churchill on September 5, 1942, stemmed from a feeling that he had been badly manipulated by the British and his own president. Marshall's efforts via Bolero to concentrate U.S. troops in England for an early cross-channel attack only made it easier to carry out Torch, an operation he opposed.[59] Marshall had intended that the British Isles would serve as a staging area for a cross-channel attack, not for operations in North Africa or the Mediterranean. Historians have noted that for political reasons President Roosevelt felt it imperative to get American troops into action against German troops somewhere—indeed, anywhere—before the end of 1942 and that this helps to explain FDR's approval of Torch.[60] However, for the president, there may have been more than politics involved. After Allied troops were ashore in northwest Africa, FDR began to feel that Allied operations in the Mediterranean might be a good way to get at Germany after all.[61] According to Mark Stoler, "Unlike the JCS, Roosevelt saw the Mediterranean as a vital part of the European theater where military gains against Germany were quite possible."[62]

The U.S. Joint Chiefs of Staff saw no value in the Torch operation. Marshall saw the CCS 94 document (see chapter 3) and Torch as a surrender to a peripheral strategy in Europe only for the time being and so that fifteen American air groups could be released from Europe to the Pacific Theater in the summer of 1942.[63] The British Chiefs of Staff, on the other hand, felt that Torch was a viable operation. Brooke had been skeptical at first about the validity of Torch but changed his mind during the summer of 1942 and joined Pound and Portal in supporting the operation.[64] Brooke's diary entries between June and September 1942 demonstrate the evolution of the thinking of the CIGS in regard to Torch.[65] British forces were already heavily engaged in North Africa, and much of British strategy in 1940–42 had been geared toward the Mediterranean area in general. A fundamental issue here was that, as Matloff and Edwin Snell put it, "Torch . . . fitted easily into British strategy; American strategy had to be fitted to Torch."[66]

In the autumn of 1943, after the date for Overlord had already been set by the Combined Chiefs of Staff as May 1, 1944, General Marshall wrote for the president a report outlining what he perceived as British reluctance to participate in an Allied campaign against the Japanese in Burma. The reasons Marshall identified go a long way toward explaining the very different approach taken by the British and American members of the Combined Chiefs of Staff to strategic planning in general, and the question of Overlord in particular. Thus Marshall's report, although primarily concerned with Burma, helps explain the bitterness of the Anglo-American debate about Overlord. In regard to Burma, and under the heading "British Pessimism Retards All-Out Support," Marshall informed FDR that British forces in India seemed to want no part of a campaign in Burma. The Chief of Staff claimed that the British had little or no faith in the fighting abilities of the Chinese and Indian infantry divisions that would be needed for such an operation and that this had made the British overly pessimistic.[67] The crux of Marshall's argument, however, was that in regard to British forces in India, "their approach appears to be that of the Quartermaster rather than that of the General. Whereas we determine upon a strategic operation as being necessary and then move heaven and earth to support it, the British staff in India appear too sensitive to logistical limitations and too indifferent to means of removing them."[68] Although Marshall intended this to be a criticism of high-ranking British military officials in India, such as Field Marshal Sir Archibald Wavell, it seems also to describe perfectly Marshall's sense of the reasons behind the reluctance of the British members of the Combined Chiefs of Staff to undertake a cross-channel invasion at the earliest possible moment.

Two qualifications should be made in regard to Marshall's complaint. In the case of operations in Burma, the great success of American forces in the Central Pacific proved that the British were most likely correct in viewing Burma as the wrong theater for full-scale operations against the Japanese. Secondly, the different approaches taken by the British and the Americans to the planning of any operation were related to the fact that the United States possessed unlimited resources while Britain did not. The latter point is well illustrated by Admiral Cunningham's experiences in the Mediterranean theater. His operations there in 1940 and 1941 had been very difficult, because ships, personnel, aircraft, and supplies were always in short supply. The situation was much different when Cunningham returned from the British Joint Staff Mission in Washington in the summer of 1942 to take up his post as Allied naval commander for Torch. Vast American resources were at his disposal in a combined operation, and Cunningham found that he could have anything he needed. This was a welcome improvement. However, it was also a situation that required Cunningham to make an adjustment in his thinking, to adapt to a new and unexpected situation.[69] General Brooke was less successful in doing so.

In his biography of Brooke, Sir David Fraser gives the impression that Pound and Portal were as dead set against an early Overlord as Brooke. This does not in fact seem to have been the case, particularly in regard to Portal. The chief of the Air Staff indicated during the spring of 1942 that he considered Sledgehammer a "real possibility" for 1942.[70] A month later, Portal indicated that he would not be opposed to undertaking Roundup/Overlord in 1943.[71] In fact, during the summer of 1942 Portal informed the COS Committee that for a 1943 cross-channel campaign, he was prepared to accept a situation in which "virtually the entire Metropolitan Air Force [i.e., RAF units based in southeastern England] will be engaged in effect on Army Support in the widest sense, including the achievement of air superiority over the battle area [in France]."[72] This open-mindedness on the question of the cross-channel invasion reflected in Portal's reports also goes against the view of his biographer, Denis Richards. According to Richards, the chief of the Air Staff agreed with General Brooke that it would be unwise for the Western Allies to launch a cross-channel attack in either 1942 or 1943.[73] It is possible, however, that Portal's enthusiasm for an early campaign in France may have been dampened somewhat once the final decision was taken in September 1942 that Operation Torch was "on" for 1942. At this point, Admiral Pound and Field Marshall Dill seemed to be the British CCS members whose views were most in accord with those of the Americans. Admiral Pound sympathized with General Marshall and Admiral King in their disappointment upon realizing that undertaking the Torch operation in 1942 meant that their would be no cross-channel attack in 1943.[74]

Field Marshall Dill and the British Joint Staff Mission in Washington, perhaps falling under American influence, seemed also to be more optimistic than Brooke in regard to a 1943 cross-channel campaign. They suggested in June 1942 that a supreme commander for such an operation should be appointed as soon as possible and that this individual should be supported by a combined, interservice, British-American staff.[75]

In the spring of 1942 Admiral King was not opposed to the Bolero transfer of American forces in the British Isles in preparation for an early cross-channel campaign. However, King did feel that it was pointless and dangerous to send American forces to Europe until the Pacific situation was at least stabilized. He saw the Pacific as more urgent, something that had to be dealt with right away. Douglas MacArthur was trying to make the same point, although his reasoning was somewhat weak—MacArthur portrayed the Pacific as a second front that would help Russia.[76] In one sense, MacArthur was accurate, in that being embroiled in a war with the United States kept the Japanese from taking advantage of the Russo-German war by invading maritime Siberia.

One reason that the American members of the Combined Chiefs pressed hard for an early cross-channel assault is that they were keenly aware of the terrible struggle in which their Russian ally was engaged. While the Western Allies allowed the summer of 1943 to pass with no cross-channel attack, the Russians and the Germans deployed between them in July some three thousand armored vehicles at Kursk in what would be the largest tank battle in history. Roughly 25,000 German soldiers were killed on the first day at Kursk (July 5)—a death toll that would rise dramatically in the next two weeks. In addition, hundreds of German aircraft and tanks were to be destroyed. The Russians' own losses were also heavy, but Kursk was a great victory for them. After the battle at Kursk ended on July 25, 1943, German forces in Russia would know only retreat until the end of the war.[77] Unlike his American CCS colleagues, however, Brooke had little sympathy for the Russians. Andrew Roberts summarizes Brooke's anti-Bolshevik sentiments nicely; after dismissing claims that the British expected the Americans to fight Hitler on their own, Roberts writes that "a much fairer criticism of Churchill and Brooke was that they were willing to fight not to the last American, but rather to the last Russian."[78] From the very beginning of Barbarossa, the Russians were compelled to engage the bulk of the troop strength of the German army. Indeed, 80 percent of the casualties sustained by the German army in World War II occurred in the war with Russia.[79] Alex Danchev illuminates this disparity by noting that "in December 1942, with the echo of Alamein still ringing in the ears, the Western Allies engaged some six German divisions. The Soviets faced 183."[80]

Allowing the defeated German forces no respite, the Russians immediately followed up their victory at Kursk by liberating Belgorod on August 5 and Kharkov on August 23. These victories were greatly aided by the fact that by summer 1943, the Russian air force was coming of age. Indeed, at the time of Kursk, the Russian air force (administratively divided into "air armies," signifying the close air support that Russian combat aircraft provided to the Red Army during the war) outnumbered Luftwaffe aircraft by a margin of almost three to one. The German air force on the Eastern Front was weakening rapidly, while greatly expanding Russian aircraft production was beginning to tell.[81] The momentum of the Russian advance would increase dramatically during 1944. In July of that year, when German Army Group Center had finally been destroyed in the Bagration campaign, Russian armies of the 1st, 2nd, and 3rd Belorussian Fronts crossed the Polish frontier. For the remarkable achievement of expelling German forces from almost all Russian territory the Wehrmacht had occupied in 1941 and 1942, the Red Army had required only two months to push the Germans four hundred miles to the west.[82]

As they rapidly moved westward during 1944, the soldiers of the Red Army found plentiful evidence of the atrocities inflicted upon Russian civilians by the German army. Historians such as Omer Bartov have vividly chronicled the barbarity of German occupation policy in Russia.[83] Indeed, the mountain of such evidence makes it difficult to know where to begin when choosing examples. For instance, in the span of just two days in late

September 1941 more than 33,000 Russian Jews from Kiev in the Ukraine were shot by SS and regular German army firing squads and were buried in a ravine at Babi Yar.[84] There is no shortage of official German documents outlining the savage occupation policy to be followed by German forces in Russia. Field Marshal Walter von Reichenau issued a chilling order to the German troops (that is, regular army troops) under his command in Russia on October 10, 1941: "In the eastern sphere the soldier is not simply a fighter according to the rules of war, but the supporter of a ruthless racial *(völkisch)* ideology and the avenger of all the bestialities which have been inflicted on the German nation and those ethnic groups related to it. . . . For this reason soldiers must show full understanding for the necessity for the severe but just atonement being required of the Jewish subhumans."[85]

Whether it was during the advances made by the German army into Russia in 1941–42 or in that same army's retreats after Stalingrad and Kursk, looting, arson, rape, and murder were indiscriminately inflicted upon Russian civilians by the Wehrmacht, to say nothing of the more than 3,000,000 Russian prisoners of war who died of abuse, starvation, and exposure in German captivity.[86] The fate of Russian prisoners in German hands is a particularly heinous crime, because prisoners of war are not supposed to die at all. They are supposed to be cared for and treated humanely. The number of Russian POWs who died in German captivity is more than six times the total number of Americans killed in the war and is still only a fraction of the 27,000,000 Russians who died. German troops often did not even bother to take prisoners, instead simply shooting out of hand any Russian soldier who tried to surrender. The ethnic groups earmarked for destruction in von Reichenau's field order quoted (in part) above went beyond Russian Jews to include Slavic peoples in general, who had been declared by Hitler to be "subhumans." This mind-set ensured that the German army, in its invasion of the Soviet Union, would be conducting a genocidal campaign that would claim the lives of millions of Jewish and non-Jewish Russian civilians, to say nothing of the millions of Russian soldiers who were killed in combat or died in squalid open-air POW camps into which they were forced in the dead of winter.[87]

Holocaust historian Richard Rhodes vividly describes how routine became mass shootings of Russian civilians, Jewish and non-Jewish, by the German invaders during Barbarossa. One eyewitness account, which mentions an SS officer named Friedrich Jeckeln, describes a mass execution of

Jews in the Ukrainian town of Schepetovka during the summer of 1941: "Women and children were among those shot. Jeckeln said: 'Today we'll stack them like sardines.' The Jews had to lie layer upon layer in an open grave and were then killed with neck shots from machine pistols, pistols and rifles. That meant they had to lie face down on those previously shot [whereas] in other executions they were shot standing up and fell into the grave or were dragged in."[88]

So terrible was the savagery of the German army toward the Russian people that, Omer Bartov suggests, after the war German veterans of the Eastern Front had to engage in a form of "collective amnesia" in order to disguise from themselves the fact "that they [i.e., regular German army troops, not just the SS] had all taken part in a huge criminal undertaking."[89] Whatever Stalin's own crimes, the Russian people certainly had done nothing to deserve such a horrific fate. Yet Churchill and Brooke were content to let them wait for their second front.

A 1943 Overlord would have been like Guadalcanal—a bitter, drawn-out campaign with a greater risk of failure than the campaign that was actually launched on June 6, 1944. The Allies had air superiority in Western Europe by June 6, 1944, but they did not yet have it a year earlier. In a 1943 Overlord, British and American fighter pilots would have had to establish air superiority over the beachhead dogfight by dogfight against the Luftwaffe. However, the proximity to the invasion beaches of the unsinkable aircraft carrier that was England would have made this task possible. The Allies had plenty of fighter aircraft in mid-1943; the problem was that most of them were deployed in the Mediterranean.[90] What the Allies did not yet have was the American long-range P-51 Mustang fighter, which throughout 1944 enabled American heavy bombers flying from England to enjoy effective protection all the way to Berlin and back. Nonetheless, and even without Mountbatten's Habbakuks but sans the Mediterranean diversion, the range handicap of the P-47, P-38, Spitfire, and Typhoon fighters the Allies would have employed in a 1943 Overlord would have been offset by the availability of refueling facilities just across the channel in England. Then, once a beachhead was established in France, forward airfields could be set up there—as was actually done when Overlord took place.

The Guadalcanal analogy seems especially apt in regard to a 1943 Overlord. One of the reasons, perhaps the most important reason, Admiral King favored undertaking the Guadalcanal operation in the South Pacific in

August 1942—a time when American forces were actually far from ready to take the offensive anywhere—was that, as he himself wrote that spring, "the best defense is offense." In the same document, King went on to say that "no fighter ever won his fight by covering up" and absorbing blows. You have to fight aggressively and offensively as best you can, regardless of how unprepared you are.[91] Marshall, Arnold, and King were willing to employ such a philosophy in regard to Overlord. Brooke definitely was not.

By the time of the Trident Conference in May 1943, President Roosevelt had come to agree with the idea put forth by the U.S. Joint Chiefs of Staff that the cross-channel assault should have precedence over any other Allied activity in Europe during 1944, but the British Chiefs were getting mixed signals from the prime minister. According to Fraser, "Churchill sometimes argued for early invasion when under great Allied or Parliamentary pressure, but he greatly feared a costly disaster in the West and he was always half-ready to be persuaded [to abandon the idea]."[92]

At the Trident Conference, the U.S. Joint Chiefs estimated that the Allies would be able to field thirty-six divisions for an April 1944 Overlord.[93] A few months earlier, the British Joint Planning Staff had pointed out that because the American Bolero buildup of forces in England had been reoriented toward the Torch operation, the bulk of the troops for any 1943 cross-channel campaign would have to be British, as would most of the landing craft and their crews.[94] This left Marshall with precious little room to maneuver, and it demonstrates how harmful the logistical inroads made by the Torch campaign were to the planning process for the cross-channel assault. As it turned out, the forces involved in the initial landings at Normandy on June 6, 1944, comprised equal numbers of British and American troops. (The "British" total included, on the first day, one Canadian division. Of the entire twenty-nine Allied divisions involved in Overlord, four were Canadian.) However, because of the massive buildup that followed, the vast majority of the Allied troops participating in the liberation of France and the invasion of Germany from the west were, in fact, American.[95]

In March 1943 the British Joint Planning Staff began to evince in regard to Overlord a guarded optimism that would become more apparent by the time of Trident. Echoing the sentiments of the British Joint Staff Mission in Washington, the British Joint Planning Staff recommended that a director of planning for a 1944 cross-channel assault be appointed forthwith. The British planners also felt that such an assault had become feasible under two possible scenarios. The Allies could carry out this operation in 1943 should Germany collapse suddenly, or in 1944 even against a vigorous defense.[96] The British Joint Planning Staff therefore seems, in this instance, to have been more enthusiastic and flexible about Overlord than were the principal British members of the Combined Chiefs of Staff. This was no doubt due at least in part to the efforts of the senior member of the British Joint Planning Staff, Captain Charles Lambe, RN, who, as we have seen in regard to the debate over strategy in the Pacific, had proven to be a very farsighted individual who, like Dill, was always capable of understanding the point of view of his American allies.

At the Quadrant Conference at Quebec in August 1943, the Combined Chiefs of Staff gave their approval to the outline plan for the cross-channel assault that had been prepared by General Morgan and his COSSAC Staff. Even then, however, it was a full-time job for the American CCS members to keep their British counterparts convinced as to the paramount stature of Overlord for 1944. The American members of the Combined Chiefs of Staff constantly pressed the point that nothing must interfere with Overlord or Anvil. (The latter operation, subsequently known as Dragoon, was the plan to support Overlord by landing Allied troops in the south of France from the Mediterranean.) Both operations were initially set for May 1944.[97] The hand of the Americans, in terms of insisting on a 1944 Overlord, had been immeasurably strengthened by the summer of 1943 by the rapid expansion of their army and the flood of supplies and weapons from their factories; the Americans could insist on controlling the Western Allied agenda for 1944 and beyond. Indeed, by January 1944, aside from the large numbers of American troops in the Pacific theater, the number of American troops deployed against the German army finally exceeded the British total.

Most importantly, the United States had not yet exhausted its manpower reserves, while Britain had. When the Teheran Conference convened in late November 1943, Stalin took the side of the Americans against Britain by insisting on a 1944 Overlord, with the Anvil invasion of southern France in support thereof. At Teheran Stalin embarrassed both FDR and Churchill by obliging them to admit that a commander for Overlord had not yet been appointed.[98] In the wake of the conference the U.S. Joint Chiefs of Staff wished to curtail operations in the Mediterranean (except, of course, Anvil/Dragoon), as soon as possible in order to counter a disturbing trend, namely, that the Mediterranean campaigns tended to absorb far more resources than the Americans had hoped. For example, to provide air cover for Torch, the Americans had been forced to strip their Eighth Air Force, based in England, of most of its aircraft, to the detriment of the American bombing campaign from England against Germany that began in January 1943.[99]

As early as November 1942, the British Joint Staff Mission in Washington pointed out to the British Chiefs of Staff that the Americans were already very nervous about exploiting the Torch campaign in North Africa, fearing that it would lead the Allies into an open-ended Mediterranean commitment. This warning to their masters in London is contained in a document that has become either legendary—or notorious, depending on one's point of view—because in it the members of the British delegation admit that the Americans "think that they have been led up the Mediterranean garden path" by their devious British allies.[100]

Until the time the Overlord landings actually took place, this fear of being saddled with wasteful Mediterranean commitments never abated for the U.S. Joint Chiefs of Staff. They wrote shortly after the Quadrant Quebec Conference that they were appalled to see the British Chiefs of Staff "renounce what they call the 'sanctity of Overlord' principle."[101] What had incensed the Joint Chiefs to this extent was a report prepared by the British Chiefs of Staff in November 1943 that in a rather convoluted fashion seemed to withdraw British backing for a firm target date, in particular, and generally for Overlord as *the* Allied campaign for 1944. The British chiefs indicated that they wanted to see Overlord reevaluated from month to month in the light of continuing Russian victories and Allied successes in the Mediterranean, such as the withdrawal of Italy from the Axis bloc. With this in mind, the British chiefs expressed reservations about withdrawing troops and equipment from the campaign in Italy in order to prepare for Overlord. The British disliked being tied to an ironclad timetable, set at Trident and reaffirmed at Quadrant, committing the Western Allies to a cross-channel assault in May 1944.[102]

The Americans viewed this news from their British colleagues as a severe affront. It seemed that the British Chiefs of Staff wanted to scrap the plans for combined operations in northwest Europe—plans that had been so difficult to formulate. The Americans called the attention of the COS Committee to the British promises that had recently been given, stating that "the British Chiefs of Staff [have recently] reaffirmed and accepted that it is part of our basic strategy that we 'concentrate maximum resources in a selected area as early as practicable for the purpose of conducting a decisive invasion of the Axis citadel' (CCS 319/5). However, the U.S. Chiefs of Staff must now construe the subject British memorandum as a denial of this principle."[103]

The British countered by claiming that they had no desire to cancel the cross-channel attack out of hand. Instead, they wanted to put it back on the limited footing that had been discussed for it in 1942 (i.e., a Sledgehammer-type operation to seize a foothold on the French coast or to hastily move large numbers of Allied troops into France to take advantage of a German collapse).[104] Brooke, Portal, and Cunningham were anxious to get out of a situation in which they claimed they were forced to "regard Overlord on a fixed date as the pivot of our whole strategy on which all else turns."[105] One aspect that particularly enraged the British was the American insistence, grudgingly accepted by the British Chiefs of Staff Committee at Trident, that seven Allied divisions be pulled out of the line in Italy in the fall of 1943 and sent back to England in order to prepare for their upcoming role in Overlord, a move that definitely tossed Mediterranean operations into the back seat as far as Allied planning was concerned. The Americans insisted at Quadrant that the wavering British reaffirm this part of the Overlord plan.[106]

The British did not seem to feel that the Allies needed one paramount campaign for 1944. They felt that there could be a limited cross-channel assault to complement Allied operations in the Mediterranean—an ironic view for the British to take, in that a limited cross-channel assault was exactly what they had refused to consider in 1942. To the British chiefs this now seemed like a good plan, because it would mean engaging German forces on a broad front, forcing the Germans to disperse their resources.[107] The American viewpoint was just the opposite. The Joint Chiefs of Staff favored concentration of the bulk of Allied resources at one point, northern France. For them, Allied operations in the Mediterranean were to be only subsidiary to, and diversions to assist, Overlord. The Americans were alarmed that as late as the Cairo Conference, which had immediately preceded Teheran, the British had seen no need to allot either a specific date or specific numbers of troops, aircraft, ships, etc., to the Overlord plan.[108] The U.S. Joint Chiefs spelled out their position as follows: "We are of the opinion that changes in the situation since Quadrant militate for, not against, the launching of Overlord on or about 1 May 1944, and we cannot agree that a firm target date is not essential to its success. . . . We believe that

extensive operations in the Eastern Mediterranean will weaken and indefi-
nitely postpone the decisive operation in northwestern France. This would
be unacceptable to us."[109]

The hand of the American members of the Combined Chiefs had been
strengthened during the Trident Conference in May 1943 by the fact that,
like them, the president had had enough of the Mediterranean and was
ready to back fully their plans for a spring 1944 cross-channel assault.[110] In
the months that followed, FDR proved willing to support all of the ideas
of the Joint Chiefs of Staff in regard to Overlord, including the operation
designed to support it by landing Allied troops in southern France (Anvil/
Dragoon). The Americans encountered opposition from the British Chiefs
of Staff and Churchill in regard to Anvil as well as Overlord. A few weeks
after the Normandy landings began on June 6, 1944, the prime minister
begged Roosevelt to reconsider the operation against southern France,
hoping to convert him to the British alternative of expanded operations in
Italy and the Balkans.[111] The president remained unmoved. He declared to
Churchill, "On balance I find I must completely concur in the stand of the
U.S. Chiefs of Staff."[112] The president went on to say that the British plan
to devote Allied resources in the Mediterranean almost exclusively to an
attempt to move through northern Italy into the Balkans was unacceptable.
He, like the U.S. Joint Chiefs, favored the principle of the concentration
of Allied forces. The British plan entailed dispersion of effort. Overlord
must have priority, said the president, and Anvil must be mounted from
the Mediterranean to support it. The Anvil/Dragoon landings in southern
France duly took place on August 15, 1944.[113]

The British made one last effort to kill the Anvil operation. The British Joint Staff Mission in Washington prepared in August 1944 a report on
behalf of Brooke, Pound, and Cunningham that proposed using the forces
detailed to the southern France operation for a descent upon the coast of
Brittany, nearer the action in Normandy.[114] The Americans prepared their
veto on the same day: the U.S. Joint Chiefs claimed that it would be reckless and unnecessary to change the landing area for the Anvil forces from
the Riviera to Brittany. They informed the British chiefs that General Eisenhower was already capable of moving reinforcements into northern France
through the Normandy beachhead that he controlled. Moving the Anvil
force to Brittany would, the Americans felt, change the character of that
operation from an independent assault designed to draw German forces

away from the Normandy beachhead area into a secondary operation that would serve only to move Allied reinforcements into northern France.[115]

It was extremely frustrating and bewildering to the Americans to find that after they had bowed to what they viewed as a British obsession with operations in the Mediterranean by delaying Overlord so as to participate in Mediterranean campaigns of questionable strategic necessity (i.e., Torch, then Sicily, then the Italian campaign), the British would so vehemently oppose the one Mediterranean operation, Anvil, that seemed to promise immediate concrete gains in the war against Germany. That such serious debates about the Overlord campaign should persist even after the operation was under way shows what a volatile issue the cross-channel campaign proved to be for the Combined Chiefs of Staff. The resiliency of the CCS organization was, in turn, displayed by the fact that despite the widely differing viewpoints of its members and the overall bitterness of the debate, an effective Overlord plan and campaign emerged. Of course, the Combined Chiefs of Staff did not operate in a vacuum. That Overlord took place at all was due to the persistence of General Marshall and his U.S. Joint Chiefs of Staff colleagues in the face of British opposition; to the support the Americans received at Teheran from Stalin; to the waning of FDR's interest in Mediterranean operations; and to the fact that by early 1944 the United States was definitely the senior partner in the Western alliance.

SIX

Keeping the Armchair Strategists at Bay

Members of the Combined Chiefs of Staff had to fend off the civilian cranks who pop up in any war with what they are certain are *the* plans for victory, or at least with supposedly prophetic warnings about how to avoid defeat. Admiral King dealt (using what was for him uncharacteristic sympathy and tact) with one such individual who wrote from Maine in the period of nationwide panic that followed in the immediate aftermath of the Pearl Harbor attack with a warning to King to be on the lookout in case Germany should attempt a Pearl Harbor–type attack of its own along the eastern seaboard. The letter, bearing no signature, reads as follows:

> German aircraft carriers as heard over radio to be completed, could take over Newfoundland via the way of Trojan Horse, (improbable, but think it over) (cut our communication off from Europe) and from there cripple air bases, ship yards [sic] lower morale by dropping bombs on N.Y. and Boston and Portland *from the rear,* then slip away into the Arctic Ocean.
>
> Remember Pearl Harbor. Nothing is too daring or too fantastic for these war mad dictators.
>
> Remember the Maginot Line.
>
> Box 14
>
> Cape Cottage, Maine
>
> Perhaps this will help in some way even if it turns out to be only a bum steer.[1]

King received this letter when he was in the last days of his posting as commander in chief of the U.S. Atlantic Fleet and just before he was promoted to command the entire U.S. Navy. Even though the scenario outlined therein was completely impossible, if only for the reason that the German navy in World War II never had an operational aircraft carrier, the admiral nevertheless believed in doing his best to calm the fears of a jittery public. Since the letter was anonymous, King was forced to address his reply to a post office box. He wrote, on December 14, 1941:

> Holder, P.O. Box #14,
> Cape Cottage, Maine.
> Sir—
>
> Receipt is acknowledged of your letter mailed December 11, 1941, relative to possible action by the enemy.
>
> Your interest in writing me is sincerely appreciated. You may rest assured that no possibility of attack on the Atlantic Coast has been minimized or overlooked; and that we are not likely to forget Pearl Harbor.
>
> Thank you for your letter.
> Very truly yours,
> E. J. King.[2]

In fact, although the specific fears expressed by King's correspondent in this instance were bizarre, to say the least, the Atlantic coast was in fact under a grave threat—one that King seems to have been slow to appreciate—namely, U-boats. For six months after American entry into the war, Admiral King failed to organize coastal convoys of cargo ships and tankers along the eastern seaboard, although transatlantic shipping was traveling in convoy even before Pearl Harbor. To make matters worse, it took King until mid-April 1942 to succeed in imposing blackouts on large cities like Boston and New York so that merchant vessels would not be backlit for prowling submarines during the hours of darkness.[3] King's biographer states that King's tardiness in organizing coastal convoys was due to the fact that he was preoccupied with so many other pressing issues in the early months of the war that he did not have time to deal with the "happy time" (as they called it) that German submariners were enjoying off the east coast of the United States in early

1942, torpedoing dozens of Allied merchant ships with relative impunity. Samuel Eliot Morison argues that there were simply not enough escort-type warships available in early 1942 to make coastal convoys feasible. The answer is probably a combination of these two scenarios.[4] Michael Gannon goes farther, ascribing extreme negligence to Admiral King, even using the word "dereliction" to describe King's tardy response to the U-boat menace off the east coast of the United States in the first half of 1942.[5] That summer, even with new escort vessels becoming available, President Roosevelt still felt that the convoy system was not being utilized enough along the East Coast. In regard to ending the practice of merchant vessels sailing alone and unprotected along the coast, FDR wrote to Admiral King in July that "frankly, I think it has taken an unconscionable time to get things going, and further I do not think that we are utilizing a large number of escort vessels which could be used. . . . We must speed things up and we must use the available tools even though they are not just what we would like to have."[6]

It is safe to say that in the early months of the war, antisubmarine warfare was not Admiral King's strong suit, although even Gannon admits that King did much better after the summer of 1942.[7]

As noted in chapter 1 above, the fact that Churchill's own army chief would refer in his diary to the prime minister as "a public menace" shows that Field Marshal Brooke did not feel that Winston Churchill's contributions to strategic debates had the sensible ring apparent in FDR's above message to Admiral King.[8] While certainly meddlesome, civilians like Churchill who thought they knew the best way to win the war served to remind the members of the Combined Chiefs of Staff that they worked for democratic governments in which civilian control of the military was (and remains today) a deeply cherished tradition.

That said, and while President Roosevelt was far more circumspect than was Winston Churchill when it came to making suggestions about strategy to Combined Chiefs of Staff members, the British feared the potential disruption that FDR's strategic views might have. This sentiment no doubt stemmed from the constant vigilance demanded of the British chiefs in their efforts to derail the wild ideas of their own prime minister. One often-quoted episode from the Casablanca Conference shows the great lengths to which the British were willing to go in order to keep *all* politicians out of the process of devising strategy. During a break after one of the contentious CCS meetings at Casablanca in which Brooke and King had argued vehemently over the conduct of the war in the Pacific, Brooke had a talk with Dill. According to Brooke, "When I replied that I would not move an inch, [Dill] said, 'Oh yes, you will. You know that you must come to some agreement with the Americans and that you cannot bring the unsolved problem up to the Prime Minister and President. You know as well as I do what a mess they would make of it.'"[9]

In general, it seems that the British members of the Combined Chiefs of Staff were saddled with highly intrusive armchair strategists to a greater extent than were their American colleagues. The most notorious of them was of course Winston Churchill. Churchill's greatness as a wartime leader lay not in the strategic plans he dreamed up—which were almost always half-baked, if not downright reckless—but in the fact that he was a fighter. Churchill's defiant spirit and his incredible energy were just what Britain needed in the crisis year of 1940. Ideas like accepting defeat, giving up, and countenancing Hitler's dominance on the continent were completely alien to Churchill. His installation as prime minister on May 10, 1940, made him the personification of the mood of the British people, a mood that had crystallized into determination to see the war through, no matter what. How they were going to see it through was less important to the British people in 1940 than was the fact that they now had a leader at No. 10 Downing Street who had the dynamic personality and the energy to forge ahead with single-minded determination.

The problem was how to harness Churchill's energy and keep that energy headed down a productive path. Left unchecked, Churchill's energies tended to scatter, like pellets from the barrel of a shotgun, in many different directions. It is an understatement to say that the new prime minister had difficulty delegating responsibility and that the petty micromanaging he engaged in was a serious impediment to those who served him. In his memoirs Churchill reprints verbatim many of the telegrams and cables he sent to members of the Combined Chiefs of Staff during the war. Many of his wartime colleagues who reviewed sections of those volumes for Churchill prior to publication suggested that he include the answers he received. Churchill's response was the replies would make his series too lengthy.[10] The real reason is perhaps a bit more complicated. The queries Churchill sent to his service chiefs give the illusion that the prime minister was in charge and on top of all the issues. The answers he received would have shown that many of his requests for information were in reality absurd wastes of time and represented an obsession with detail that undeniably hampered the work of his service chiefs.

A March 1943 reply by Portal to one such query from the prime minister regarding a recent transatlantic flight to Newfoundland by Foreign Secretary Anthony Eden, who was being flown to Washington by Churchill's personal pilot (a young American named William J. Van der Kloot), illustrates this point accurately. Portal wrote Churchill, "You asked me about the time taken over Mr. Eden's flight to Gander. I find that it was only 27 minutes longer than Captain Van der Kloot had expected when making his flight plan, i.e. 13 hours 36 minutes instead of 13 hours 9 minutes. The ground speed average was 140 knots, and the contrary wind averaged a strength of 34–45 knots except at the start of the flight when it was between 30 and 40 knots. . . . There is therefore nothing abnormal about the time taken."[11]

The man entrusted with directing the wartime efforts of the Royal Air Force both at home in England and throughout the British Empire, in addition to his responsibilities as a CCS member for planning and directing overall Allied strategy, should never have been forced by the prime minister to waste his time responding to such trivial enquiries, of which there were many.[12] It was not uncommon for the prime minister's obsessiveness to extend to correcting the grammar of his subordinates. For instance, in late October 1942, Churchill minuted to Sir Edward Bridges of the War Cabinet Secretariat and to General Ismay as follows: "For general convenience it will be better in future to use the words 'aircraft' and 'airfields' instead of 'aeropolanes' and 'aerodromes.' The former method is better English, is shorter, is more in accord with American practice and, on the whole, in more general use."[13]

The prime minister's interest in military affairs caused difficulties for all of the British members of the Combined Chiefs of Staff. In the fall of 1942, Brooke was furious when Churchill and Secretary of State for War Sir James "P.J." Grigg had proved unable to keep quiet after Brooke filled them in on the blow that was about to fall on Erwin Rommel's Afrika Korps at El Alamein. Churchill and Grigg promptly told Eisenhower and his chief of staff, Lieutenant General Walter Bedell Smith, as well as two other persons—one of whom was a public relations administrator.[14] Brooke concluded from this that "it is absolutely fatal to tell any politician a secret, they are incapable of keeping it to themselves."[15]

General Brooke's visit to Washington in June 1942 was the occasion of his first meeting with FDR. While he found President Roosevelt to be a charming man, the CIGS quickly became convinced that the president's forte was politics, not strategy. Brooke felt that FDR tended to make suggestions about strategic planning that took little or no account of the implications the proposed course of action would have on the war effort as a whole.[16] Also during this visit Brooke had a rare moment of agreement with Marshall and King, in that all three men became worried when the prime minister and the president left their military advisers in Washington and went off to spend a weekend at FDR's Hyde Park estate. At this time, Brooke had not yet given up his initial opposition to Torch and therefore shared the worry of his American colleagues that Torch might be part of what, in Brooke's words, "the PM and the President had been brewing up together at 'Hyde Park'!"[17] As we have seen, these fears were completely justified, in that Torch was one of the rare occasions during the war when President Roosevelt went against the opinion of his military advisers.

A few months earlier, Brooke had spelled out in his diary quite clearly the doubts he had about the leadership ability of politicians in general in wartime: "Politicians still suffer from that little knowledge of military matters which gives them unwarranted confidence that they are born strategists! As a result they confuse issues, affect decisions, and convert simple problems and plans into confused tangles and hopeless muddles. . . . It is all desperately depressing."[18] Brooke understood clearly that the prime minister had a combative personality. The key to handling such a person, Brooke believed, was to choose one's fights carefully. The CIGS therefore decided early on that it was futile to protest against all of Churchill's idiosyncrasies.[19] As he explained to one of his wartime assistants, "We mustn't argue with Winston on small things, but only on things that really matter."[20] This philosophy no doubt proved to be a useful survival skill for Brooke. Yet further proof that no detail was too small to escape the prime minister's eye is the following March 1944 telegram from Churchill to the Minister of Works, Lord Wyndham Portal (not to be confused with the chief of the Air Staff): "Just below the Foreign Office, on the grass opposite St. James's Park lake, there is a very untidy sack with holes in it and sand leaking out, a sandbag structure, and some kind of obstacle formerly used as a practice ground by the local Home Guard. It does not seem to have been used for a very long time. Such a conspicuous place ought not to look untidy, unless there is some real need which can be satisfied in no other way."[21] Churchill's concern for the appearance of London's public parks is, of course, to his credit. However, in the midst of a global war the minister of works surely had more important business to attend to, such as attempting to alleviate the wartime housing crunch in London, than the removal of a few sandbags.[22]

The need to argue selectively with Churchill may help to explain why Sir John Dill had not been a success as Brooke's predecessor in the post of Chief of the Imperial General Staff. According to Sir James Grigg, Dill was a more brilliant strategist than Brooke.[23] However, the inability of Dill and Churchill to work together effectively may have been due to the fact that Dill, as CIGS, "had let himself be drawn into endless argument, and been worn down in debate, and in the end given in."[24] This made Dill's tenure as CIGS a miserable experience. With his defenses eroded by the prime minister's endless harangues, Dill had ended up going along (reluctantly) with costly adventures of the prime minister to which Dill was adamantly opposed. One of these was the British defense of Greece in April 1941.[25]

While better able than Dill to find ways of managing Churchill, Brooke nevertheless would have been happier if Britain's wartime ruling coalition had included a greater number of forceful politicians who might have acted as counterweights to the prime minister. In the spring of 1942 Brooke wrote in this regard that "a government with only one big man in it, and that one a grave danger in many respects, is in a powerless way."[26]

The prime minister's keen interest in military affairs and the fact that he clearly felt himself to be a gifted strategist certainly created a problematic situation for the Combined Chiefs of Staff as a whole, and its British component in particular. The COS Committee did, however, enjoy one major advantage in dealing with Churchill's attempts to interfere in the realm of strategic planning. This was, as Sir James Grigg stated, the fact that "since Gallipoli Churchill, despite his manner, was uneasy at taking a decision on operations. He would never pursue a course of action which he could not afterward tell the House of Commons, had had the full support of the Chiefs of Staff. He might bully and argue and try to win their support by wearing down their defences, but he would never over-rule them."[27]

As troublesome as they found him, the British Chiefs of Staff were not necessarily opposed to every initiative put forward by the prime minister. For instance, Sir Charles Portal claimed that the British Chiefs of Staff were sympathetic to Churchill's designs in the Balkans. Although his American

Combined Chiefs of Staff colleagues disagreed with him on this issue, Portal himself felt that Allied operations in the Balkans would have provided a viable opportunity for an Allied advance toward Germany through Austria.[28] According to Portal, "The British Chiefs of Staff were always strongly in favour of operations in the Balkans as a corollary to the Italian campaign, and as a means of dissipating the Axis forces."[29] Portal also felt that the Balkan strategy would prevent the creation of postwar Russian satellites there. He and the other British Chiefs of Staff felt that getting Allied troops on the ground in the Balkans would be a better way to support Overlord than would be the Anvil/Dragoon landings in southern France that the Americans favored.[30] As we have seen, the Americans won this dispute. The Allies put troops ashore on the Riviera on August 15, 1944, to support Eisenhower's ongoing campaign in Normandy.

Like Brooke, Portal apparently had no objection to Churchill's penchant for communicating directly with Portal's subordinates, such as Air Chief Marshal Sir Arthur Harris and other RAF commanders.[31] However, it is true that the prime minister and his inner circle of civilian advisers proved to be the most troublesome group of armchair strategists with whom Portal was forced to deal during the war.

In late 1942 and early 1943, as the Allies were gaining air superiority on all fronts with highly advanced aircraft that were entering service in ever-increasing numbers, Portal began to encounter difficulties with civilian policy makers in London in regard to which British aircraft designs should receive priority in production. Two such individuals with whom Portal came into conflict during this time period were the minister of production, Oliver Lyttelton, and the minister of aircraft production, Sir Stafford Cripps.[32] The chief of the Air Staff was apparently also concerned that such civilian administrators were exercising a detrimental effect upon the judgment of the RAF personnel who had been assigned to work in their offices as advisers.[33]

Several of Winston Churchill's civilian confidants from the 1920s and 1930s found themselves in positions of considerable influence once Churchill's political fortunes had been restored in September 1939, when he once again became First Lord of the Admiralty, and in May 1940, when he became prime minister. Lord Beaverbrook, Desmond Morton, and Frederick Lindemann (Lord Cherwell) were included in this group.[34] In his authoritative history of Churchill's relations with the navy, Stephen Roskill sides with other historians' unflattering descriptions of these civilian advisers: "As one surveys that band it is difficult not to accept both Anthony Storr's view that [Churchill] was attracted by 'energetic adventurers' and Liddell-Hart's that he was 'only comfortable with men of lesser calibre than himself.'"[35] This criticism may be somewhat harsh in the case of Beaverbrook. While admitting that Beaverbrook was not an easy person to work with, A. J. P. Taylor casts him in a more favorable light. In regard to Beaverbrook's tenure as minister of aircraft production during the Battle of Britain, Taylor writes that "at the moment of unparalleled danger, it was Beaverbrook who made survival and victory possible."[36] Undoubtedly, the tremendous output of fighter planes from British factories under Beaverbrook's stewardship was a miraculous achievement. Nevertheless, Beaverbrook's relations with the chief of the Air Staff were poor. Portal resented what he perceived as Beaverbrook's vainglorious and devious nature. This fact takes on added significance when it is remembered that almost everyone who came in contact with the CAS found Portal to be easygoing, well mannered, and a pleasure to work with.[37]

Although his official title from December 20, 1942, onward was that of paymaster-general, Lindemann/Cherwell served unofficially as the prime minister's scientific and statistical adviser. One reason why Cherwell, a distinguished Oxford physicist, became a controversial figure is that his faith in his own intellectual ability convinced him that he deserved to be in a position of great power. In short, he was arrogant. However, it should be noted that Cherwell's desire for power was tempered by a sincere wish to be of whatever assistance he could to the prime minister.[38] While he made many enemies, Cherwell is not without his supporters. One of these is his biographer, the Earl of Birkenhead, who claims that Cherwell's persistence enabled him to fight and win some difficult bureaucratic battles that aided the Allied war effort. For example, in the summer of 1940 Cherwell came to the assistance of the British intelligence services in their efforts to form an accurate picture of German strengths and weaknesses. He helped to demonstrate that the Battle of Britain was winnable by proving that the German air force was not as powerful as two London bureaucracies, the Air Ministry and the Ministry of Economic Warfare, had made it out to be.[39]

Birkenhead also points out that Cherwell "was usually at his best in matters where he had no preconceived ideas."[40] One such instance had to do with deficiencies in British ordnance. In the autumn of 1943 Cherwell quickly carried out a study proving that British high-explosive aerial bombs were less effective than those being used by the Germans. He urged (successfully) that the British armaments industry concentrate upon aluminized explosives rather than the older types. The results were good.[41] Even C. P. Snow, one of Lord Cherwell's harshest critics, concedes that Cherwell had an amazing ability to get things done.[42] Birkenhead, while a sympathetic biographer, hints that what many found to be so infuriating about Cherwell was that where Cherwell *did* hold preconceived ideas, he could not be budged from those ideas even if he was wrong.[43]

Like Churchill, Lord Cherwell was fascinated by technology. This proved to be unfortunate for Portal, Pound, and Cunningham, as wartime improvements in aircraft design and in antisubmarine equipment were to attract a great deal of attention from Cherwell. As an officer in the comparatively low-tech army, Brooke seems to have spent less time fending off Cherwell than did his colleagues on the COS Committee. The latter were forced to waste a great deal of their time responding to unwarranted criticisms and unwanted suggestions from him (as routed through the prime minister). Cherwell's brisk one-page notes could always get a hearing with Churchill who inevitably made follow-up queries. Consequently, Portal was forced to write detailed refutations of Cherwell's critiques. The chief of the Air Staff (CAS) did not have the luxury of the kind of provocative statements, vague generalities, and complete lack of supporting detail that characterized Cherwell's reports to the prime minister.

Portal treated Lord Cherwell warily, giving both qualified approval of Cherwell's statistics and subtly masked criticisms of the flawed techniques that were invariably used to gather them.[44] For instance, in one report that was forwarded to Portal by the prime minister with a request that the CAS comment on it, Cherwell was clearly stacking the evidence to support his own conclusions. Lindemann/Cherwell had found a 14.6 percent loss rate among Handley-Page Halifax bombers for the month of April 1942, as compared with 4.3 percent in March 1942. Portal made clear that Cherwell's figures had been skewed by including special operations—in this case, a raid on the German battleship *Tirpitz* at Trondheim in Norway on March 30, 1942.[45] Portal informed the prime minister that "the corrected figures are 10% and 9.2% for March and April."[46]

Cherwell's technique seems to have always been to go for the quick and sensational, knowing that this would have an impact on Winston Churchill, who liked to do the same thing. It was left for others, usually the British members of the Combined Chiefs of Staff, to come up with the detailed information that, more often than not, showed the fallacy of the arguments. For instance, Lord Cherwell's original report to Churchill on the above-mentioned Halifax loss rates consisted of a single sheet of paper (just the way the prime minister liked reports to be written) that made no mention of his faulty source base—that is, the raid against the *Tirpitz*.[47]

Although he certainly found such unwarranted criticism to be time-consuming and irritating, Portal was certainly not in the habit of digging in his heels and categorically denying that there were ever problems with the performance of British aircraft. In the summer of 1942, Portal made clear to the prime minister that he was aware of the fact that a lack of proper exhaust dampers and inability to maintain stability during evasive action made Halifaxes vulnerable to attack by enemy night-fighter aircraft. Portal assured Churchill that he was working to correct these difficulties.[48]

Lord Cherwell fancied himself to be an expert in the field of aircraft design. However, in this he proved to be no match for the chief of the Air Staff. In the summer of 1942 Cherwell informed the prime minister of a comparison he had made in regard to the relative merits of the German Focke-Wulf (FW) 190 fighter plane and the current British fighter types. Cherwell focused upon how well the Hawker Typhoon I, an excellent British fighter and ground-attack aircraft, stacked up against the German machine. The results, Cherwell informed the prime minister, showed that it was imperative to accelerate the development of the Napier Sabre-type engine, which he felt would revitalize the Typhoon and allow it to keep current with any aircraft that the Germans could put up. At this point, Cherwell had all but written off the superb Supermarine Spitfire of Battle of Britain fame, which he felt had reached the end of its operational life span.[49]

As always, the prime minister wanted Portal to comment on Cherwell's assertions.[50] Portal could see that as fine a machine as the Typhoon was, it had limitations. For one thing, it was heavy. Portal explained that he wanted to continue the development of new fighters like the Hawker Tempest or an advanced design from the Folland company to replace the Typhoon.[51] Portal was thinking ahead, placing the issue in a framework wholly different from what Cherwell envisaged—merely improving the engine of an existing airplane, although Portal realized that it was always a good idea to continue to develop promising new engines. Portal began by explaining to the prime minister, as a way of assuring him that the British fighter situation was not as bad as Cherwell made it seem, that "although the Merlin [a Rolls-Royce twelve-cylinder, in-line engine] in the Spitfire is nearing the end of its development, there is still something to come, and the Minister of Aircraft Production informed us yesterday that he hoped to keep up with the B.M.W. [the Focke-Wulf power plant] development in the near future."[52] The operational life of the Spitfire was in fact extended considerably by the introduction of the Griffon 61 engine, which became that airplane's new power plant in the spring of 1943.[53] (Interestingly, it would not be until April 1954 that the Spitfire would finally be retired from frontline service with the Royal Air Force.[54] This shows how little Cherwell knew when he dismissed the type as practically obsolete in 1942.)

Improved versions of the Sabre engine were becoming available in mid-1942 for use in the Typhoon II.[55] Portal agreed that the Typhoon II should be rushed into production as soon as possible. However, he pointed out to Churchill that even the upgraded Typhoon would, because of its greater weight, be at a disadvantage when compared to the FW 190 in terms of climbing ability and maneuverability.[56] The chief of the Air Staff felt that the best way to keep ahead of the FW 190's performance was to develop a new fighter "of the lightest weight possible, designed for the same characteristics as the 190, i.e., maximum rate of climb from ground to medium altitude."[57] A short time later, Portal and the Air Ministry delivered to the Ministry of Aircraft Production their performance requirements for the new fighter plane.[58]

The case of Cherwell/Lindemann also shows what harm could occur when the ideas of an armchair strategist were allowed to influence strategy. Cherwell's March 1942 "de-housing" report to Churchill is a prime example of this. As usual, it was a one-page document in which Cherwell proposed that Britain should concentrate its bombing campaign against the fifty-eight largest German cities. Lindemann's idea was that instead of attacking individual industrial targets, the Allied war effort would be materially advanced if the workers in those cities could, through indiscriminate nighttime area bombing, "be turned out of house and home."[59]

Cherwell had not initiated the idea of bombing German cities at night. The British had been engaged in such activity on and off since 1940. It was a policy that Portal supported. As a policy it was revitalized in February 1942 (before Cherwell's paper was written) when Air Vice Marshal Sir Arthur Harris, fresh from his duties with the British Joint Staff Mission in Washington, became Commander in Chief, RAF Bomber Command. Harris was a vigorous proponent of nighttime area bombing. His appointment to Bomber Command happened to occur when the aircraft to carry out such a campaign were becoming more readily available. Early 1942 saw the beginning of a transformation of RAF Bomber Command in which twin-engine aircraft such as the Whitley and Hampden were being replaced by large, four-engined, long-range bombers of the Halifax, Stirling, and Lancaster types.[60]

Postwar analysis of the results of the strategic bombing campaign would show that British nighttime raids caused heavy German casualties, did a great deal of damage, and tied up a considerable amount of German resources for such things as antiaircraft defense and large labor detachments needed to repair damage after each raid. However, the inaccuracy of British bombing was a grave flaw. It was to be the conclusion of the U.S. Strategic Bombing Survey that the American campaign of daylight strategic bombing of specific German industrial targets (particularly oil refineries) had a much greater impact upon the German war economy than did the British policy of destroying homes via nighttime area bombing. In addition to reducing German oil output, American daylight raids also caused considerable disruption in the munitions industry. This was due largely to the fact that the oil plants that were being bombed regularly by the Americans were also the producers of chemicals, such as nitrogen and methanol, that were vital ingredients in the production of all types of explosive ordinance, from artillery shells to rifle cartridges.[61]

Another aspect of daylight bombing by the Americans that proved devastating to Nazi Germany is that it forced the German air force to come up and fight to protect the homeland. This provided many benefits for the Allies. It forced the Germans to withdraw fighter aircraft from the Russian front and obliged the German aircraft industry to concentrate on building fighters for defense instead of bombers for offense. Most importantly, because American B-17 and B-24 bombers each carried at least ten heavy (.50-caliber) machine guns for defense and from December 1943 onward enjoyed long-range fighter escort, the German air force was utterly destroyed in aerial combat with the Americans (and by the simultaneous severe mauling the Luftwaffe was receiving at the hands of Russian fighter pilots in the East) by the summer of 1944.[62] This had been a vital prerequisite for a successful Allied cross-Channel invasion.

In the last year of the war, American daylight bombing raids against synthetic-oil facilities had a devastating effect upon the German war effort.

As oil output thus declined precipitously, the operational sorties (and even training programs) of the German air force had to be drastically curtailed.[63] Indeed, it would be the conclusion of the U.S. Strategic Bombing Survey that "the greatest single achievement of the air attack on Germany was the defeat of the German Air Forces."[64] That achievement was due primarily to American daylight bombing. Even "Bomber" Harris admitted that in the British night campaign dropping bombs upon German factories was secondary to the primary goal of creating generalized chaos in German cities and that British bombing had almost no role whatsoever in the reduction of the German air force.[65] A good example of the ineffectiveness of the British bombing campaign is a series of four massive raids carried out by Harris' command against Hamburg in July and August 1943. These raids resulted in some 77,000 casualties among the city's residents, including 40,000 dead. However, within three months Hamburg's munitions factories were producing at almost three-fourths of their former capacity.[66]

At the Casablanca Conference, Portal had supported the Americans in their desire to expand and develop the idea of the daylight precision bombing of Germany, although he had doubts about its feasibility. The CAS became more enthusiastic when the Americans began to get results. In fact, Portal began to believe that the two Allied bombing campaigns should coordinate their activities to a greater extent. By mid-1943, Portal felt sure that the British were capable of hitting precision targets at night. He became disenchanted with Harris, who preferred area bombing, when the latter did not support this idea. Indeed, Portal became so angry when Harris refused to follow up the second American daylight raid against the ball-bearing factories at Schweinfurt in October 1943 with a British raid the same evening that he seriously considered firing Harris.[67]

The fairly successful American policy of daylight strategic bombing of German industrial targets had been pressed vigorously by General Arnold and his staff. British nighttime area bombing had backing within the RAF from figures like Portal and Harris. However, due to his influence with the prime minister, Cherwell may have helped to give that flawed policy undue weight. While he was to become a wholehearted enthusiast of the British bombing campaign and one of its most ardent champions, Winston Churchill had, it should be remembered, initially harbored doubts about its potential effectiveness. In the autumn of 1941 he had warned Portal not to overestimate the effectiveness of the aerial bombardment of German cities, that in his view it was far from clear that bombing cities would have any kind of large-scale effect upon the German military or upon munitions production.[68] The prime minister went on to say, "Before the war we were greatly misled by the pictures [the Air Staff] painted of the destruction that would be wrought by Air raids. . . . This picture of Air destruction was so exaggerated that it depressed the Statesmen responsible for the pre-war policy, and played a definite part in the desertion of Czecho-Slovakia in August 1938."[69]

Cherwell's interference in the debate over the bombing campaign against Germany seems to have given Churchill, FDR, and the Combined Chiefs of Staff the erroneous impression that bombing, whether of the American precision type by day or British nighttime "carpet" bombing, could have a detrimental impact upon the morale of the German people. This turned out to be a misguided idea—rather than weakening morale, dropping bombs on people tends to have the opposite effect of making them very angry. It was defeat on the battlefield (particularly on the Russian front), the destruction of its navy, air force, and industrial infrastructure, and finally invasion by Allied ground forces that caused the defeat of Germany. German civilian morale did not "crack" under the weight of Allied bombing. However, as late as February 1943, in the wake of the Casablanca Conference, the Combined Chiefs felt that it might. The "Casablanca Directive" that provided a list of target priorities for the British-American Combined Bomber Offensive devoted considerable attention to German morale:[70]

1. Your primary object will be the progressive destruction and dislocation of the German military, industrial, and economic system, *and the undermining of the morale of the German people to a point where their capacity for armed resistance is fatally weakened.*

2. Within that general concept, your primary objectives, subject to the exigencies of weather and tactical feasibility, will for the present be in the following order of priority:
     (a) German submarine construction yards.
     (b) The German aircraft industry.
     (c) Transportation.
     (d) Oil plants.
     (e) Other targets in enemy war industry.[71]

Of interest in this list of target priorities for the bombing campaign is that morale, which proved to be the wrong objective, ranks far higher than oil plants. The latter turned out to be the real answer to the question of how to destroy the German war economy through aerial bombardment.[72] Without interference from such armchair strategists as Lindemann and Churchill, the Combined Chiefs of Staff might have come to this realization earlier than they did.

Armchair strategists were less of a problem for the American members of the Combined Chiefs of Staff. For example, General Marshall and Secretary of War Henry Stimson worked quite well together. There were, however, some exceptions to this general rule. Admiral King's relations with navy secretary Frank Knox had been quite cordial;[73] however, the same could not be said of the situation that developed upon Knox's death in April 1944 and his replacement by James Forrestal. As undersecretary to Knox from 1940 to 1944, Forrestal had been heavily involved in the naval procurement programs that had flourished in those years.[74] Upon becoming secretary of the navy, Forrestal resented King's influence in production issues, which the secretary apparently regarded as his own private preserve. Shortly after Knox's death, Forrestal issued the following terse and sharp warning to King in regard to the Naval Office of Procurement and Material: "Any memorandums or Directives relating to or dealing with the functions of subject office will be cleared with the Office of the Secretary of the Navy before transmission."[75] Such bitterness between the navy secretary and the Chief of Naval Operations would have been unthinkable during the tenure of Knox. King's own view of his relations with Forrestal was characteristically succinct: "I didn't like him, and he didn't like me."[76]

President Roosevelt intervened far less often in strategic matters than did Churchill and Churchill's cronies. The evidence shows that after the founding of the U.S. Joint Chiefs of Staff in February 1942 the president went against their recommendations on only two occasions. In one, the decision to proceed with Torch, Roosevelt courted disaster by thus causing the delay of the cross-Channel assault until 1944. This choice, while keeping American casualties to a minimum, allowed Russian casualties to continue to skyrocket and caused a marked deterioration in the relations between the Soviet Union and its Western allies. The president's other wartime incursion into strategic decision making was far more enlightened. As mentioned previously, the president placed severe constraints upon the Allied campaign to retake Burma from the Japanese by canceling the Buccaneer/Andamans campaign at the time of the Cairo/Teheran discussions in November and December 1943. The U.S. Joint Chiefs of Staff opposed the president on this matter.[77] However, the dramatic success of the American advances in the Pacific theater, which in early 1944 began to exceed the expectations of all Allied planners, made it abundantly clear that the war against Japan was not going to be decided in Burma anyway. Thus, it must be admitted that in regard to Buccaneer, the president got one right.

Admiral King remarked in a 1949 interview that "the British Chiefs of Staff had to do what Churchill wanted done, whether they liked it or not. The Joint Chiefs of Staff had little trouble with President Roosevelt. . . . 'If one would fight F.D.R. he would quit.'"[78] In fact, as his biographer James MacGregor Burns has pointed out, Franklin Roosevelt's greatness as a wartime leader stemmed largely from his willingness to delegate strategic decision making to the Joint Chiefs of Staff and the Joint and Combined Planning Staffs. FDR did not feel threatened by the military talent represented by the presence in Washington of the Joint and Combined Chiefs of Staff. Rather, he took pride in the fact that he almost never had to overrule the decisions of the Joint Chiefs, people whom *he* had had the wisdom to appoint to their commands.[79] In terms of their respective temperaments, FDR was much more comfortable with a "hands off" management style than Churchill, who was happy only if he could interfere everywhere and anywhere.

Another reason that armchair strategy was less of a problem for the American CCS members than for their British colleagues is that in the United States some of the potential offenders neutralized each other by mutual antagonism and suspicion. For example, on orders from the president, the U.S. State Department was not represented at either Casablanca or Teheran.[80] The president also seemed to attract most of the ire of American isolationists, to such an extent that they became a headache for him instead of the Combined Chiefs of Staff.

The Pearl Harbor attack greatly weakened the isolationist movement in the United States, but isolationism never quite went away. Some of the more radical isolationists, such as the "radio priest" Father Charles Coughlin, were never reconciled to America as an active belligerent. Others, such as press baron "Colonel" Robert McCormick, owner of the *Chicago Tribune,* and Republican senators Hiram Johnson (of California) and Arthur Vandenberg (of Michigan), became troublemakers of a different stripe, by attempting after Pearl Harbor to force FDR to repudiate the "Germany first" strategy in favor of devoting all of America's military resources to the war against Japan. This sentiment went so far as to convince Senator Vandenberg in 1944 that he had found the perfect Republican presidential candidate to challenge FDR, in the person of General Douglas MacArthur. The constant complaints from the paranoid MacArthur that his Southwest Pacific command was being maliciously deprived of resources fit perfectly into the new cause of the isolationists—that liberating Europe was far less important than defeating the Japanese. Suggesting MacArthur, whose idea of a great president was Herbert Hoover, as a presidential candidate in 1944 shows how the sentiments of the isolationists–turned–"Pacific firsters" had by then become combined with the "anything to get rid of Roosevelt" desperation of the Republican Party.[81] The idea of MacArthur as a candidate did not progress very far, and it would be Thomas E. Dewey who went down to inevitable defeat in the 1944 presidential election.

Another reason why President Roosevelt was less dangerous as an armchair strategist than Churchill was that FDR made more of an effort to keep the focus of the Allies upon military, rather than political, aims during the war. He was not entirely successful in this, however. The president felt compelled to attempt to formulate postwar political plans for Asia to a greater extent than for Europe.[82] One result of this was the formulation of the Pacific War Council, which met on thirty-six occasions between April 1942 and February 1944. FDR served as chairman, thus entertaining another group of potential armchair strategists and keeping them out of the way of the Combined Chiefs of Staff. Besides those of the United States, the members of the Pacific War Council consisted of representatives from Canada, China, Australia, New Zealand, the Philippines, Great Britain, the Netherlands, and the Free French. The issues discussed at meetings of the Pacific War Council included supply, strategy, and, according to Timothy Maga, "what the post-war Pacific should look like."[83]

Roosevelt shared some of his own racial views with the members of the Pacific War Council. For instance, the president approved of a plan, which had been decided upon as far back as 1935, to grant independence from the United States to the Philippines in 1945. Rather paternalistically, he felt that a long period of American tutelage had prepared the people of the Philippines for independence. However, FDR dismissed the peoples of Borneo and Indochina as "headhunters," not yet ready to be released from

European colonial rule.[84] Such a statement was at odds with the anticolonial sentiment that manifested itself in the United States during the war.

The Pacific War Council had no binding power to decide anything. It was solely a forum for inter-Allied discussion in regard to the war against Japan. In this regard, it provided a service to the Combined Chiefs of Staff. Admiral King and General Marshall promoted the Pacific War Council vigorously. For them it represented an ideal method for dissipating the frustration felt by nations that were part of the Allied camp but had no representation in the deliberations of the Combined Chiefs of Staff—where the real decisions about strategy were being made.[85] It should be noted, however, that the fact that the council lacked real power did not go entirely unnoticed by its delegates, such as China's Dr. T. V. Soong.[86]

In marked contrast to the trust placed in his military chiefs by President Roosevelt was the relationship between Winston Churchill and the British Chiefs of Staff Committee. Even an inveterate meddler like Churchill was reluctant to flatly overrule his military advisers. However, he appears to have devoted a great deal of energy to attempting to bring those advisers around to his point of view, rather than accepting their views at the outset. The controversy over the Pacific strategy described in chapter 3 is a good example of this. Meetings between Churchill and the COS Committee occurred far more frequently than did FDR's meetings with the Joint Chiefs of Staff. Not only did Churchill attend many of the regular COS Committee meetings in London, but Brooke had to give up the chair to him when he did.[87] It is interesting to note, however, that if he chose to surround himself with civilian advisers who, like Lindemann/Cherwell, were sometimes problematic, Churchill's judgment was considerably more sound when it came to *military* advisers.

All of the British Chiefs of Staff were subjected to the micromanaging tendencies of the prime minister. With varying degrees of success, each struggled to devise strategies to deal with this situation. Even though Churchill and Admiral Pound were friends—or perhaps *because* they were friends—Churchill's temper tantrums and odd working habits (such as scheduling meetings at midnight, not because of any great crisis but simply because he liked working at midnight) took a greater physical toll on Pound than on the other British chiefs. Churchill's written messages to Pound and Portal were invariably rude and accusatory. Such treatment seemed to sap Pound's strength. The chief of the Naval Staff was physically a wreck even at the start of the war, seeming tired and prematurely old, as well as suffering severe arthritis in his left hip. Pound took Churchill's criticisms to heart, overworking in his determination to provide dedicated service to the prime minister and the nation. In the end, Churchill wore Pound out.[88]

Air Chief Marshal Portal proved to be more successful in handling Churchill. The prime minister admired Portal for his tact, modesty, and determination.[89] Portal conceded that what he referred to as Churchill's "brainwaves on strategy" were highly problematic for the COS Committee. He felt, however, that Churchill made up for these with his courage, energy, and stamina and by supporting the British Chiefs of Staff when things went wrong.[90] Portal's biographer is undoubtedly correct in writing that upon receipt of one of the Churchill's frequent and strongly worded criticisms, "Portal would reply in studiously courteous terms, avoiding polemics, but citing solid facts and figures to rebut the Prime Minister's accusations."[91]

Churchill's attempts to impose his own strategic views upon the British Chiefs of Staff infuriated Admiral Cunningham after he took over the position of First Sea Lord in October 1943.[92] Cunningham's biographer, Oliver Warner, claims that Churchill and Cunningham got along well together.[93] Archival evidence, however, does not bear this out. Cunningham's diary entries in regard to the debates over the Pacific strategy (covered in chapter 3) indicate that Cunningham in fact developed an intense dislike for Churchill.[94]

The misguided Bay of Bengal strategy was not by any means the only wild idea of Churchill's that the British chiefs were forced to attempt to neutralize. Brooke did not share Churchill's enthusiasm for a campaign against the German forces in northern Norway (Operation Jupiter).[95] Brooke wrote in September 1942, "It is quite impossible at the same time as the North African expedition. Shipping alone will make it impossible."[96] His colleagues on the COS Committee shared Brooke's doubts.[97] To the American CCS members, any ideas of landing in Norway were simply additional manifestations of the British reluctance to undertake Overlord. In the fall of 1943, however, Churchill had still not given up hope of an operation to drive the Germans out of Norway. This type of operation fit perfectly into the prime minister's penchant for peripheral military operations, concepts that while imaginative had little or no strategic validity. (Gallipoli in World War I and Churchill's obsession with the Dodecanese in World War II are other examples.) The disaster of the British Norwegian campaign of 1940, in which Churchill had played such a large role, seems only to have whet his appetite for a second go-around. As the plans for Overlord were becoming finalized, the British Joint Planning Staff echoed Brooke's sentiments that Jupiter was simply not a practical or efficient use of Allied resources.[98] General Marshall was in complete agreement with the Brooke and British planners in this regard.

There were civilians whom the American members of the Combined Chiefs of Staff found to be quite helpful. One of these was Harry Hopkins, who, in addition to being a close adviser to the president, served as the director of the American branch of the Munitions Assignment Board. Hopkins never questioned the right of the Combined Chiefs of Staff to have final say over Anglo-American munitions distribution.[99] Hopkins was on excellent terms with the U.S. Joint Chiefs of Staff. In a letter written a few weeks after the Japanese surrender, Admiral King wrote the ailing Hopkins, "I shall never forget—nor do I intend to let others forget—how much the Joint Chiefs of Staff owe to your unfailing interest, your keen analysis, and your practical advice. In fact, the people of the United States owe you more than they know, but I am confident they will, in due course, come to realize the scope and importance of your services to the country throughout the conduct of the war."[100]

Because the production of munitions was so closely associated with military strategy in World War II, there was always the danger that civilians involved with industrial mobilization might indirectly exert a harmful influence upon Allied strategy. Maintaining control over weapons production was therefore of great concern to the Combined Chiefs of Staff. In the United States this was difficult, because there was no single "production czar." However, the elements of the somewhat decentralized American munitions-production system did have one common basis, namely, that the federal government had taken control over all basic aspects of the wartime economy. This included providing the bulk of the money to build munitions factories, controlling the manufacture and distribution of machine tools and raw materials, and purchasing the finished products.[101]

Therefore, while the U.S. Joint Chiefs of Staff were forced to deal with civilian organizations, such as the War Production Board (WPB) and the Reconstruction Finance Corporation, in regard to munitions production, Marshall, King, Arnold, and Leahy were able to maintain a dominant influence over what, and how much, was produced. One factor that allowed this to be accomplished was that the American services, and their chiefs, were all heavily involved in the procurement process. For example, through Lieutenant General Brehon Somervell, head of the Army Service Forces, General Marshall was able to maintain army control over the materiel produced for the Army Ground Forces. As stated in the official U.S. Army history, under the March 9, 1942, reorganization of the War Department that created the Army Service Forces/Services of Supply, "Somervell now found himself in command of the Army's entire machinery for procurement, economic mobilization and supply."[102]

As such, General Somervell sometimes clashed with (and acted as a brake on) Donald Nelson, chairman of the WPB. The board controlled the distribution of raw materials, but the Army Service Forces controlled the procurement of weapons and supplies for the Army Ground Forces. This included artillery, tanks, ammunition, and medical equipment. Somervell and Nelson disagreed as to the extent to which the American economy should be converted to war production. Nelson feared that Somervell wanted the virtual elimination of the production of any civilian goods whatsoever and felt that this would cause the economy as a whole to become dangerously unbalanced. As it turned out, Nelson's view of what Somervell wanted was unduly harsh. The head of the Army Service Forces did not wish to shut down the civilian economy. He simply wanted to be sure that munitions production had priority until victory was achieved.[103] General Somervell's biographer summarizes the rivalry between Nelson and Somervell nicely, writing that General Somervell "saw Nelson as an errand boy, whose primary job was to see that army requirements were satisfied, and thus, he pushed for more efficient management in the WPB and a stronger voice for the military in the field of production. Jealously guarding the army's prerogatives, Somervell refused to accept the WPB as a superior agency and aggressively asserted military claims to scarce raw materials."[104]

Another player in the confusing tangle of American weapons procurement management was William S. Knudsen, a former president of the General Motors Corporation, who in January 1942 was commissioned directly from civilian life as an army lieutenant general and made "Director of War Production for the War Department."[105] Exactly where this placed Knudsen vis-à-vis General Somervell was not made clear, which seems to have been the way FDR liked to do business.

The Combined Chiefs of Staff worked with many forceful civilian personalities during the war (and had a few of their own strong personalities on tap, in the form of subordinates like General Somervell). There are several reasons why the Combined Chiefs were highly successful in keeping the armchair strategists at bay. Among these, Churchill's fear of another Gallipoli (for which he might have to take the blame if he forced a strategic issue) and bureaucratic infighting among civilian agencies in Washington and London are certainly important. However, the most important reason seems to have been that because the Combined Chiefs of Staff were an unusually talented group of individuals, the politicians, the bureaucrats, and the general public were content to leave strategic decision making in their hands.

SEVEN

Delegation versus Control from the Center

During the war it was not always apparent to the public, to politicians, or to military personnel just how important the Combined Chiefs of Staff was to the war effort of the Western Allies. Part of the reason for this was that a bureaucratic organization like the Combined Chiefs of Staff was a brand-new way of running a war. There were lingering doubts that war could be controlled by a central authority removed from the immediacy of the battlefield. Also partly responsible for this situation is the fact that none of the members of the Combined Chiefs of Staff had the publicity-seeking mentality of, say, Douglas MacArthur. In fact, its principal members all shared an active dislike for publicity. During the war, news that emanated from the battlefront (from the headquarters of the theater commander) had a more immediate hold upon the imagination of the public than did the decisions quietly being made by the Combined Chiefs of Staff in the Public Health Building on Constitution Avenue in Washington. To the public, the Combined Chiefs of Staff principals were better known as service chiefs rather than as members of a grand-strategy-manufacturing entity.

One result of the incomplete understanding of the value of central direction of the British-American war effort that existed at the time was that there were periodic efforts to move CCS members out of Washington and London and into large field commands of their own. This line of thinking was a reversion to the World War I idea that warfare should be controlled from a headquarters near the front line and was therefore the antithesis of the reasoning behind the creation of the Combined Chiefs of Staff. Happily, these efforts failed. From the time that Admiral Leahy arrived in Washington in July 1942 until the end of the war, the only changes in the composition of the principal membership of the Combined Chiefs of Staff were the resignation of the then seriously ill Admiral Pound in September 1943, his replacement the following month by Admiral Cunningham, and the death of Field Marshal Dill in November 1944. Therefore, the Combined Chiefs were able to continue unhindered in their role as the primary strategic planning organization for the Western Allies.

Perhaps the primary reason that good sense prevailed in the matter of not breaking up the Combined Chiefs of Staff team by sending its members out to field commands is that, as Richard Overy has pointed out, the British and the Americans had learned the critical lesson from the Great War that grand strategy was too important to be left to frontline commanders, who might be too caught up in what was happening on their respective fronts to see the big picture. Politicians had to get involved in active oversight of military campaigns to avoid the type of military disasters brought on during World War I by the decisions of such frontline commanders as those two bumbling incompetents Sir Douglas Haig and Robert Nivelle.[1] I would add to this that with rare exceptions, such as the decision to green-light Torch and then to cancel Buccaneer, Churchill and FDR felt compelled to delegate the direction of grand strategy for the Western Allies to the Combined Chiefs of Staff. As stated in chapter 6, this was not a concession that the prime minister and the president made willingly. In Churchill's case, the terrible memory of Gallipoli was a constant reminder of his very real fallibility as a strategist.[2] The oversight provided by Churchill and Roosevelt during World War II consisted largely of approving decisions arrived at by the Combined Chiefs of Staff, although, as stated previously, the Combined Chiefs had to fend off numerous attempts by their political overlords, especially Churchill, to influence strategic decision making by putting forward half-baked pet schemes, such as the Jupiter plan to drive the Germans out of Norway.

The activities of the Combined Chiefs of Staff represented a sort of board of directors, corporate style of running a war. Such a system invariably forced the Combined Chiefs to delegate a great deal of responsibility to their theater commanders in Europe, the Pacific, the Mediterranean, and Asia. The question of how much authority to delegate was a difficult one. Throughout the war, the Combined Chiefs attempted to strike a balance between, on one hand, allowing their on-the-scene commanders enough discretion to modify CCS directives to suit local conditions without, on the other, appearing to be totally detached from the day-to-day activities of the Allied forces that were deployed at the various fighting fronts. On the whole, this system worked well. This was largely due, no doubt, to the fact that Allied theater commanders, such as Admiral Nimitz and General Eisenhower, were not afraid to exercise the considerable authority that had been delegated to them. There were, however, instances in which the Combined Chiefs of Staff delegated either too little or too much responsibility to their theater and other top commanders.

As mentioned earlier, both Marshall and Brooke had been considered for the Overlord command. That was not the only instance during the war in which there was talk of giving a field command to a member of the Combined Chiefs of Staff. Churchill had earlier tried to give Brooke a theater command in the Middle East. This was apparently something of a sudden inspiration, one that took hold of Churchill while he and Brooke were visiting the front in North Africa. During the course of this visit to the Western Desert in August 1942, the prime minister had decided to replace the Middle East commander, General Sir Claude Auchinleck, as well as his top field commander, Major General Neil Ritchie, then commanding the British Eighth Army. Churchill initially wanted Brooke to become part of the new command team that would, he hoped, reverse recent British setbacks in North Africa, such as the fall of Tobruk on June 21, 1942. Brooke describes, in his diary entry for August 6, his first intimation of the prime minister's plans in a quote that nicely encapsulates the essence of the Brooke-Churchill working relationship for the entire war: "P.M. suddenly burst into my room. Very elated and informed me that his thoughts were taking shape and he would soon commit himself to paper! I rather shuddered & wondered what he was up to!"[3]

What Churchill had in mind was to make Egypt into a subtheater of the Middle East command and give it to Brooke. Serving under Brooke would have been General Bernard Montgomery, who was being considered for the Eighth Army command.[4] In the end, Montgomery got the Eighth Army, but the new theater commander in Egypt was not Brooke but General Sir Harold Alexander. This was a relief to Brooke, who had declined the offer of the theater command primarily because he lacked firsthand experience in desert warfare. He was also aware that as CIGS he was in a position to act as a restraint upon the more grandiose of Churchill's schemes; Brooke was convinced that in this way he was providing a valuable service to the Allies.[5] Future events were to prove him entirely correct.

That Brooke, Marshall, and Dill could have been considered for top Allied field commands during the war shows the high esteem in which the individual members of the Combined Chiefs of Staff were held. It also shows that it took some time for the true value of the Combined Chiefs of Staff, as an integral unit that should not be tampered with, to sink in. In the end, it proved far more beneficial to the Allies to retain Brooke, Marshall, and Dill in their Combined Chiefs of Staff roles, from which they were able to continue to supervise overall American-British strategy. To carry out that strategy, they would rely upon their theater commanders, to whom they would delegate the responsibility for specific operations.

Clearly there were instances in which top Allied field commanders failed to measure up to the expectations of the Combined Chiefs of Staff. The crisis in the Western Desert in the summer of 1942 is a case in point. Technically, the decision to replace Auchinleck and Ritchie was made by Churchill, but Brooke, traveling with the prime minister at the time, concurred. As far as the replacements, Brooke and Churchill were agreed on General Alexander as the new Middle East commander, but Brooke had doubts about Churchill's first choice as the new commander of the British Eighth Army, Lieutenant General William "Strafer" Gott. Shortly after being appointed, Gott was killed when the plane he was traveling in was shot down by a German fighter plane. Gott had been a friend of Brooke, and the CIGS was certainly distraught over his death. However, it did clear the way for Montgomery, whom Brooke preferred over Gott, to be named Eighth Army commander.[6] In the 1950s, Brooke reflected on Gott's death in an interesting sentence: "It seemed almost like the hand of God suddenly appearing to set matters right where we had gone wrong."[7]

Another high-ranking field commander who had to be relieved was an American vice admiral, Robert L. Ghormley, who cracked under the strain of commanding the South Pacific Area during the Guadalcanal campaign in the summer and fall of 1942. Ghormley was not quite a theater commander, his command being a subset of the Pacific Ocean Areas theater command of Admiral Nimitz. However, Ghormley's sector was an active one, and his breakdown could not have come at a worse time—the height of the fighting on Guadalcanal. Admiral Nimitz, who visited Ghormley at his headquarters at Noumea on New Caledonia on September 28, 1942, to confer with him, was shocked by what he found. Nimitz's biographer records that Ghormley "was occupying a small hotbox of an office in his headquarters ship, the *Argonne,* which had no air-conditioning. He had scarcely left the vessel since he arrived at Noumea just before the invasion of Guadalcanal. Nimitz wondered why Ghormley had not taken more comfortable and commodious headquarters ashore. It appeared that the local French authorities had offered nothing of the sort and Ghormley had not insisted."[8]

Indeed, Ghormley was physically wasting away under the strain of command. He seems to have fallen into a deep depression, due mainly to the pressures of the Guadalcanal campaign that he was supposed to be supervising. Ghormley's teeth had become severely decayed, due most likely to a combination of the tropical climate and his own neglect, owing to his depression, of personal hygiene.

General Arnold, who was visiting the South Pacific Area at the same time, was also surprised that Ghormley almost never went ashore, though his ship was anchored in a protected harbor. Ghormley was working too hard and getting no exercise. In classic workaholic fashion, Ghormley worked all the time but got nothing done. A good example, at which both Arnold and Nimitz were aghast, was that some eighty merchant ships were anchored in the roadstead at Noumea and not being unloaded. Allied merchant ships, not to mention their precious cargoes of supplies and munitions, were in terribly short supply the world over, and such a bottleneck at Noumea represented managerial negligence that was practically criminal. Ghormley claimed that it was impossible to know what was in each ship and thus the order in which they should be unloaded, because nobody had prepared proper manifests when they had been loaded in the United States. That, if true, was something beyond Ghormley's control. However, the solution was within his control, and his idea about how to solve the problem was simply not rational. Ghormley spoke of possibly sending the ships to Wellington, New Zealand, more than a thousand miles to the south, there to be unloaded, provided with manifests, packed up again, and sent back to Noumea.[9] Meanwhile, the situation on Guadalcanal was getting worse and worse, and the American marines there were short of supplies of all kinds. What Ghormley should have done was to send those eighty ships to Guadalcanal immediately. Certainly doing so would have meant running the risk of sending something totally unneeded—say, perhaps, a consignment of typewriters—to the marines there, but no matter. Those ships undoubtedly also contained ammunition, medicine, and food that the marines did desperately need. There was no time for something so outrageous as sending the ships to New Zealand for sorting out.

With Admiral King's approval, and not a moment too soon, Nimitz relieved Ghormley and appointed Vice Admiral William F. Halsey as the new commander of the South Pacific Area, effective October 18, 1942.[10] The decision was a difficult one for Nimitz, since Ghormley was an old friend. Nimitz wrote to his wife, "Today I have replaced Ghormley with Halsey. . . . Ghormley was too immersed in detail and not sufficiently bold and aggressive at the right times."[11] When Ghormley visited Admiral King in Washington in late 1942, King became convinced that the pain caused by bad teeth had been the explanation for Ghormley's poor performance in the South Pacific.[12] However, it is more likely that the teeth were a symptom of Ghormley's problems, not the cause.

One of Halsey's first moves was to get off that infernal headquarters ship in the harbor and commandeer, not without complaints from the French, living and working quarters ashore in Noumea.[13] The manner in which the rank and file of the Pacific Fleet found out about the change in command at Noumea is interesting. On October 26, 1942, barely a week after Halsey had arrived in Noumea, American ships, including the aircraft carriers *Enterprise* and *Hornet,* preparing to halt a Japanese naval force that was approaching Guadalcanal received a most un-Ghormley-like radio message. The impact of that message is perhaps best described by Edward Stafford in his biography of the *Enterprise,* which like the *Lexington,* was a very "happy" ship. The "Big E" had been Halsey's flagship during the first six months of the war, but its crew had lost track of Halsey when the admiral was hospitalized just prior to Midway. Now, as they prepared to fight what would become known as the battle of the Santa Cruz Islands, the crew of the *Enterprise* found out what had happened to their beloved old admiral. As Stafford writes:

> Before daylight on the twenty-sixth . . . a message was received from the headquarters of the commander, South Pacific Force, at Noumea. It was in a familiar style. Three words:
>   ATTACK, REPEAT, ATTACK
> Only one man could have sent it and the Big E's men knew him well. Bill Halsey was back in the war. . . . It was by his order that Kinkaid's task force

was engaged in the northwestward sweep which had found the enemy. A new confidence stirred through the *Enterprise*.[14]

Halsey also visited the marines on Guadalcanal, something Ghormley had failed to do. Halsey then cleared up the supply logjam that he had inherited by seeing to it that ships were unloaded quickly at Noumea and sent on their way. While Halsey's performance when he returned to seagoing command in 1944 was to be decidedly less than stellar, his fighting spirit was just what the doctor ordered for the South Pacific area in late 1942. The vigor that Halsey brought to his new job as South Pacific commander was critical to the eventual American success in driving the last Japanese troops off Guadalcanal in early February 1943.[15]

As Army Chief of Staff, General Marshall too had to deal with field commanders who did not measure up under pressure. The most difficult such situation for Marshall developed in the always-troublesome Italian campaign shortly after the Allied landings at Anzio in January 1944, a campaign that was supposed to provide the Allies a shortcut to Rome. Instead of a shortcut, the Anzio campaign, for which Churchill had pressed vigorously, became a deadly stalemate. The senior Allied commander, American major general John P. Lucas of VI Corps, decided to dig in and fortify the beachhead rather than move quickly toward Rome. The results were deeply disappointing, even tragic—German troops rushed to the area and laid siege to the beachhead. For weeks, the British and American troops there were shelled by artillery and strafed and bombed by aircraft. With Marshall's concurrence, Lieutenant General Mark Clark replaced Lucas with Major General Lucien K. Truscott Jr. The change of command did not immediately reverse the Allied fortunes at Anzio, but Truscott proved to be much more of a fighter than was Lucas.[16]

Historians have noted that during the war General Marshall read the memoirs of Field Marshal Sir William Robertson, who had been Chief of the Imperial General Staff during World War I when Alan Brooke had been a young officer serving in the trenches on the western front. In his book *Soldiers and Statesmen*, Roberts deplored such wasteful diversions as Churchill's Gallipoli campaign and stressed the importance of concentrating strength on the Great War's vital front—northern France and Belgium. For Marshall, the book was a vindication of his insistence, over British objections, on an early cross-channel invasion.[17] Another work of military history that made a profound impression on General Marshall during World War II was Douglas Southall Freeman's *Lee's Lieutenants: A Study in Command,* the first volume of which was published in 1942. Freeman sent a copy to Marshall, who read it with interest, as did Admiral King. Reading *Lee's Lieutenants* reminded Marshall (and presumably King as well) that he was not the first high-ranking military officer who was sometimes disappointed in officers to whom he had delegated responsibility for action in the field.[18] While many Civil War histories focus on the shocking incompetence of the successive commanders of the Union's Army of the Potomac prior to the appointment of General George Gordon Meade in late June 1863, just a few days before Gettysburg, Freeman's book is an excellent reminder that Robert E. Lee's Army of Northern Virginia was not exactly the finely tuned Swiss watch that it is often characterized as having been. For instance, Marshall would have read Freeman's postmortem on the performance of Lee's subordinate commanders during the Seven Days' battles in the summer of 1862. Freeman records how Confederate brigadier general Robert Toombs, an arrogant braggart, was so insubordinate that on one occasion early in the war General Joseph E. Johnston felt compelled to have him arrested. Later, at Malvern Hill, the last engagement of the Seven Days, the brigade Toombs was commanding performed poorly—a performance witnessed by Major General D. H. Hill. When Hill reprimanded Toombs sharply, the latter proceeded to challenge Hill, his superior officer, to a duel.[19] Hill declined, informing Toombs that "when we have a country to defend and enemies to fight, [a duel] would be highly improper and contrary to the dictates of plain duty."[20]

Even Lee's most able commanders gave him trouble. For instance, in the wake of the Seven Days, Major General James Longstreet felt that "the other" and somewhat more famous Hill, Major General Ambrose Powell Hill, was allowing newspaper columnists to give him, Hill, too much credit for Confederate successes at Mechanicsville and Frayser's Farm, at the expense of Longstreet, under whom A. P. Hill was then serving. A. P. Hill and Longstreet were both divisional commanders, and they were two of the Confederacy's brightest stars in terms of military talent. Tension mounted between the two men, during which period Longstreet decided that A. P. Hill was being insubordinate. As with Johnston and Toombs, Longstreet had A. P. Hill temporarily arrested, but almost certainly with less reason than Johnston had had with Toombs. Again there was talk of a duel. Finally,

Robert E. Lee had to step in and settle the dispute, by sending A. P. Hill and his division off to serve under Thomas J. "Stonewall" Jackson.[21]

Marshall, incidentally, was a fast reader. *Lee's Lieutenants* weighs in at over seven hundred pages, and Marshall, who did not have much time for recreational reading during the war, apparently finished it in a week or two.[22] In December 1942, having read the book, Marshall wrote to Freeman that "my griefs over the personal feelings of leaders and subordinate leaders these days shrank into insignificance beside those of Lee. . . . The miracle of the rapid and quiet adjustments effected by Lee between Malvern Hill and Second Manassas is possibly the strongest evidence of his capacity to command citizen-soldiers."[23] Lee's "adjustments" to which Marshall refers included settling the Longstreet–A. P. Hill feud and getting rid of incompetent generals like "Prince" John Magruder and Benjamin Huger. The politically well connected Toombs, a former senator from Georgia, was kept on for a time.[24] Freeman's assessments may have been colored somewhat by the fact that highlighting the deficiencies of some Confederate generals makes the achievements of Freeman's true hero, Robert E. Lee, stand out in bold relief. Nevertheless, the book was an interesting read for General Marshall.[25] Similarly, reading *Lee's Lieutenants* may have helped Admiral King to feel less guilty about the Ghormley situation.

The rare occasions in World War II when the Combined Chiefs of Staff decided to bypass theater commanders and become involved in day-to-day operations in the field did not always end happily. The disastrous fate of convoy PQ 17, which was eviscerated by German submarine and air attack in July 1942 while en route from Iceland to Archangel, is a case in point. Admiral Pound bears much of the responsibility for the fact that twenty-three out of the thirty-four Allied merchant ships in the PQ 17 convoy were sunk by enemy action, with heavy loss of life. On July 4, when the convoy had been at sea for six days and had just passed south of Spitzbergen, Pound became convinced that heavy German surface ships based in Norway, including the battleship *Tirpitz,* had sailed to attack the convoy. He therefore issued a direct and highly controversial order to Rear Admiral L. H. K. Hamilton, one of two British admirals at or near the scene, that the Allied covering force of cruisers and destroyers had to be withdrawn and that the ships of the convoy were to scatter.[26] Once they had done so, the ships of the convoy were virtually defenseless against German aircraft and submarines. It is a wonder that any ships reached Archangel at all.

The other British admiral near the scene was Sir John Tovey, the commander in chief of the British Home Fleet. Tovey commanded a separate inter-Allied striking force that was deployed along the northern convoy route for the very reason that it had been well known beforehand that the *Tirpitz* might appear and attack a passing convoy. The force that Admiral Tovey had at his disposal—which included the aircraft carrier HMS *Victorious* and two battleships, HMS *Duke of York* and USS *Washington*—almost certainly would have proven more than a match for the *Tirpitz*. The Allied battleships were at some distance from the convoy, however, and thus intercepting the *Tirpitz* would not have been easy. It would probably have been necessary for torpedo planes from *Victorious* to attack the German battleship and slow it down so that *Duke of York* and *Washington* could catch up, in a fashion similar to that in which the *Bismarck,* sister ship to the *Tirpitz,* had been destroyed a year earlier. Even to put the British carrier's aircraft within striking distance might have required turning PQ 17 around and having it steam westward, away from the Russian ports and toward the Allied heavy ships, an idea to which Pound was opposed.[27] In a sort of savage irony, the German battleship never appeared, having turned back to its base long before reaching the convoy. According to Stephen Roskill, Tovey, when informed of Pound's orders to Hamilton, issued a "prophetic warning that to order the convoy to scatter would be 'sheer bloody murder.'"[28]

Overruling his commanders on the scene was, in this instance, clearly a mistake on the part of Pound. It is especially surprising that Pound would overrule Tovey, who had a great deal of experience at sea and in combat. For instance, Tovey had been in command of the Home Fleet when it had finally tracked down and sunk the *Bismarck*. Tovey had been on hand for the final battle of that episode on May 27, 1941, on board his flagship, the battleship HMS *King George V*. However, Tovey was more than a hundred miles away from PQ 17 when the order to scatter was given. At least part of Pound's decision to micromanage the situation from London was that the senior naval officer actually with the convoy was Captain Jackie Broome, RN, who commanded a force of destroyers and other small escorts. Pound felt it would be unjust to force a relatively junior officer to make such a momentous decision on his own.[29] Thus, Pound's motives were more benign than those of many people, like Pound, who cannot bring themselves to delegate. Rather than feeling himself superior and the only one capable of making an informed decision, Pound seems to have been trying to protect his underlings by taking the heaviest responsibilities upon himself. Nonetheless, the results of Pound's decision were disastrous. He would have done better to order Broome to break radio silence (so as to confer with Hamilton and Tovey) and allow Tovey to make the final decision as to whether or not to scatter the convoy. Pound could have better protected his officers, not to mention the crews of the PQ 17 merchant ships that were sunk (in freezing Arctic waters, where there was almost no chance of survival for men who went into the water even if picked up quickly), by promising Tovey that he would support whatever decision Tovey made.

There were, however, occasions when Pound's intervention in day-to-day operational matters seemed more enlightened and helpful. For example, the First Sea Lord never felt that enough was being done about the U-boat menace in the Atlantic. In July 1943, therefore, he curtly instructed the Naval Staff that "no vessel at present employed in the battle against the U-boats is to be diverted from this purpose or paid off without my approval."[30] A year earlier, Pound had worked out an arrangement with Air Chief Marshal Portal by which some additional long-range aircraft, such as Lancaster bombers, would be diverted from the bombing of Germany in order to concentrate on antisubmarine patrols over the Atlantic.[31] Also, during the hunt for the *Bismarck* in May 1941, Pound made a significant contribution by realizing that Admiral Tovey's staff aboard *King George V* had plotted the *Bismarck*'s position incorrectly and had thus for some hours inadvertently taken the Home Fleet *away* from the *Bismarck*. The Admiralty in London had the correct bearing, and Pound used it to enable Force H, hurrying north from Gibraltar, to find and damage the German battleship using carrier-based aircraft from HMS *Ark Royal,* slowing the *Bismarck* down so that Tovey was able to catch up the next morning and sink the German raider.[32]

Admiral Pound certainly believed in delegating responsibility, even though in practice he found it difficult to do so. He valued field commanders who were able to delegate. For example, Pound admired the way that General Eisenhower was able to successfully delegate responsibility to his commanders during Torch. In regard to Admiral Cunningham, who was then serving as the Allied naval commander for Torch, Pound noted that "Cunningham is co-operating with Eisenhower and has not received one single order from the latter."[33]

Air Chief Marshal Portal was no exception to the general preference of CCS members to delegate whenever possible. However, Portal did score some notable successes when he decided that he had to intervene in day-to-day matters. For example, it was Portal who created the Pathfinders in August 1942. This was an elite unit composed of the air crews in RAF Bomber Command who had the best records for consistently finding their targets, night after night. By placing them all in one group and sending them out ahead of the main bombing force to identify the target area by dropping flares, Portal hoped to improve the accuracy of British nighttime bombing raids against Germany—which had hitherto been rather dismal.

Portal's intervention in this matter differed from Pound's action in regard to convoy PQ 17 in that Portal was attempting to find a long-term solution to a major problem, while Pound had acted to overrule a field commander during one specific operation. CCS members were entitled to act in such instances with the authority of the entire group, because the Combined Chiefs often appointed individual members to act on its behalf for a particular issue. For instance, Portal had been given the responsibility for supervising the Anglo-American combined bomber offensive on behalf of the Combined Chiefs of Staff. General Arnold performed a similar role in the operations of the American B-29 bombers based in the Mariana Islands for firebombing raids against Japanese cities. Such a system is similar to the manner in which, under the legal system of the United States, appeals to the U.S. Supreme Court are sometimes heard by one or two justices rather than by the entire Court.

Results were to prove that the Pathfinders were a successful organization. Portal's biographer points out that while Group Captain S. O. Bufton of the Air Staff and Lord Cherwell had supported the idea of the Pathfinders, "it was Portal who insisted on its creation."[34] "Bomber" Harris was, along with his air group commanders, bitterly opposed to what he referred to as a "corps d'elite" within Bomber Command. Nonetheless, in June 1942, Portal politely informed Harris that he was being overruled; the chief of the Air Staff pointed out that the new organization would serve Bomber Command in the same manner that specialized reconnaissance units serve the infantry during ground campaigns. Rather than hurting the overall efficiency of Bomber Command as Harris feared by robbing the average squadron of its best pilots and air crew, Portal pointed out that the Pathfinders were sure to set a new standard of excellence that would have a ripple-down effect benefiting Bomber Command as a whole.[35]

Portal was capable of occasionally exchanging his good manners for ruthlessness when dealing with his subordinates.[36] This is apparent in

Portal's desire for discipline in his command. The chief of the Air Staff was not afraid to prod his commanders. In July 1944 Portal wrote to Air Chief Marshal Sir Trafford Leigh-Mallory, General Eisenhower's air commander for Overlord,

> It is stated in the report that an officer who failed to decipher a 5-Z message for four hours was "working under very difficult conditions due to enemy action." If this means that the poor man had been blown up and was trying to collect his ciphers etc. in the dark, it is a perfectly good excuse. If, however, it means that the man who ought to have been deciphering a 5-Z message was cowering in a dugout because a few bombs were falling at intervals in the neighborhood then even under our rather milk and water arrangements he should be punished. In Russia he would be shot and I cannot help noticing that the Russians do seem to make a success of their war.[37]

According to his biographer, Admiral King "never entirely trusted Nimitz's judgement. In King's mind, Nimitz took bad advice and was too willing to compromise with the Army in the interests of harmony."[38] This may be an overly harsh assessment of the relationship between King and Nimitz. The two men kept in close touch with cables and telegrams on a daily basis and face to face in two-or-three-day conferences in San Francisco every two months. The Chief of Naval Operations allowed Admiral Nimitz, from the time of Trident (May 1943) onward, to move troops and ships around in the Pacific as he saw fit without prior permission from the U.S. Joint Chiefs of Staff.[39] As described in chapter 3, the U.S. Joint Chiefs of Staff determined overall strategic objectives in the Pacific theater under CCS auspices, such as the seizure of the Gilbert and Marshall island groups in the Central Pacific. Once these objectives had been identified, however, Admiral King allowed Nimitz to carry out a great deal of the detailed planning for each operation. For instance, while fulfilling his CCS directive to plan for the seizure of bases in the Marshalls, it was Admiral Nimitz who decided to jump straight to the heart of the group and land first at Kwajalein. It was a daring plan, and King was impressed with the nerve displayed by his Pacific commander.[40]

As First Sea Lord, Admiral Cunningham gave considerable latitude to his subordinates, as is apparent in a spring 1944 dispute between Cunningham and Admiral Sir Bruce Fraser, who had succeeded Admiral Tovey as commander in chief of the Home Fleet, over an attack by naval aircraft against the *Tirpitz*, which had continued to take refuge in Norwegian coastal waters. The operation, code-named Tungsten, was carried out in April 1944. The German battleship was damaged but not sunk. Cunningham urged Fraser to make an immediate follow-up attack to finish the job. Fraser objected, knowing that it would be impossible to achieve surprise in a second attack following immediately upon the first.[41] The debate got ugly. The minor mutiny on the part of Fraser that ensued is best described in Cunningham's diary:

> I called up Bruce Fraser about repeat Tungsten and found him in a most truculent and obstinate mood. He had . . . made the decision that Tungsten was not to be repeated. I reasoned with him and pointed out that C in C decisions were not irrevocable & that the Admiralty must be allowed some voice in what operations were to be carried out. He did not admit this & said if we were not satisfied we must get another C in C, and in fact indicated that he would haul his flag down if ordered to repeat Tungsten. I told him to sleep on it & call me up in the morning.[42]

The next day Fraser was still refusing and threatening to resign his command. Cunningham was not about to let this state of affairs continue. However, while he was determined that the second raid against the *Tirpitz* would in fact take place, Cunningham was prepared to allow Fraser to argue his case personally at the Admiralty. Cunningham reasoned that this would give Fraser the opportunity to back down in a dignified fashion. In the end it proved to be unnecessary; Fraser soon cooled down and agreed to carry out his orders.[43] Admiral Cunningham had the wisdom to regard the entire episode with some humor. He seems to have dismissed Fraser's outburst as nothing more than the result of the strain and frustration inherent in carrying out command responsibilities over an extended period in a long war.

As we have seen, the Combined Chiefs tried to steer clear of day-to-day operations but were not averse to occasionally getting involved in such activities if they felt that commanders in the field were not measuring up. One area in which the Combined Chiefs of Staff intervened in day-to-day operations was the use of airborne troops. The Combined Chiefs of Staff felt that there was a great deal of room for improvement in the Allied use of this new element of warfare. The Combined Chiefs were informed in March 1944 by the Combined Planning Staff that Allied commanders in the field were not following the procedures outlined by the CCS for the use of airborne forces.[44] Therefore, the planners concluded, "we are not fully exploiting our inherent airborne potential or capability."[45] Such criticisms from the Combined Planning Staff struck a responsive chord among the Combined Chiefs. For example, General Marshall was a firm believer in the necessity for the Allies to utilize airborne troops aggressively and on a large scale.[46]

Marshall's enthusiasm about the potential of Allied airborne troops to land quickly and unexpectedly behind enemy lines was seconded most strongly among the British chiefs by Field Marshal Brooke.[47] This seems surprising, in that the two men did not often see eye to eye on strategic issues. Also interesting in regard to Brooke is that in spite of his conservative and cautious nature, he seemed to have had greater faith in the necessity for large airborne forces than did the "air man" Portal.[48] This seems to be out of character for Brooke in that initiating new strategic ideas was not ordinarily considered to be one of Brooke's strong points.

As chief of the Air Staff, Portal had doubts about the troop-and-equipment-carrying gliders that were to be towed behind troop-filled transport planes in an airborne operation as large in scale as Overlord promised to be. Portal remarked in a telegram to the British Joint Staff Mission in Washington in April 1943 that "the difficulties attending the use of [the gliders] are certainly formidable."[49] Portal had doubts about the readiness of American airborne forces and their commanders. In particular, Portal mentioned in the spring of 1943 that he felt Major General Mathew Ridgway, commander of the U.S. 82nd Airborne Division, was still learning about the proper employment of airborne troops.[50] Portal was probably right, in that everyone was still learning about airborne troops in 1943, when moving troops by air was a very new idea.

It was some time before Portal came around to accepting the necessity for large Allied airborne forces. Six months before mentioning his doubts about the gliders, Portal had expressed unease about the entire airborne enterprise. This, it seems, was due to the serious shortage of transport aircraft faced then by Britain. In fact, the British had to rely heavily upon American transport aircraft throughout the war. The large aircraft being manufactured in Britain during the war were almost exclusively bombers, not transports. With their greater industrial capacity, the Americans were able during the war to produce more than 20,000 transport aircraft, as well as some 30,000 long-range bombers.[51] Consequently, prompted by a nervous "Bomber"

Harris, Portal initially opposed the creation of large British airborne forces, for fear that they would have to be transported in bombers, thereby largely curtailing the British bombing campaign against Germany.[52] Faced with such a harsh choice, Portal informed the British Chiefs of Staff in September 1942 that "I regard the bombing of German industry as an incomparably greater contribution to the war than the training and constant availability of an airborne division and, as the two things at present seriously conflict, I would certainly accord priority to bombing."[53]

At the same time, Portal had not forgotten his earlier pledge to support a cross-channel attack with all of the resources of the metropolitan air force. Because of that promise (mentioned earlier in regard to CCS deliberations regarding Overlord) Portal left the door open to the possibility that British bombers might have to be temporarily reassigned to troop-carrying duty.[54] However, Portal's conclusion at that time (September 1942) was that British airborne forces currently in training and those being planned for the future should be reduced in size. He did not then feel that England needed more than four thousand parachute troops and "a small glider-borne force."[55]

Portal's attitude toward the use of large airborne forces became more optimistic as time went on, most likely due to the enthusiasm for large-scale airborne operations shown by Brooke and Marshall and to the growing availability of American transport aircraft, which made it unnecessary for British bombers to desist from dropping bombs to carry troops. Allied bombing activity was, however, temporarily diverted from attacks on German cities in order to bomb railway installations in northern France, as well as other tactical targets, in support of Overlord.

The Combined Staff planners had become alarmed by sentiments like Portal's 1942 views, expressed also by some Allied field commanders, that airborne troops should be organized into relatively small groups, that an airborne *division* might be "too heavy logistically."[56] Prior to the D-Day landings, Allied airborne and parachute troops had been used in North Africa, in Sicily, and on New Guinea. However, the troops transported to the battle zone by air in these operations had been organized in small units, such as regiments. Almost the entire U.S. 82nd Airborne Division, having arrived by air, had fought at Salerno in Italy in September 1943. Instead of landing behind enemy lines before the Allied ground troops had been put ashore, however, the troops of the 82nd landed within the Salerno beachhead seven days after the seaborne landings began, in order to provide much-needed support to the hard-pressed Allied forces, which had been pinned down near the water's edge since coming ashore on September 8. Because such a supporting role was not the intended use for an airborne division, the Combined Planning Staff felt justified in concluding, in March 1944, that "the airborne division as such has never yet been tested in combat. The policy of organizing airborne troops into divisions should not be changed unless and until tests in combat show that this policy is unsound."[57]

The Combined Planning Staff recommended, as a means of increasing the overall awareness as to the potential benefits to be derived from the imaginative use of airborne troops, that all Allied planning agencies, theater commanders, and other high-ranking field commanders appoint to their staffs officers experienced in troop carrier and airborne operations.[58] The criticisms made and remedies suggested in regard to airborne troop deployment by the Combined Planning Staff were approved by the Combined Chiefs of Staff.[59] The wisdom of the Combined Planning Staff was demonstrated shortly thereafter when three complete airborne divisions were used more or less successfully in the vicinity of the invasion beaches during the first wave of the Normandy assault. It is possible to speculate, however, that Marshall and Brooke would probably have liked to have seen the airborne troops landed farther inland than they actually were.

The Combined Chiefs of Staff as a group occasionally took a personal hand in other air-related matters as well. For example, while the CCS did not ordinarily plan individual bombing missions, usually delegating this responsibility to local commanders (such as Air Chief Marshal Harris of RAF Bomber Command or Lieutenant General Ira C. Eaker, the commander of the U.S. Eighth Air Force, based in England), there were a few exceptions. One was the low-level raid against Romanian oil refineries at Ploesti carried out by American B-24 bombers of the U.S. Eighth and Ninth Air Forces on August 1, 1943. Two months previously the Combined Chiefs had ordered that this attack take place. It had taken direct action after becoming convinced of the vital importance of Ploesti as a primary source of oil for Germany. General Eisenhower, as Allied commander in North Africa (from where the raid was to be launched), was consulted; however, the initiative for the raid came from the Combined Chiefs of Staff.[60]

During the Torch landings in North Africa, the Combined Chiefs of Staff gave as much latitude as possible to General Eisenhower, in his capacity as the Allied commander in chief of the operation, in the interpretation of their directives. For example, while he knew that the Combined Chiefs expected him to land in North Africa before the end of 1942, Eisenhower had been informed by the CCS in September 1942 that he was free to choose the actual landing dates.[61] However, once the date was set for November 8, the Combined Chiefs did not want any last-minute changes. The Combined Chiefs became aware, one week before the assault was to begin, that Eisenhower was considering a delay until the 20th.[62] On November 2, Sir John Dill informed the British Chiefs of Staff that "United States Chiefs of Staff recognize impossibility of altering date now and are so informing Eisenhower with my concurrence in name of Combined Chiefs of Staff."[63]

General Eisenhower was also given retroactive latitude by the Combined Chiefs in regard to negotiating the "Darlan deal," which allowed for an early halt to hostilities between Allied and French forces in North Africa. Under this agreement, which took effect on November 10, 1942, and was formally ratified by Eisenhower three days later, French forces in North Africa ceased all armed resistance to the Allied landings. In return, Admiral François Darlan was allowed to exercise command of French military forces in the region. He therefore came to overshadow General Henri Giraud, who had been handpicked by the Allies to be the top French civil and military official in North Africa. This agreement was made by Eisenhower on the spot, time constraints preventing him from consulting the Combined Chiefs of Staff. Because Darlan was the second most powerful politician in the collaborationist Vichy regime in France, there were public outcries against this deal in both Britain and the United States.[64]

On the situation in North Africa, Lord Halifax, the British ambassador in Washington, informed Foreign Minister Anthony Eden about the misgivings of the U.S. Joint Chiefs of Staff about Darlan. Halifax stated that Admiral Leahy "has no confidence in Darlan and thought if by any unhappy chance the military situation were to turn sour on us, Darlan might well walk out on any agreement. . . . Leahy did not see how we were going to get quickly out of Darlan."[65] Admiral Leahy was in a position to know about the difficulties involved in dealing with Vichy politicians, having served as American ambassador to Vichy France before joining the U.S. Joint Chiefs of Staff. While he was glad that the shooting had stopped at Oran and Casablanca, Leahy nevertheless felt that the best policy for the Western Allies would be to somehow extricate themselves from their agreement with Darlan as soon as possible. Leahy was aware that the

Darlan deal was a public-relations nightmare for the Allies but felt that there was no easy solution.[66]

Darlan's assassination on December 24, 1942, thus got the Western Allies out of a tight spot.[67] Eden informed Halifax that the death of the French admiral had created a general feeling among the Allies that a great burden had been lifted. According to Eden, "Darlan's assassination has aroused no emotional stories. The general reaction was relief that the chief obstacle to French unity has disappeared. There is also considerable satisfaction and even delight. . . . De Gaullists and other elements critical or hostile to Darlan privately sum up the situation by saying 'that is one fewer.'"[68]

Allied administration of North Africa, however, continued to be a very difficult problem. Under an agreement worked out a week after the landings, the Combined Chiefs had determined, in conjunction with the president and the prime minister, that for the purposes of civil administration, North Africa would be divided into American and British zones.[69] Perhaps because of their discomfort over the Darlan deal, the U.S. Joint Chiefs of Staff decided to assert themselves more forcefully in North Africa after the assassination. In late December 1942, after Darlan's death, General Marshall sent a revised directive to Eisenhower that read, "With the approval of the president, you are authorized to appoint General Giraud provisionally in charge of both Civil and French Military Authorities in your area."[70] Eventually, the Allies arranged a power-sharing system for North Africa between Giraud and Brigadier General Charles de Gaulle, the leader of the Free French. This system quickly led to a power struggle between the two men, a struggle in which de Gaulle was the winner.[71]

In allowing Eisenhower a great deal of leeway to run the Torch campaign (and later Overlord) as he saw fit, the Combined Chiefs demonstrated that they preferred to trust the judgments of their theater commanders when it came to managing the day-to-day operations on distant battlefronts. The freedom of action that was granted to Nimitz in the Pacific is another example of this. After setting overall objectives and allocating supplies, equipment, and personnel, the Combined Chiefs were more likely to intervene directly only in smaller-scale operations (such as creating the Pathfinders or scattering convoy PQ 17) that were not directly under the jurisdiction of a particular theater commander.

Delegation of as much responsibility as possible to their theater commanders and other high-ranking field commanders, such as Air Chief

Marshal Harris, was absolutely essential to the success of the Combined Chiefs of Staff. This was the only way in which it could maintain a global perspective. By focusing on the broad outlines of operations, such as the Central Pacific drive, while leaving the detailed planning to subordinates in the field, the Combined Chiefs operated a very efficient command system. Such a system allowed the CCS to discuss many different issues, such as the Burma Road, the Mediterranean, weapons production schedules, and the supply of morphine in military hospitals in the course of a single day. Its members did not have to concentrate all of their time and energies upon a specific campaign, such as Overlord. Also, by allowing their field commanders to carry out the detailed planning of operations, the Combined Chiefs were able to take advantage of the knowledge gained by those commanders of local conditions the world over. The Combined Chiefs of Staff did sometimes feel compelled to become involved in details. Sometimes their intervention was helpful, sometimes not. On the whole, however, the balance struck by the Combined Chiefs of Staff between delegation and control from the center was highly effective.

EIGHT

Production and Diplomatic Tasks
for the Combined Chiefs

The members of the Combined Chiefs of Staff were forced to deal with many issues that fell outside the strict definition of generating and supervising campaign plans. For instance, the American members needed to be able to express in an effective manner their views to members of Congress in order to secure approval for military budgets. In addition, as service chiefs, members of the Combined Chiefs of Staff were responsible for overseeing the wartime growth of their respective services. Two of the most important of the additional duties with which the Combined Chiefs of Staff were concerned were the production of munitions and the conduct of wartime diplomacy. Certainly, weapons procurement would have been an activity that these men would have had to undertake anyway as service chiefs had the Combined Chiefs of Staff never been formed. However, it is to the credit of CCS members that they could successfully handle huge wartime weapons procurement activities on top of their global strategy-making responsibilities.

Wartime diplomacy, on the other hand, is an area in which the Combined Chiefs of Staff compiled a somewhat mixed record. In some diplomatic episodes with which the Combined Chiefs of Staff were forced to involve themselves, such as the "Darlan deal" mentioned earlier, there seemed to be no good option. In other instances, such as the passage of Allied and Axis hospital ships through combat areas, the Combined Chiefs of Staff acted with wisdom. There were occasions, however, such as in regard to the use of the Azores as an air base, when the American members of the Combined Chiefs of Staff could be a bit heavy-handed.

Production

Because so many different civilian and military bureaucracies—the U.S. War Production Board, the U.S. Office of War Mobilization, the British Ministry of Aircraft Production, the U.S. Army Service Forces, and the British Air Ministry, to name a few—had a hand in production issues in Britain and the United States, the Combined Chiefs of Staff could not exert absolute control over the production of military equipment. They did, however, have a great deal of influence over what and how much was produced. One of the key roles played by the Combined Chiefs of Staff in regard to production during the war was to balance the production goals put forth by the prime minister, the president, themselves, and the various production bureaucracies. The Allies were vastly more effective at achieving a balanced production program with which to wage war than were the Germans.

A great many new and advanced weapons became available to the Allies early in World War II. For example, several of the finest British aircraft of the war, such as the De Havilland Mosquito, the Hawker Typhoon, and the Avro Lancaster, first became available in 1942. There were also the American-built, small, escort carriers (or "baby flattops"), which proved to be crucial to the Allied victory in the war against the U-boats. The first American escort carrier, the USS *Long Island,* entered service in June 1941. By early 1943 the escort carriers (or CVEs) were being mass-produced, fifty of them entering service that year.[1] Allied antiaircraft defense was greatly enhanced by the introduction in January 1943 of ammunition detonated by proximity fuses—highly sophisticated devices that proved very effective. Between 1940 and 1942 the British and the Americans put into service the new battleships of the *King George V, North Carolina,* and *South Dakota* classes. These ships incorporated, in addition to heavy firepower and thick armor, many improvements—such as high speed, dozens of defensive antiaircraft guns, and radar direction for the big guns—over the World War I–era battleships in use by both nations in 1939.

The creation of the *Long Island* through the conversion of a merchant ship hull had predated King's appointment as Commander in Chief, U.S. Fleet, as did the planning for the new 27,000-ton fleet aircraft carriers (CVs) of the *Essex* class. Admiral Emory S. Land, director of the Maritime

Commission, was responsible for the construction of merchant shipping in the United States during the war. Land's involvement in the process that created the *Long Island*–type CVE resulted from the fact that although these were warships, they were hybrids, created by "nailing down" flight decks on top of merchant-ship hulls. The approval to go ahead with the creation of the first CVE was given at a meeting that, according to Land, took place "sometime in 1940 or early 1941" between Admiral Harold R. Stark (then Chief of Naval Operations), Admiral William. V. Pratt (himself a former CNO), and three other admirals—Frederick J. Horne, Royal Ingersoll, and Land himself.[2] Land gives most of the credit for the very important decision to build the *Long Island* to Admiral Pratt.

The American fleet was augmented also during the war by eighteen new, full-sized aircraft carriers. These ships, such as the *Essex* and the *Bunker Hill,* were more than eight hundred feet in length and capable of carrying a hundred aircraft each. They were much larger than the escort carriers and were designed to engage an enemy battle fleet. The smaller escort carriers, however, were ideal for protecting convoys from submarines by projecting air cover out into the Atlantic. In April 1942 the *Long Island* was still the only escort carrier in the American navy, although the Americans had seven of the large, fleet-type carriers at that time. By then, King had been the fleet commander for four months. There were plans to build thirty-one new CVEs during 1942, but such plans were being brought to the attention of the Combined Chiefs of Staff by people like Admiral Land and Admiral Joseph Mason Reeves (the latter of the Munitions Assignment Committee), not by King. Reeves understood the urgency of the German submarine menace and made ceaseless efforts to provide more and better escorts for Allied Atlantic convoys.[3]

The Combined Chiefs of Staff had no control over what was being produced in Russian armament factories. However, as with British and American industry, Russian industry was fully mobilized for war production right away. It became clear long before the war ended that the Allies were going to win the war of production. In addition to the impressive quantity of weapons produced in Russian factories mentioned in chapter 4, the *quality* of Russian weaponry was quite high. For instance, it was quite a shock for Hitler and his generals, not to mention for the ordinary German foot soldier, to learn that Russian weapons technology was considerably more advanced in several critical respects than was the arsenal of German weapons with which Hitler embarked on Barbarossa. The Russians possessed the superb T-34 and KV-1 tanks at the outset of Barbarossa, albeit not yet in the necessary quantity, while the Germans were forced to rely on inferior light and medium tanks until the first heavy Tiger tanks appeared on the battlefield in late 1942.

In terms of the production and distribution of war materiel, the Combined Chiefs of Staff dealt with an extremely wide variety of items. For example, one report sent in August 1942 by the Admiralty in London to the British Joint Staff Mission in Washington dealt with distribution schedules for many different types of munitions, including escort vessels (corvettes) built in Canada, antiaircraft guns (40-mm Bofors and 20-mm Oerlikon), torpedoes, depth charges, and carrier-based fighter aircraft.[4]

By mid-1944 the German Ministry of War Production, which since February 1942 had been under the direction of Albert Speer, had finally and belatedly succeeded in placing German industry on something approaching a "total war" footing. Consequently, German war industry was now producing munitions at a vastly increased tempo. Great numbers of tanks and aircraft were produced in Germany during the last year of the war; however, the industrial situation was badly out of balance. The soaring production totals of tanks and aircraft achieved under Speer's guidance dazzled Hitler. However, the armaments minister was going for quick and sensational items that would impress the Fuehrer while ignoring less glamorous but critical production problems. For example, by late 1944 there was nowhere near enough oil being produced in Germany to supply fuel for the aircraft that were rolling out of factories. Nor were enough new pilots being trained to fly them.[5]

One CCS action that served to help place the Allied production program in balance occurred in late 1942, when the U.S. Joint Chiefs of Staff attempted to scale down President Roosevelt's 1943 production goals for American aircraft. Thus it is obvious that the Combined Chiefs of Staff, unlike Speer, realized that while it was urgent for the Allies to produce as many aircraft as possible, it was equally essential that the aircraft production program take into account other pressing wartime production needs. The U.S. Joint Chiefs of Staff showed a keen understanding of production issues when, in the fall of 1942, they were forced to rebut the president's claims that the planned production program for American factories the next year did not provide for enough aircraft. In offering their rebuttal, the Joint Chiefs were doing their part to keep the Allied production program in balance.

Specifically, in October 1942, the president declared to the U.S. Joint Chiefs of Staff that he did not see how the Western Allies could carry out their strategic plans for 1943 unless the United States could produce at least 100,000 combat airplanes in that year.[6] FDR had been informed of the more modest aircraft production goals proposed by the War Production Board. The president found these "totally inadequate to meet our obvious requirements."[7] He felt it was well within the industrial capability of the United States to produce 100,000 combat aircraft in 1943 without detriment to other production schedules, such as those for shipping and tanks. FDR wanted the views of the U.S. Joint Chiefs in regard to which types of aircraft would be produced and what the monthly totals for each type would be in order to reach the 100,000 threshold.[8] He did not want to know whether they thought the goal of 100,000 aircraft was feasible, having already decided for himself that it was.

The Joint Chiefs of Staff had other ideas, however. The reply of the U.S. Joint Chiefs of Staff to FDR was written by Marshall and sent to the president over Leahy's signature as a JCS document. Marshall wrote that in the opinion of the Joint Chiefs, "The program that calls for 100,000 tactical and 31,000 training planes in the desired types, is *unobtainable* in 1943, even if given first call on the entire resources of the nation. Furthermore, to attempt this program would almost certainly result in a reduction in output under the present . . . program."[9] The U.S. Joint Chiefs did, however, feel that it would be possible to build the 82,000 combat and 25,000 training planes that had initially been planned for 1943 under the existing program. In the opinion of the Joint Chiefs, even under their more modest proposal, the production of aircraft would have to be given immediate priority status, in regard to such things as raw materials and labor allocation, over that of other military equipment. Marshall's letter pointed out to FDR that the views of the U.S. Joint Chiefs of Staff in regard to aircraft production in the United States for 1943 had the support of Army and Navy production planners, as well as that of Donald Nelson and the War Production Board.[10]

There were several reason why the U.S. Joint Chiefs of Staff felt that the president's program would result in a net *loss* rather than increased output among American aircraft factories. First, a program calling for 100,000 combat aircraft and 31,000 training planes would require that the government build thirteen new assembly and subassembly plants in the United States. Due to the difficulties involved in getting any new factory up and running, the Joint Chiefs were convinced that these new plants would not be able to produce more than five thousand airplanes between them during their first year of operation (i.e., 1943). The diversion of resources that these proposed new factories would require, in terms of raw materials, labor, and machine tools, would handicap the aircraft (and other munitions-oriented) production plants that were already in existence, thereby decreasing their output.[11] Therefore, Marshall wrote, among the U.S. Joint Chiefs of Staff here was "general unanimity in the belief that if we set our program beyond our capacity, and give that program priorities accordingly, we will actually get fewer planes than we would produce if the objective were within practical striking distance."[12]

Marshall conceded that the confused state of production schedules in the aircraft industry in the United States was preventing production quotas from being met. There was a great need for clarification of this vital issue. The U.S. Joint Chiefs of Staff, however, were convinced that the president's plan did not represent the correct answer. By way of Marshall's report, they therefore requested the president to agree to a 1943 aircraft production schedule that provided for 82,000 combat planes and 25,000 training planes as the best means of keeping American war production on a sound and balanced basis.[13]

The views of the U.S. Joint Chiefs of Staff seem to have prevailed on this issue, although the output of combat planes ultimately proved lower than they had anticipated. The record shows that the United States produced 85,898 aircraft in 1943. Of these 53,343 were combat aircraft, and 7,012 were transports; the remainder consisted of training, communications, reconnaissance, and special-purpose aircraft. While the 85,898 figure was less than what the president desired, it was still more than double the combined figure for the production of German and Japanese aircraft (41,500) during 1943.[14]

For Air Chief Marshal Portal, the key issue in British aircraft production seems to have been which aircraft types to put into production rather than how many to produce. Portal was determined to secure the best possible aircraft for British pilots to fly. He always placed the highest premium upon producing *quality* aircraft, even at the risk of slowing down the production schedules somewhat. In his constant search for better aircraft designs, Portal wrote in July 1942, to Sir Archibald Sinclair, the secretary of state for air, that one promising idea that he wanted to see followed up vigorously was that of fitting the P-51 Mustang fighter plane with a British Rolls-Royce Merlin

61 engine. The Merlin-powered Mustang turned out to be one of the most important decisions of the war in regard to air warfare. Portal may not have been the first one to think of this idea, but he did see its merits early on and quickly became a convert. In the same letter, Portal showed himself to be an early advocate of jet-powered aircraft.[15] His early and firm backing in this area is one of the reasons why the British were able to get a jet-powered fighter plane, the Gloster Meteor, into production and into service in 1944— long before the United States was to have an operational, combat-ready jet fighter of its own.

Portal became involved in an interesting production debate with the Ministry of Aircraft Production in regard to a highly advanced fighter plane designed by Folland Aircraft in response to a requirement known as Air Ministry Specification F. 6/42. Portal felt the Folland to be an excellent design that could be a worthy successor to the Hawker Typhoon. He became involved in a running argument over the Folland fighter with Air Chief Marshal Sir Wilfrid R. Freeman, the chief executive of the Ministry of Aircraft Production under Sir Stafford Cripps, minister of aircraft production. Portal respected Freeman due to the latter's considerable experience in aircraft development gained during high-level tours of duty at the Air Ministry in the prewar and early wartime periods. From 1936 to 1938, Freeman had been Air Member for Research and Development at the Air Ministry. From 1938 to 1940, he had been Air Member for Development and Production. In May 1940, Freeman's entire Development and Production Department was removed from the Air Ministry and placed in the new Ministry of Aircraft Production (MAP).

This is the reason for Britain's aircraft production miracles that followed during the Battle of Britain. Lord Beaverbrook as minister of aircraft production at that time had a ready store of technical expertise to draw upon from RAF personnel like Freeman whom he (Beaverbrook) inherited in 1940. From May to November 1940, Freeman worked for Beaverbrook at the Ministry of Aircraft Production. The two men did not get along. In November 1940, shortly after Portal became chief of the Air Staff, Freeman returned to the Air Ministry as vice chief of the Air Staff. In 1942, the year in which Freeman and Portal began to debate the Folland fighter design, Freeman retired from the RAF, but he retained the title of Air Chief Marshal. The reason for his retirement was to be able to return to the Ministry of Aircraft Production in October 1942, after Beaverbrook was gone, this time as chief executive, under Sir Stafford Cripps. In this capacity, Freeman ran the day-to-day operations of the Ministry of Aircraft Production under Cripps during the midwar period. Freeman and the MAP staff felt the Folland fighter plane was too heavy. They favored the Hawker Tempest, a design Portal thought inferior to the Folland F. 6/42.[16]

The chief of the Air Staff informed Sinclair that the Ministry of Aircraft production should press ahead with the Folland fighter, a new design, and regard the Tempest (which, in two variants, was an upgraded Typhoon) as a stopgap.[17] Portal agreed with Sinclair and Freeman that "the Tempest is an altogether better fighter than the Typhoon, and we are counting on it to replace the Typhoon as soon as possible."[18] He urged Freeman to see that the MAP placed both the Tempest I and II into production immediately.[19] This did not mean, however, that the Tempest was a good enough airplane to satisfy Portal's exacting standards.

In explaining the need for Britain to develop a new high-performance fighter plane, such as the Folland F. 6/42, Portal wrote to Sinclair that "the trend of German design as exemplified by the F.W. 190, is towards a light, high powered, heavily armed machine with good climbing qualities and manoeuverability. If this development is to be adequately matched we need a new type with similar characteristics, designed *ab initio*. So much may depend on this type that the best designers in the industry should be asked to concentrate on it."[20] One reason Portal felt the Folland to be such an advanced design was that though a single-engine airplane, it had two contra-rotating propellers, mounted one immediately behind the other on telescoped shafts, giving extra pulling power.[21]

Freeman informed Portal in December 1942 of another reason (in addition to the question of weight) for the reluctance of the Ministry of Aircraft Production to put the Folland fighter into production. Freeman felt sure that it would take more than two years to get the Folland F. 6/42, as a new airplane, into production. He was equally sure that the Tempest II would be rolling off assembly lines by early 1944.[22] Quite bluntly, Freeman thus told Portal that "I expect therefore that you will prefer to drop any idea of the Folland as an F. 6/42 aircraft."[23]

Portal lost this argument. The Folland fighter never went into production. In retrospect, the Royal Air Force might well have been better served if Portal's advice had been heeded. Freeman's confidence in the ability of the Ministry of Aircraft Production to get the Tempest II quickly into full production proved to be unfounded. It was October 1944 before the Royal Air Force received its first Tempest IIs, and then only in small quantities. Fewer than 175 Tempest IIs were produced before the end of the war. None of these ever saw combat. A different version of the airplane, the Tempest V, encountered fewer production problems and was available earlier and in greater numbers. Between April 1944 and the war's end, several hundred Tempest Vs saw action in RAF service. The Tempest V was, in fact, the only version of the Tempest to engage enemy forces during the war. When the Tempest II finally began to operate with the Royal Air Force in the postwar era, the influence of the Folland fighter was evident in its design.[24] For example, like the Folland, the Tempest II incorporated an air-cooled radial engine, a power plant Portal felt would be better able to withstand battle damage than a liquid-cooled, in-line engine.[25] The effect of the Folland upon the design of the Tempest II went beyond the choice of an engine, as Portal explained in frustration to an unimpressed Freeman: "Here was a design [the Folland] so much ahead of its competitors that we have been compelled to incorporate as much of it as possible into the most promising of the contemporary fighters. . . . Surely it [the Folland] must have shown outstanding merits if it was the cause of the complete redesign of the Tempest II."[26]

Whether at the Ministry of Aircraft Production or as Portal's deputy at the Air Ministry in the role of vice chief of the Air Staff, Freeman was highly loyal to Portal, and the two men were good friends. Freeman advised Portal on personnel issues as well as aircraft designs. Portal felt Freeman to be a brilliant man, even when they disagreed. Portal admired Freeman for always giving his true opinions, without feeling any need to be polite.[27]

Portal and his American CCS counterpart, General Arnold, did not always recognize the potential of new aircraft that they examined, however. The commanding general of the U.S. Army Air Forces exercised virtually complete control of the American aircraft industry during the war. For example, shortly after the Pearl Harbor attack the chief executive officer of the Republic Aircraft Corporation was fired on Arnold's orders because the general regarded him as a stumbling block on the road to the increased production of P-47 fighter aircraft. In 1938, Arnold had informed Harry Hopkins that the new government-financed aircraft factories then being planned for construction in the United States would have to use modern production-line methods instead of the old handcrafted processes by which aircraft had hitherto been produced. It is therefore ironic that Arnold was slow to appreciate the merits of the North American P-51 Mustang, which was destined to be the war's greatest fighter plane.[28] Similarly, in late 1940 Portal indicated that he saw little use for the De Havilland Mosquito, which was also to attain immortal status as a superb and versatile combat aircraft.[29] To his credit, however, it seems that Portal was not the only one to underestimate this new type. Sir Archibald Sinclair, the secretary of state for air, also expressed grave doubts about the Mosquito at that time.[30] Portal's friend and adviser, the aforementioned Air Chief Marshal Sir Wilfrid Freeman, was right about this one. Freeman had pressed relentlessly and eventually successfully to get the Mosquito into production.[31]

While the U.S. Joint Chiefs of Staff were attempting to get the president's approval for a balanced aircraft production program for 1943, the British Joint War Production Staff (JWPS) was, ironically, informing the British Chiefs of Staff that the Americans were not doing nearly enough to achieve balanced production. Specifically, the British felt that virtually all of the various American munitions production programs were adopting goals far beyond the actual production capabilities of the United States. The blame for this turn of events was, according to the British production planners, shared by all the American services. They did, however, feel that the U.S. Army was the worst offender in setting overly ambitious production goals not related to strategic needs. To the British it seemed that the unbalance and decentralization of the American production system would, if not rectified immediately, have a detrimental effect upon Allied strategy as a whole. On a more specific note, the British planners also felt that the overextended priorities and goals of munitions production in the United States would deprive Britain (and other Allied nations) of finished military equipment and raw materials that had been promised to them by the Americans.[32]

To illustrate their concerns, the British JWPS cited several examples. They mentioned that it was the intention of the president to see that the American Maritime Commission produced in American shipyards 24,000,000 deadweight tons of new merchant shipping during 1942 and 1943. However, the Maritime Commission was not being given nearly enough steel to accomplish this objective. One reason for this disparity between goals and raw materials was that the Americans were also planning to build 90,000 tanks during 1943. The British found this to be astonishing—under such a program the Americans would have enough tanks to equip two hundred armored divisions. At its peak strength during the war the American army never contained more than ninety divisions, the majority of which were infantry.[33] The British noted that in terms of steel allotments "tank production is directly competitive with shipbuilding."[34]

Another area in which the Americans were, according to the British Joint War Production Staff, badly out of step in regard to matching production goals with strategic reality was in the matter of ordnance. The Americans hoped to produce in 1943 enough aerial bombs to enable their aircraft to drop 180,000 tons each month. The British had found that between the outbreak of the war and June 1942, the Royal Air Force had never dropped more than seven thousand tons of bombs in a single month.[35] While it is true that at that time the full weight of the combined bomber offensive had yet to be felt, the British already had some large-scale raids behind them. For example, in May 1942 RAF Bomber Command had carried out the famous "thousand bomber" raid against Cologne.

The conflicts within the Allied production program as it stood in October 1942 were summed up by the British JWPS as follows:

> The result of the absence of combined strategic requirements, therefore, is that a vast American production of war equipment is being developed, which bears no relationship to the amounts required for effective use against the enemy. . . . The seriousness of the situation lies in the fact that in the pressure which is developing upon United States supplies of raw materials and productive facilities, strategically necessary requirements are being squeezed out in favour of requirements for forces which cannot conceivably be engaged against the enemy in 1943.[36]

They felt that the situation could be rectified if the British and the Americans adhered to what the British planners referred to as "a combined Order of Battle." Such a document could serve as a blueprint of production requirements for the Allies on a theater-by-theater basis. By determining the equipment, munitions, and troop needs of each individual theater of operations, the British JWPS felt, a much more precise picture of Allied production needs could be obtained than was possible under the current system. As it was, production requirements were based upon the anticipated needs of Allied forces the world over, regardless of whether those forces were stationed in highly active theaters, such as the Central Pacific, or relatively quiet ones, such as the Caribbean Defense Command.[37]

A semblance of order seems to have been brought to the Allied production situation by the following summer—at least according to the U.S. Joint Chiefs of Staff. They informed the president in July 1943 that in their opinion the military production programs in the United States "are in an excellent state of balance at present."[38] Munitions production schedules were being met, the shipping situation had improved dramatically, and the threat of the U-boats was waning. Allied merchant ship convoys now enjoyed heavy escort from warships. This meant that Allied forces overseas were receiving all the supplies and equipment they required in order to undertake offensive operations.[39] In order to allow this favorable state of balance to continue, the Joint Chiefs of Staff noted, "shipping must not be permitted to get ahead of the flow of munitions or beyond the capacity of the Navy to provide appropriate escort."[40]

The problem of naval escorts was crucial. A key Allied strategy in the war against the German submarines that haunted the Atlantic shipping lanes was simply to build freighters and tankers faster than the Germans could sink them. In June 1942, the Combined Staff planners warned their CCS superiors that such a policy was far more complicated than it appeared to be. The Combined Staff planners had themselves been advised by two admirals, the American Joseph Mason Reeves and British rear admiral J. W. S. Dorling, that it would be reckless to concentrate simply on building more and more merchant ships unless this building was accompanied by corresponding construction of escort vessels, such as corvettes and destroyers, with which to protect merchant shipping from submarine attack.[41] Admiral Reeves (not to be confused with Rear Admiral J. W. Reeves, a carrier-division commander in the famed Task Force 58, the "muscle" of the U.S. Fifth Fleet)[42] had served as Commander in Chief, U.S. Fleet during the 1930s.[43] Admiral Dorling was attached to the British Joint Staff Mission in Washington.

Reeves and Dorling constituted the Munitions Assignment Committee (Navy) of the Combined Munitions Assignment Board—the latter being one of the ten subcommittees of the Combined Chiefs of Staff organization. They warned that should the Allies reduce the number of escorts built in order to concentrate on merchant ships, the gap between new tonnage being built and losses due to U-boat attack would never be completely closed. Indeed, Reeves and Dorling stated that under such a scenario there would actually be a net loss (due to sinkings) in the American merchant fleet of over 5 percent by the end of 1943 despite a projected building program that would most likely have delivered 26,500,000 tons of new merchant shipping by that time. They wanted twenty new escort vessels for every one hundred new cargo ships, instead of the 7.3 escorts per hundred cargo ships then prevailing in American convoys.[44]

Reeves and Dorling found a receptive audience in the Chief of Naval Operations. Admiral King fully supported their efforts to get more escorts built quickly. King had felt in the summer of 1942 that a previous report from the Combined Staff planners had been overly optimistic in predicting that, even without drastic measures, Allied merchant sinkings would soon begin to decline. He feared that such unfounded optimism might divert attention from the pressing need to build more escorts.[45] King urged that all Allied convoys be given adequate escort and that "killer groups" be allowed to branch off "to destroy submarines once contact has been made"—a tactic that would demand even more escorts, in addition to those earmarked for convoy duty.[46] He felt that escort vessels should be given an even higher priority than merchant ships in Allied building schedules.[47] In June 1942 King stated that he was "of the opinion that the war cannot be won until the submarine menace has been removed. Escort vessels in adequate numbers are absolutely vital to the defeat of the enemy's submarine campaign."[48] King's views on this issue were entirely in agreement with those of his British CCS counterpart, Admiral Pound. As we have seen in his order to the Naval Staff in July 1943 that he be notified in advance of any plan to remove any British warship from convoy escort duty, Pound was determined that the Allies maintain as many submarine-hunting ships as possible on duty in the Atlantic sea-lanes.[49]

King and Pound were not, it seems, immediately successful in convincing their colleagues on the Combined Chiefs of Staff of the urgency of the Battle of the Atlantic. It took some time for escort vessels to receive the priority in regard to production that they deserved. A January 1943 message on the subject from Leahy to the Combined Production and Resources Board (CPRB) probably should have been sent six months earlier. In it Leahy informed the board that the Battle of the Atlantic was in a critical phase, with sinkings at an alarmingly high level.[50] In spelling out the need for urgent Allied action against the U-boats, Leahy informed the CPRB that the Combined Chiefs of Staff "desire that you adopt every means possible to effect an immediate acceleration and expansion of the escort vessel construction program, and also that you submit a report to them as to the effects of such expansion on other critical items of munitions."[51]

Admiral King's role as Chief of Naval Operations in the production and distribution of munitions and supplies was often, but not always, helpful. In February 1943 King dispatched a memo to his commanders of the U.S. Pacific and Atlantic Fleets (Admirals Chester W. Nimitz and Royal Ingersoll, respectively) stating that the emergency that had begun with the Pearl Harbor attack had set off a dizzying increase in the production and distribution of all kinds of munitions and supplies. Now that the situation had stabilized, King felt that it was time to find out exactly what was in the supply pipeline and to get that material out to the fighting areas.[52] He urged the two commanders to "take all steps to eliminate the stagnation in the reservoirs of materials of all kinds—munitions, supplies, stores, spare parts, etc.; reduce the size of the reservoirs of materials to the practicable minimum; and, generally, see to it that the *flow* of materials through the pipelines—to the operating forces—is as direct and as adequate as naval efficiency can make it."[53]

King's approach to other logistical issues did not always have such a sensible ring to it. Waiting until the summer of 1942, as we have seen, to organize the merchant ships traveling up and down the east coast of the United States into coastal convoys was a major error on King's part. Consequently, the six months following the Pearl Harbor attack saw marauding packs of U-boats sinking American ships at will a few miles off the beaches from Cape Cod to Florida.[54] Also, in regard to the aforementioned escort carriers, King's biographer has noted that the impetus for their construction did not come from King.[55]

Wartime Diplomacy
The diplomatic skills of the Combined Chiefs were much in demand during the war, especially in the case of the Americans. In London, Foreign Secretary Anthony Eden was kept abreast of all important war information by Churchill and the British Chiefs of Staff. The American situation was somewhat more muddled. In addition to its absence, noted earlier, from big wartime conferences such as Teheran, the U.S. State Department in general lacked influence during the war and was in disarray. For example, the American ambassador in London, John G. Winant, was

forced to get most of his war information from the British, due to the fact that his superiors in Washington failed to keep him informed of new developments.[56]

Perhaps it would have been better if the U.S. State Department had been kept more in the loop during the war. The U.S. Joint Chiefs of Staff were at times heavy-handed diplomats, to say the least, intervening in diplomatic matters without consulting the State Department or their British CCS colleagues. This characteristic is nowhere more apparent than in the enthusiastic response in September 1943 by the U.S. Joint Chiefs of Staff to the news that the government of Portugal had agreed, effective October 8, 1943, to allow the British to use the Azores as an air base. The Americans were eager to use the Azores themselves as a staging and refueling base on their aircraft ferry route, and the U.S. Joint Chiefs of Staff wishfully concluded that the United States was automatically included in the agreement for the use of the islands. The actual situation was far more complicated and called for delicate handling. Even General Marshall appears to have been uncharacteristically blind to the delicacy of the Azores situation as the Americans plowed ahead like bulls in a china shop.

American aircraft were already using a northern ferry route (Newfoundland–Greenland–Iceland–Scotland), as well as a southern route that involved flights from Brazil to West Africa. The Joint Chiefs of Staff were certain that an Azores base would allow a more expeditious transfer of American aircraft to the European theater than the rather circuitous southern route. Accordingly, the Americans wanted to put the Azores into their ferry air route right away and on a large scale. The British chiefs urged a more cautious and gradual approach, in which the activities of the Americans would initially be cloaked "under British cover."[57] There were good reasons for caution on the part of the British Chiefs of Staff. The government of António de Oliveira Salazar in Portugal had not known that through its deal with the British it was granting the United States a major air base. The agreement governing the use of the islands had been negotiated by Britain and Portugal alone, having been made possible by the existence of a formal treaty of alliance between the two nations dating back to 1373. Even with the alliance, the negotiations over the use of the islands as a British base had been quite delicate, owing to Portugal's neutrality in the war. The completed agreement (signed by a representative of the British Chiefs of Staff, Air Vice Marshal C. E. H. Medhurst, and Vice Admiral Alfredo Botelho De Sousa of

Portugal) therefore stipulated that Britain was to keep the size of its Azores garrison force to an absolute minimum.[58]

The British were proud of the fact that they had reached this agreement all on their own, without any help from the United States. They did not, therefore, appreciate the overzealous attitude of the Americans.[59] After the British had done all of the negotiating, the U.S. Joint Chiefs of Staff were proceeding with what would essentially constitute American annexation of the islands.[60] For example, in regard to the island of Terceira, the Americans urged the immediate construction of "one landplane base at Lagens Field with two 7,000 ft. runways for air transport and ferry operations, and accommodations for 3,500 personnel."[61] British anxiety was heightened further by the fact that the Americans also wanted to station four squadrons of long-range maritime patrol aircraft on Terceira for hunting German U-boats in the Bay of Biscay.[62] For the islands as a whole, the Americans intended to station 6,800 army and 1,400 naval personnel.[63] All this when the entire British garrison for the Azores was to number no more than two thousand.[64] In reaction to the extensive American demands in regard to the use of bases in the Azores, the British Joint Staff Mission in Washington lamented that "the whole principle of the permanent stationing of U.S. ground forces in the islands is one that will cause great difficulty with the Portuguese."[65] George Kennan was stationed in Lisbon at the time and was horrified at the manner in which the U.S. Joint Chiefs of Staff were running roughshod over the Portuguese government. It is interesting to speculate how far his firsthand knowledge of the heavy-handedness of the U.S. Joint Chiefs of Staff and Secretary of War Henry Stimson during this particular foray into wartime diplomacy may have influenced Kennan in his determination three years later, when he wrote the Long Telegram, to be sure that policy makers in Washington understood what was really going on overseas.[66]

One of the more interesting episodes of CCS wartime diplomacy had to do with the unusual career of the *Gripsholm,* an 18,000-ton passenger liner of the Swedish American Line. As we have seen, the American members of the Combined Chiefs of Staff exercised considerable control over the allocation and utilization of American merchant shipping. For the most part, this shipping consisted of troopships, freighters, and tankers. The *Gripsholm,* whose prewar career had been devoted to carrying passengers back and forth across the Atlantic between Stockholm and New York, as well as occasional cruises to the Bahamas or the Mediterranean, was used for a different purpose: between March 1942 and March 1946 the ship was chartered by the U.S. government at a cost of $17,000 per day to serve as a mercy ship in affiliation with the International Red Cross.[67] In this role, the *Gripsholm* was used by the Americans "to carry exchange prisoners-of-war, children, diplomats, repatriated seamen and Allied nationals with neutral status."[68] Typical of the wartime voyages of the *Gripsholm* was one in March 1944 in which the ship carried more than six hundred Americans from the Far East to New York. Some of these passengers were American POWs. The remainder were American women and children trapped in Japan by the outbreak of the war.[69]

To carry out these voyages safely, the *Gripsholm* was entitled to the same kind of immunity from attack that was granted under international law to hospital ships. To receive this protection the *Gripsholm* was forced to adhere to the same sort of rules that governed the passage of hospital ships through combat areas. The entire ship was given a coat of white paint, and along each side the word "Diplomat" was spelled out in large black letters, more than five feet from top to bottom. This brightly marked hull was fully illuminated during the hours of darkness, in sharp contrast to the blackouts imposed on convoys and combat vessels.[70] Other rules governing the use of hospital and mercy ships stipulated that such vessels could not travel in convoy, were forbidden from steaming in a zigzag pattern, and could not be used to carry military equipment, munitions, or combat troops.[71]

The U.S. Joint Chiefs of Staff faced a pressing problem in regard to the *Gripsholm* in the autumn of 1943. By that time, the Joint Chiefs had been made aware of the mistreatment of American prisoners of war, such as the survivors of the Bataan Death March, who were suffering terribly in Japanese camps. Marshall, King, Arnold, and Leahy were also aware of the potential propaganda value these atrocity stories held for the American war effort. The difficulty lay in the fact that the *Gripsholm* was then in the midst of a voyage carrying Japanese civilians home from the United States. In return for the safe passage of its own citizens on board the *Gripsholm*, the Japanese government had agreed to release a group of American citizens and to distribute Red Cross parcels and food being carried by the *Gripsholm* to American prisoners of war being held in the Philippines. (This exchange took place at Mormugao, a Portuguese-controlled port on the west coast of India approximately 250 miles south of Bombay.) The Joint Chiefs felt that once the ship docked, it would take from three to six months for the supplies to reach the American POWs.[72]

The president wanted the views of the Joint Chiefs of Staff as to when it might be advisable to publicize the atrocity stories brought back by American POWs who had escaped from Japanese camps without detriment to the ability of the *Gripsholm* to deliver its present cargo, and any future cargoes, of food and medicine to American prisoners being held by the Japanese. FDR also wanted to be certain that such stories, if and when they were made available to the American public, did not cause the Japanese to react by worsening the conditions under which American prisoners were living. Interestingly, the president sought the views of Stimson, Knox, and the Joint Chiefs of Staff but *not* of the State Department on this issue.[73]

The U.S. Joint Chiefs of Staff agreed with the president that the best course of action for the immediate future was to refrain from informing the American public as to the conditions under which American prisoners of war were living. Like him, they felt that it was imperative that the mercy missions of the *Gripsholm* be continued without interference.[74] The Joint Chiefs were aware of how acute was the need of American prisoners of war for relief supplies. According to Admiral Leahy, "American officers who have escaped from Japanese prison camps have stated that conditions in these camps could scarcely be much worse and that unless such conditions are improved within a short time very few of the American prisoners will survive. They agree that Red Cross food and supplies are of paramount importance to these prisoners at the present time."[75] General Marshall felt that the Joint Staff planners should periodically review the situation with a view toward ascertaining the appropriate time when the atrocity stories in regard to Japanese treatment of American prisoners of war could be released to the American public without detriment to the safety of those prisoners.[76]

The subject of the *Gripsholm* presented the Combined Chiefs with problems similar to those encountered in regard to the related issue of hospital ships. For example, after the Australian hospital ship *Centaur* was torpedoed and sunk by a Japanese submarine in the Pacific, the Combined Chiefs of Staff opposed immediate retaliation in kind. In urging restraint in the form of allowing continued safe passage for Japanese hospital ships, the CCS was certainly motivated by a desire to keep from giving the Axis the opportunity to produce effective anti-Allied propaganda. Its members had other reasons as well, however. The Americans conceded the possibility that the attack on the *Centaur* might have been accidental. The Americans themselves had accidentally attacked four Italian hospital ships; upon realizing their error, the Americans had issued a formal apology to the Italian government. The American members of the Combined Chiefs felt that the best way to respond to the *Centaur* incident would be to continue to refrain from attacking Japanese hospital ships unless and until the Japanese should sink any more Allied hospital ships. The primary reason that the Joint Chiefs of Staff opposed retaliatory attacks against Axis hospital ships was the pragmatic one that, as they were aware, the Allies were operating more hospital ships than Germany and Japan combined. Those ships would, of course, have been themselves endangered if the Allies began making retaliatory attacks against Japanese hospital ships to avenge the *Centaur*.[77]

An additional problem for the Combined Chiefs in this regard was that as the tide of the war turned against Japan there were rumors that the Japanese might, out of desperation, be using their own hospital ships for military purposes. Specifically, the U.S. Joint Chiefs of Staff reported in June 1943 that "there have been numerous reports, not verified, that [Japanese] hospital ships have been used to transport troops and materials of war. . . . Some [of same] are reported to have been steering zig-zag courses."[78] In December 1943, the Japanese government lodged a formal complaint against the United States stating that American forces had attacked four Japanese hospital ships in the Pacific. The U.S. State Department, to which this document had been forwarded by the Spanish embassy in Washington, sought an advisory opinion from the Joint Chiefs of Staff as to how to reply. The British government had also received a copy of this complaint. Both the Americans and the British customarily issued formal replies to the Japanese in these instances, whether or not they admitted guilt in the specific attacks concerned.[79]

That there was any diplomatic activity between the Western Allies and Japan is surprising in view of the ferocity of the conflict in the Pacific and Far East. For instance, British troops captured when the Japanese army overran Burma, Malaya, and Singapore in 1942 suffered terribly for the remainder of the war. They were used for forced labor under intolerable working conditions on projects like the Burma–Siam railway; the death toll among the POWs due to abuse and neglect was very high.[80] The bitterness with which the two sides fought each other in the Pacific is apparent in the island campaigns, such as at Tarawa, where when the smoke cleared in November 1943 the victorious Americans took only seventeen prisoners out of a Japanese/Korean garrison of 4,500 that had been on the island when the assault began.

The diplomatic skills of the British Chiefs of Staff were repeatedly put to the test by the difficulties of British personnel serving in the Soviet Union with No. 30 Mission. Its commander, Lieutenant General Giffard Martel, appealed to the British Chiefs of Staff Committee in July 1943 on behalf of two British soldiers under his command who were facing the prospect of harsh disciplinary action from Russian authorities for an unnamed, but apparently minor, offense. The British chiefs got to the point quickly in their reply to Martel: "Reference your Mil. 9522 Foreign Office have decided in first instance approach Americans with view to joint representation to Russians that service personnel should be tried by their own Authorities. Meantime do *not* hand over Pte. Spencer or Sgt. Ryan without further instructions. . . . Hoping to obtain Foreign Office approval instruct you embark these men for U.K. earliest."[81]

One highly volatile diplomatic crisis into which the Combined Chiefs of Staff were drawn began during the final days of the war in Europe. At that time it seemed possible that British and American troops might actually come to blows with the Yugoslav forces of Marshal Josip Broz Tito. The American, British, and Russian governments were most anxious that this not happen, especially since Tito's forces had been an effective part of the anti-German wartime coalition. In the final days of the European war, in early May 1945, as the inter-Allied 15th Army Group was driving German forces out of northern Italy, it became apparent that Tito's forces were intent upon installing themselves in as much Italian territory as they could. The Western Allies found it highly objectionable that Tito should seize Italian territory. Particularly sensitive in this regard was the port of Trieste, which the Allies badly needed for supply purposes. Eventually, the Trieste issue was settled peacefully to Allied satisfaction.[82] However, the Combined Chiefs of Staff had prepared a number of documents outlining strategies that Allied forces should adopt should the Trieste situation escalate. These documents show that while the Combined Chiefs hoped to avoid armed conflict with Yugoslav troops, they were determined nevertheless to secure Allied interests at all costs. One such CCS directive, written by the British Joint Staff Mission in Washington, informed British Field Marshal Sir Harold Alexander, the Allied theater commander in the Mediterranean, "In the event of refusal by Marshal Tito to comply with demands of His Majesty's Government and United States Government you will, on instructions from us, eject (using force if necessary) all Yugoslav forces from southern Austria, Trieste, Gorizia,

Montfalcone, Pola and such areas of Venezia Giulia as are necessary in order to secure and protect your lines of communication to Austria."[83] Although this directive never had to be carried out, the Combined Chiefs of Staff were clearly in the thick of the crisis over Yugoslav forces in northern Italy and the Balkans.[84]

In both the production and diplomatic spheres, then, the members of the Combined Chiefs of Staff proved that they were a farsighted and multitalented group of individuals—although they were capable of overstepping, as in the case of Portugal and the Azores. Their ability to take on such responsibilities in addition to developing campaign strategies serves as evidence that the Combined Chiefs were uniquely suited to operating within a modern coalition at war.

CONCLUSION

The Combined Chiefs of Staff was the most essential element for the conduct of successful Anglo-American coalition warfare. Both nations were in great need of such an organization, and both nations brought unique and essential elements to it. The British needed a combined command structure because, having hoped for American intervention for so long, Churchill and his military advisers wanted to be certain that the American war effort maintained the proper orientation. That is, it was essential to prevent the United States from scrapping the "ABC" decisions in order to concentrate exclusively on the war against Japan. In this regard it was necessary to counter American public opinion, which dearly desired immediate revenge for the Pearl Harbor attack. The Americans needed the Combined Chiefs of Staff organization because, with Hitler's declaration of war against the United States, it was clear that all Allied military effort in Western Europe and the Mediterranean would center upon England. The crucial nature of the British Isles as a staging area for all Anglo-American combined operations in this area (Torch, Sicily, Italy, Overlord, and the combined bomber offensive) certainly bears this out. Also apparent was the fact that for some time to come in the war against Germany, British troop strength in the field would exceed that of the United States. At the time of the German surrender on May 7, 1945, the strength of the American army in Western Europe outnumbered British troops by a ratio of three to one. However, American troops deployed in Europe did not begin to outnumber British troops there until January 1944.[1] Therefore, the U.S. Joint Chiefs of Staff were aware that it would have been ludicrous for the Americans to even consider conducting autonomous military operations in Europe in the manner of the American Expeditionary Force of World War I.

In addition to the talents of Dill, Brooke, Pound, Portal, and Cunningham, the British brought to the Combined Chiefs of Staff an organizational structure. The British Chiefs of Staff Committee served as the model for the creation of both the U.S. Joint Chiefs of Staff and the Combined Chiefs of Staff as a whole.[2] The strength of the influence of the example of the British Chiefs of Staff in this regard is exemplified by the fact that during the war Marshall, King, Arnold, and Leahy were often referred to as the "United States Chiefs of Staff" rather than by their official title of "Joint Chiefs of Staff."[3] By introducing such an organizational structure, the British undoubtedly did much to improve interservice cooperation in the American military.

What the Americans brought to the Combined Chiefs of Staff organization, in addition to the strategic gifts of the Joint Chiefs of Staff, was an unlimited store of resources in the form of troops, ships, aircraft, and supplies. This made possible powerful offensive operations, such as a return to the continent, which would have been impossible for Britain to undertake alone. Therefore, while the Americans sometimes found it difficult to work under a British-style command structure, the British members of the Combined Chiefs, in turn, found it difficult to discard a policy of attrition and short-term planning for the process favored by the Americans of long-term planning for large-scale offensive operations.[4] Thus, in explaining the inter-Allied difficulties involved in planning Overlord, American general Omar Bradley writes that "while the British, by instinct, played cautiously and safe in their strategic planning, [the] Americans could afford to bet the works on one climactic invasion."[5]

Despite their differences of opinion regarding strategic planning, the individual members of the Combined Chiefs of Staff had many things in common. They all understood the need to run the Anglo-American war effort from a central headquarters, rather than from the field. Each proved to be highly adaptable to operating within such a "board of directors" system for the direction of a coalition war effort. In addition, in a war in which (unlike World War I) the power of the offense again became capable of overcoming defensive fortifications and weapons, the members of the Combined Chiefs of Staff proved themselves quite open to understanding and planning for the utilization of modern tactics and weapons. The advocacy of Brooke and Marshall for the vigorous use of airborne divisions, as well as Portal's efforts to get jet fighter planes into service, exemplify this common characteristic. This is significant in view of the fact that all of the principal members of the Combined Chiefs of Staff had been born before the Wright brothers' airplane first flew at

Kitty Hawk in 1903. Undoubtedly, the Combined Chiefs were aided in adopting a modern outlook in such matters by the fact that they had been young officers during World War I—a conflict that had taught them the folly and the tragedy of a static, defensive-oriented war.

CCS members showed their adaptability in other ways as well. For example, they willingly took on tasks outside of the strict definition of military science that had suddenly become necessary aspects of the role of members of a high command in modern warfare. Wartime diplomacy and production issues fall into this category. Indeed, in addition to serving as the head of the British Joint Staff Mission in Washington and as senior British representative on the Combined Chiefs of Staff, Field Marshal Dill was something of a second British ambassador to the United States. One of Dill's unofficial responsibilities was to assist Lord Halifax in the latter's dealings with the U.S. State Department and the president.[6] The efforts of the Combined Chiefs of Staff in the field of munitions production were essential to keeping production programs in balance and to making certain that the highest quality weapons were produced.

To be sure, the Combined Chiefs of Staff organization was not without its faults. The absence of Russian representation is a complicated issue. As mentioned in chapter 4, until the time of the Cairo/Teheran Conferences in November–December 1943, the Western Allies did not feel a great need for closely coordinated planning between Anglo-American forces, on the one hand, and Russian forces, on the other. That may have been true in a literal sense. However, the difficulties encountered by General Deane upon his arrival in Moscow in October 1943 as head of the U.S. Military Mission might have been mitigated somewhat if the Western Allies had done more up to that point to coordinate their diplomatic, if not their military, activities with those of their Russian ally. For example, the Russians regarded as a severe affront the failure of the Americans and the British to allow Russian representation at the discussions that led to the surrender of Mussolini's Italy in September 1943. Under this agreement, the Russians were not allowed any effective influence in Allied-occupied portions of Italy.[7] This certainly seemed to violate the spirit of the Declaration of the United Nations, in which the Allied nations had pledged each other not to make separate peaces with any Axis nation.

Of course, any diplomatic overture made by the Western Allies to the Russians would have been hampered in its effectiveness by the failure of the

Americans and the British to provide what the Russians wanted and needed most—an early cross-Channel invasion of Western Europe. The fact that that campaign was delayed until June 6, 1944, was the cause of the most damaging rift among the Allied nations during the war.

Another shortcoming of the Combined Chiefs of Staff was that they sometimes delegated either too much, or too little, responsibility to theater commanders. The invasion, by Nimitz's Central Pacific forces, of Peleliu in the Palau Islands in October 1944 demonstrates what can happen when too much discretion is left to a field commander. This campaign required six weeks of heavy fighting in which two thousand American marines and infantry were killed. In addition to the horrendous casualties, Peleliu was controversial because by taking over unoccupied Ulithi in the western Carolines at the same time, the Americans had provided themselves with an excellent alternative base at no cost.[8] In regard to the American landings on Peleliu, Nimitz's biographer has written that "it is questionable whether the advantages gained offset the terrible cost."[9] Because Admiral King kept a close watch on operations in the Pacific, he probably should have rejected Nimitz's plan to seize Peleliu. The converse problem of not enough responsibility being delegated to a field commander has been described in chapter 7, in regard to Admiral Pound and Convoy PQ 17.

In attempting to assess its precise role in the Allied victory in World War II, perhaps the greatest praise that can be lavished upon the Combined Chiefs of Staff organization is that all of the military campaigns planned and conducted under its auspices, with the exception of the abortive ABDA effort, ended in victory. Of these victorious campaigns, Overlord and the war in the Pacific exhibited the most dramatic successes. Italy, on the other hand, was perhaps the most disappointing for the Combined Chiefs, due to the long periods of stalemate endured by Allied forces there. In all of these campaigns, the Combined Chiefs of Staff did their utmost to support their field commanders by providing as much as they possibly could in the way of solid advance planning, adequate troops and supplies, and air and naval forces.

It is perhaps best to end where I started—by stating that never before or since in history has one military staff been responsible for the planning and ongoing supervision of as many simultaneous, large-scale military operations as was the Combined Chiefs of Staff in World War II. The successes achieved by British and American forces in the field attest to the wisdom, discipline, breadth of vision, and stamina of that military staff.

NOTES

Introduction

1. Gordon Harrison, *United States Army in World War II: Cross–Channel Attack* (Washington, D.C.: Office of the Chief of Military History, 1951), 4n.

2. For example, when General Sir Hastings Ismay was reading an early draft of the third volume of Winston Churchill's memoirs, he was astounded to find that Churchill's account of the ARCADIA Conference, which began in December 1941 and extended into January 1942, did not include any description of the establishment of the Combined Chiefs of Staff. Apparently it was only due to Ismay's protest against this oversight that the published version of Churchill's memoirs does, in fact, mention the creation of the CCS. (Ismay to Churchill, October 31, 1946, Ismay Papers, 2/3/10, Liddell Hart Centre for Military Archives, King's College, London [hereinafter LHC]. For comparison, see Winston S. Churchill, *The Second World War*, vol. 3, *The Grand Alliance* [Boston: Houghton Mifflin, 1950], 686–88.) Ismay referred to that aspect of the ARCADIA discussions as "one of the really decisive decisions of the war." (Ismay to Churchill, October 31, 1946, Ismay Papers, 2/3/10, LHC.) Indeed it was.

3. Sally Lister Parker, *Attendant Lords: A Study of the British Joint Staff Mission in Washington, 1941–1944* (PhD dissertation, University of Maryland, College Park, 1984), 187; William D. Leahy, *I Was There* (New York: Whittlesey House / McGraw–Hill, 1950), 97. Sally Parker's dissertation (which, sadly, has never been published) provides a great deal of information in regard to the vital nature of the British Joint Staff Mission, and of Field Marshal Dill as its leader, to the Combined Chiefs of Staff organization.

4. Albert C. Wedemeyer, *Wedemeyer Reports!* (New York: Henry Holt, 1958), 3–6, 163–67; Forrest C. Pogue, *George C. Marshall*, vol. 2, *Ordeal and Hope* (New York: Viking, 1966), 140–41. See also, Andrew Roberts, *Masters and Commanders: How Four Titans Won the War in the West, 1941–1945* (New York: HarperCollins, 2009), 223–24.

5. Alex Danchev, *Very Special Relationship: Field Marshal Sir John Dill and the Anglo-American Alliance, 1941–1944* (London: Brassey's Defence, 1986), 32–56. See also, Hastings Ismay to Churchill, "The Combined Chiefs of Staff Organization," Ismay Papers, 2/3/10/2A/1, LHC.

6. Omer Bartov, *Hitler's Army: Soldiers, Nazis, and War in the Third Reich* (New York: Oxford University Press, 1992), 29. For more on German casualties in Russia, see Bartov, p. 45, and Alex Danchev, "God Knows: Civil–Military Relations with Allies," in *On Specialness: Essays in Anglo-American Relations* (New York: St. Martin's, 1998), 65.

7. U.S. Joint Chiefs of Staff, CCS 228/11, June 27, 1944, CAB 88/11/1–2, The National Archives of the UK [hereinafter TNA].

8. Thomas M. Coffey. *HAP: The Story of the U.S. Air Force and the Man Who Built It, General Henry H. "Hap" Arnold* (New York: Viking, 1982), 262.

9. Forrest C. Pogue, *George C. Marshall,* vol. 3, *Organizer of Victory* (New York: Viking, 1973), 336.

10. Danchev, *Very Special Relationship,* 23, 32–33. As Dill's biographer, Danchev deftly examines the personal, off-the-record diplomacy that helped an alliance to work.

11. Parker, *Attendant Lords,* 154–156; Danchev, "God Knows," 57, 64; Roberts, *Masters and Commanders,* 106.

12. Hastings Ismay to Churchill, "The Combined Chiefs of Staff Organization," Ismay Papers, 2/3/10/2A/1, LHC.

Chapter 1. The Combined Chiefs of Staff

1. Mark A. Stoler, *Allies in War: Britain and America against the Axis Powers, 1940–1945* (London: Hodder Arnold, 2005), 43–45; Andrew Roberts, *Masters and Commanders: How Four Titans Won the War in the West, 1941–1945* (New York: HarperCollins, 2009), 103, 110.

2. Forrest C. Pogue, *George C. Marshall,* vol. 2, *Ordeal and Hope* (New York: Viking, 1966), 283.

3. Larry I. Bland, ed., Sharon Ritenour Stevens, assoc. ed., *The Papers of George Catlett Marshall,* vol. 3, *"The Right Man for the Job:" December 7, 1941–May 31, 1943* (Baltimore: Johns Hopkins University Press, 1991), 590.

4. Henry H. Arnold, *Global Mission* (New York: Harper and Brothers, 1949), 15–20, 26–27.

5. Obituary, *New York Times*, January 16, 1950, 25.

6. Thomas M. Coffey, *HAP: The Story of the U.S. Air Force and the Man Who Built It, General Henry H. "Hap" Arnold* (New York: Viking, 1982), 344, 343–44, 382.

7. Ibid., 304–7, 312–13, 343–45, 358–62, 376.

8. Arnold, *Global Mission,* 500–2, 606–7; Coffey, *HAP,* 1, 312, 358–61; Alex Danchev and Daniel Todman, eds., *War Diaries 1939–1945: Field Marshal Lord Alanbrooke* (Berkeley: University of California Press, 2001), xlvii.

9. Sally Van Wagenen Keil, *Those Wonderful Women in Their Flying Machines: The Unknown Heroines of World War II* (New York: Rawson, Wade, 1979), 253–54, 226–27; Molly Merryman, *Clipped Wings: The Rise and Fall of the Women Airforce Service Pilots (WASPs) of World War II* (New York: New York University Press, 1998), 6–7, 77–80, 124–26, 129.

10. King interview, August 26, 1950, King Collection, 37/7/31/2–3, Naval War College.

11. Forrest C. Pogue, *George C. Marshall,* vol. 3, *Organizer of Victory* (New York: Viking, 1973), 7. The same volume contains numerous references to the friendship between the two men.

12. Marshall to Arnold, December 23, 1942, Marshall Papers, 56/41, George C. Marshall Research Library, Lexington, Virginia.

13. Thomas B. Buell, *Master of Sea Power: A Biography of Fleet Admiral Ernest J. King.* (Boston: Little, Brown, 1980), 72–76; Coffey, *HAP,* 260.

14. Coffey, *HAP,* 197, 319, 334–36, 342–43. For Arnold thinking ahead, see Douglas quote therein on 113; King interview, August 26, 1950, p. 2, 4.

15. Coffey, *HAP,* 346.

16. Arnold as quoted in Bland and Stevens, eds., *Papers of George Catlett Marshall,* vol. 3, 687.

17. For the quotation, Coffey, *HAP,* 2.

18. Ibid., 61–64, 71–73, 77–78, 84–87.

19. Ibid., 84–87.

20. Bland and Stevens, eds., *Papers of George Catlett Marshall,* vol. 3, 589–90.

21. Arnold, as quoted in Coffey, *HAP,* 346.

22. Arnold to King. September 7, 1944, King Papers, Man. Div., box 9, Arnold file, LC; King interview, July 30–31, 1949, King Collection, 37/7/25/1–2, Naval War College; King interview, July 4, 1950, King Collection, 37/7/2, Naval War College.

23. King to Rear Admiral J. W. Greenslade, February 19, 1942, King Collection, 37/5/12/1–2, Naval War College.

24. King to Rear Admiral C. S. Freeman, March 27, 1942, 37/5/12/1, ibid.

25. Grace Person Hayes, *The Joint Chiefs of Staff in World War II: The War against Japan* (Annapolis, Md.: Naval Institute Press, 1982), 590–96, 660–62.

26. Obituary, *New York Times,* January 16, 1950, p. 25.

27. Sir James Grigg, interview with M. C. Long, Alanbrooke Papers, 12/11/1/4/1–2, LHC; Sir David Fraser, *Alanbrooke* (New York: Atheneum, 1982), 246.

28. Alex Danchev, *Very Special Relationship: Field Marshal Sir John Dill and the Anglo-American Alliance, 1941–1944* (Washington, D.C.: Brassey's Defence, 1986), passim.

29. Sally Lister Parker, *Attendant Lords: A Study of the British Joint Staff Mission in Washington, 1941–1944* (PhD dissertation, University of Maryland, College Park, 1984), 155.

30. Brooke (an undated, late 1950s) reply to letters from Butler and Howard, Alanbrooke Papers, 10/3/12/1, LHC.

31. Fraser, *Alanbrooke,* 14–15, 37, 38–40.

32. Alex Danchev, "Great Britain: The Indirect Strategy," in *Allies at War: The Soviet, American, and British Experience, 1939–1945,* ed. David Reynolds, Warren F. Kimball, and A. O. Chubarian (New York: St. Martin's, 1994), 3–4.

33. Ibid., 3.
34. Brooke diary entry, March 31, 1942, Alanbrooke Papers, 5/5/87, LHC.
35. Ibid.
36. Fraser, *Alanbrooke,* 315.
37. Ibid., 325.
38. Roberts, *Masters and Commanders,* 20–22.
39. Brooke diary entry, September 10, 1944, reprinted in Fraser, *Alanbrooke,* 442.
40. See Lord Moran comment quoted in Brian Bond, "Alanbrooke and Britain's Mediterranean Strategy, 1942–1944," in *War, Strategy, and International Politics: Essays in Honour of Sir Michael Howard,* ed. Lawrence Freedman, Paul Hayes, and Robert O'Neill (Oxford, UK: Clarendon, 1992), 192–93.
41. Grigg, interview; Col. P. Earle, interview with M. C. Long, Alanbrooke Papers, 12/11/2/17/2, LHC.
42. Grigg, interview.
43. Lord Louis Mountbatten, interview with M. C. Long, 1952, Alanbrooke Papers, 12/11/1/2/1, LHC.
44. Earle, interview.
45. Portal, interview with M. C. Long, Alanbrooke Papers, 12/11/1/1/1–2, LHC.
46. Ibid., p. 2.
47. Ibid.
48. Ibid.
49. Stilwell diary entry, as quoted in Alex Danchev, "Being Friends: The Combined Chiefs of Staff and the Making of Allied Strategy in the Second World War," in Lawrence Freedman, Paul Hayes, and Robert O'Neill, eds., *War, Strategy, and International Politics: Essays in Honour of Sir Michael Howard.* (New York: Oxford University Press, 1992), 208.
50. Brooke diary entry, June 26, 1942, Alanbrooke Papers, 5/5/137, LHC.
51. Ibid., p. 138.
52. Michael Simpson, *A Life of Admiral of the Fleet Andrew Cunningham* (London: Frank Cass, 2004), 174, 179–80.
53. Ibid., 2.
54. Stephen Fox, *Transatlantic: Samuel Cunard, Isambard Brunel, and the Great Atlantic Steamships* (New York: HarperCollins, 2003), 398–400.
55. Simpson, *Life of Admiral of the Fleet Andrew Cunningham,* 3.
56. Robert K. Massie, *Castles of Steel: Britain, Germany, and the Winning of the Great War at Sea* (New York: Random House, 2003), 636–37, 642–46.
57. Simpson, *Life of Admiral of the Fleet Andrew Cunningham,* 3.
58. Obituary, *Times of London,* June 13, 1963, 17; Simpson, *Life of Admiral of the Fleet Andrew Cunningham,* 2, 5–14, 25–26, 90, 175.
59. Roberts, *Masters and Commanders,* 419–20; Winston S. Churchill, *The Second World War,* vol. 3, *The Grand Alliance* (Boston: Houghton Mifflin, 1950), 265–66; Simpson, *Life of Admiral of the Fleet Andrew Cunningham,* 73–74, 89–94; Barrie Pitt, ed., *The Military History of World War II* (New York: Military, 1986), 43.

60. Simpson, *Life of Admiral of the Fleet Andrew Cunningham,* 127–32.

61. Pogue, *Organizer of Victory,* 258.

62. For Churchill's desire to recapture Singapore and Hong Kong, see Roberts, *Masters and Commanders,* 313. See also, Warren F. Kimball, *Forged in War: Roosevelt, Churchill, and the Second World War* (New York: William Morrow, 1997), 133.

63. Alex Danchev, "Field Marshal Sir John Dill," in *Churchill's Generals,* ed. John Keegan (New York: Grove Weidenfeld, 1991), 51–52, 59.

64. Ibid., 59.

65. Ibid., 52–53, 63.

66. Roberts, *Masters and Commanders,* 76–78.

67. Alex Danchev, "Good Boy: Field Marshal Sir John Dill," in *On Specialness: Essays in Anglo-American Relations* (New York: St. Martin's, 1998), 81–82, 181n.

68. Danchev, "Field Marshal Sir John Dill," in *Churchill's Generals,* ed. John Keegan (New York: William Morrow, 1992), 66.

69. Danchev, *Very Special Relationship,* passim; and Parker, *Attendant Lords,* passim.

70. Nancy Dill to Marshall, December 22, 1944, Dill Papers, 5/2, LHC.

71. Marshall address, Yale University, February 16, 1944, 5/2/4, ibid.

72. Parker, *Attendant Lords,* 155–56, 189; Sir John Dill to E. J. King, December 13, 1943, King Papers, Man. Div., box 10, Dill file, LC; Nancy Dill to E. J. King, November 13, 1944, King Papers, Man. Div., box 10, Dill file. LC.

73. JSM to COS October 12, 1942, "Personal from Field Marshal Dill," JSM 423, CAB 122/31/1, TNA.

74. Gordon Harrison, *United States Army in World War II: Cross-Channel Attack* (Washington, D.C.: Office of the Chief of Military History, 1951), 4n; Danchev, "Being Friends," 200; Danchev, "Good Boy," 86.

75. FDR to Churchill, January 10, 1945, Dill Papers, 5/2, LHC.

76. See Robert Albion quote in Buell, *Master of Sea Power,* 234. See also, Simpson, *Life of Admiral of the Fleet Andrew Cunningham,* 130.

77. Robert W. Love Jr., "Ernest Joseph King," in *The Chiefs of Naval Operations* (Annapolis, Md.: Naval Institute Press, 1980), 140; Buell, *Master of Sea Power,* 41–42, 88–89.

78. Buell, *Master of Sea Power,* 17–24, 89.

79. Ibid., 17–24, 261; Love, "Ernest Joseph King," 160; Ernest J. King and Walter Muir Whitehill, *Fleet Admiral King: A Naval Record* (New York: W. W. Norton, 1952), afterword by Whitehill, 651–52.

80. King and Whitehill, *Fleet Admiral King,* 306, 413 (for the blowtorch quote); Buell, *Master of Sea Power,* 222–23. For additional proof that King did indeed have a sense of humor, see Love, "Ernest Joseph King," 161.

81. Buell, *Master of Sea Power,* 17–24, 43–44, 47–53, 58–64, 67–70, 76–78, 80–81, 199–202; Samuel Eliot Morison, *History of United States Naval Operations in World War II,* vol. 4, *Coral Sea, Midway and Submarine Actions: May 1942–August 1942* (Boston: Little, Brown, 1949), 44–45n, 54–55, 59, 60n, 79–82; John B. Lundstrom,

Black Shoe Carrier Admiral: Frank Jack Fletcher at Coral Sea, Midway, and Guadal-canal (Annapolis, Md.: Naval Institute Press, 2006), 208–09, 501–02; E. B. Potter, *Nimitz* (Annapolis, Md.: Naval Institute Press, 1975), 77, 86, 185, 241; Love, "Ernest Joseph King," 156–57.

82. Vice Admiral Harry Sanders, USN (Ret.) to Thomas Buell, November 16, 1974, "Assorted Notes re FADM King," King Collection, 37/2/1, Naval War College.

83. Buell, *Master of Sea Power,* 232.

84. Buell, *Master of Sea Power,* 155. For more on Edwards' personality, see Love, "Ernest Joseph King," 147.

85. Buell, *Master of Sea Power,* 232.

86. For King as gentleman, Buell, *Master of Sea Power,* 260.

87. King interview, July 30–31, 1949.

88. Spruance to King, January 22, 1947, King Papers, Man. Div., box 18, Spruance file, LC.

89. Ibid.

90. King interview, August 26, 1950, 2, 4.

91. King and Whitehill, *Fleet Admiral King,* 493n.

92. King interview, August 26, 1950, 2, 4.

93. Ibid.

94. John Major, "William Daniel Leahy: 2 January 1937–1 August 1939," in Love, *Chiefs of Naval Operations,* 101–2.

95. Ibid., 101. See also William D. Leahy, *I Was There* (New York: Whittlesey House / McGraw-Hill, 1950), 87–93; obituary, *New York Times,* July 21, 1959, 29.

96. Major, "William Daniel Leahy," 116; Pogue, *Ordeal and Hope,* 298–300; Roberts, *Masters and Commanders,* 96–97.

97. Love, "Ernest Joseph King," 147; Roberts, *Masters and Commanders,* 96–97.

98. Pogue, *Ordeal and Hope,* 298–300; Major, "William Daniel Leahy," 116; Buell, *Master of Sea Power,* 243.

99. Buell, *Master of Sea Power,* 227.

100. Ibid., 242–43.

101. Steven T. Ross, "Chester William Nimitz: 15 December 1945–15 December 1947," in Love, *Chiefs of Naval Operations,* 181.

102. Buell, *Master of Sea Power,* 209.

103. Major, "William Daniel Leahy," 102–3, 107; Ian Sturton, ed. *Conway's All the World's Battleships: 1906 to the Present* (Annapolis, Md.: Naval Institute Press, 1987), 178, 181. Information on American battleships therein is by Norman Friedman.

104. Ibid.

105. Buell, *Master of Sea Power,* 332–33, 471.

106. John Kennedy Ohl, *Supplying the Troops: General Somervell and American Logistics in WWII* (DeKalb: Northern Illinois University Press, 1994), 105.

107. Forrest C. Pogue, *George C. Marshall*, vol. 1, *Education of a General* (New York: Viking, 1963), 164, 323; Pogue, *Ordeal and Hope*, 23; Roberts, *Masters and Commanders*, 27; Sir Hastings Ismay, *The Memoirs of General Lord Ismay* (New York: Viking, 1960), 251; Mark A. Stoler, *George C. Marshall: Soldier Statesman of the American Century* (Boston: Twayne, 1989), 121.

108. Ismay, *Memoirs of General Lord Ismay*, 251.

109. Obituary, *New York Times*, October 17, 1959, 12; Pogue, *Education of a General*, 327, 342. See also, Roberts, *Masters and Commanders*, 27–28.

110. Buell, *Master of Sea Power*, 187.

111. Pogue, *Education of a General*, 284–85, 292–99.

112. Larry I. Bland, ed., and Sharon Ritenour Stevens, assoc. ed., *The Papers of George Catlett Marshall*, vol. 4, *"Aggressive and Determined Leadership:" June 1, 1943–December 31, 1944* (Baltimore: Johns Hopkins University Press, 1996), 345–46, text and notes.

113. Ibid., 345.

114. Bland and Stevens, eds., *Papers of George Catlett Marshall*, vol. 3, 668n.

115. Ibid (text of letter).

116. Pogue, *Education of a General*, 55–57, 67–69, 97, 126, 151–54, 226, 236, 245–46, 262–63; Roberts, *Masters and Commanders*, 11–12, 23–24.

117. Bland and Stevens, eds., *Papers of George Catlett Marshall*, vol. 4, pp. 9, 17; Pogue, *Organizer of Victory*, 44–47.

118. Bland and Ritenour Stevens, eds., *Papers of George Catlett Marshall*, vol. 4, 9; Pogue, *Organizer of Victory*, 221.

119. Bland and Ritenour Stevens, eds., *Papers of George Catlett Marshall*, vol. 4, 9.

120. Pogue, *Organizer of Victory*, 44.

121. Pogue, *Ordeal and Hope*, 12, 24 (quote); Pogue, *Education of a General*, 35, 302; Pogue, *Organizer of Victory*, 43, 53–54.

122. Pogue, *Organizer of Victory*, 53.

123. Ibid., 46–52.

124. Bland and Ritenour Stevens, *Papers of George Catlett Marshall*, vol. 4, 473–74.

125. Ibid., 474.

126. Ibid., 474n, 473.

127. Denis Richards, *Portal of Hungerford* (London: Heinemann, 1977), 4–5.

128. Ibid., 5.

129. Obituary, *Times of London*, April 24, 1971, 14.

130. Parker, *Attendant Lords*, 154–55.

131. Richards, *Portal of Hungerford*, 183, 214–15.

132. Portal, as quoted in Richards, *Portal of Hungerford*, 207–8.

133. Ibid., 595–596. For more information on both of the Canadian fishing trips, see Richards, *Portal of Hungerford*, 207–9.

134. Danchev and Todman, eds., *War Diaries*, 596.

135. Ibid., 596.

136. Richards, *Portal of Hungerford*, 199.

137. Portal to Harris, October 10, 1942, Portal Papers, 9/63/1, Christ Church, Oxford.

138. Parker, *Attendant Lords*, 184.

139. Portal, interview with M. C. Long.

140. Ibid.

141. Richards, *Portal of Hungerford*, 261, 265; Brian Bond, "Alanbrooke and Britain's Mediterranean Strategy, 1942–1944," in Freedman et al., *War, Strategy, and International Politics*, 184.

142. Danchev, "Great Britain," 7–8; Roberts, *Masters and Commanders*, 102–3.

143. Brooke diary entry, April 2, 1942, Alanbrooke Papers, 5/5/89, LHC.

144. Robin Brodhurst, *Churchill's Anchor: Admiral of the Fleet Sir Dudley Pound, OM, GCB, GCVM* (Barnsley, South Yorkshire, UK: Leo Cooper, 2000), 17.

145. Peter Kemp. "Admiral of the Fleet: Sir Dudley Pound," in *Men of War: Great Naval Leaders of World War II*, ed. Stephen Howarth (New York: St. Martin's, 1992), 25, 40.

146. Roberts, *Masters and Commanders*, 44, 419.

147. Danchev, "Great Britain," 7.

148. King interview, July 30–31, 1949.

149. See, for example, King to Pound, March 28, 1943 and June 4, 1943, King Papers, Man. Div., box 14, Pound file, LC.

150. King-Pound correspondence, passim, King Papers, Man. Div., box 14, Pound file, LC.

151. Robin Brodhurst, "Admiral Sir Dudley Pound (1939–1943)," in *The First Sea Lords: From Fisher to Mountbatten*, ed. Malcolm Murfrett (Westport, Conn.: Praeger, 1995), 192–94.

152. Brodhurst, *Churchill's Anchor*, 95–96, 218.

153. Ibid., 120.

154. Ibid.

155. Kemp, "Admiral of the Fleet Sir Dudley Pound," 20.

156. Ibid., 20–24. See also, Brodhurst, *Churchill's Anchor*, 116–17, 210–13.

157. Brodhurst, *Churchill's Anchor*, 37, 58, 105 (on delegation in general), 248–49 (on PQ-17).

158. Parker, *Attendant Lords*, 160, 187.

159. Pogue, *Ordeal and Hope*, 310–12; Winston S. Churchill, *The Second World War*, vol. 5, *Closing the Ring* (Boston: Houghton Mifflin, 1951), 69–70.

160. Roberts, *Masters and Commanders*, 103.

161. Pogue, *Ordeal and Hope*, 311.

162. Stoler, *Allies in War*, 124–25; Churchill, *Closing the Ring*, 81.

163. For a good description of this incident, see Roberts, *Masters and Commanders*, 405–6. For the details of the design, see Susan B. M. Langley, "Habbakuk," in *Encyclopedia of Underwater and Maritime Archaeology*, ed. James P. Delgado (New Haven, Conn.: Yale University Press, 1997), 186.

164. Langley, "Habbakuk," 186.
165. Bland and Stevens, eds., *Papers of George Catlett Marshall,* vol. 3, 225–26, text and notes.
166. Ibid., 226.
167. Ismay, *Memoirs of General Lord Ismay,* 169.
168. Pogue, *Organizer of Victory,* 6; Roberts, *Masters and Commanders,* 110–11; Ismay, *Memoirs of General Lord Ismay,* 355–56.
169. Ismay, *Memoirs of General Lord Ismay,* 168.
170. Ibid., 168–69, 317–18.
171. Ibid., 171–72.
172. Parker, *Attendant Lords,* 175–94.
173. Ibid., 175.
174. Love, "Ernest Joseph King," 143.
175. Pogue, *Ordeal and Hope,* 261.

Chapter 2. Organization, Anatomy of a Summit Conference, and Home Base

1. Sally Lister Parker, *Attendant Lords: A Study of the British Joint Staff Mission in Washington, 1941–1945* (PhD dissertation, University of Maryland, College Park, 1984), 104–15.
2. Ibid., pp. 17–21, 104–26.
3. Arnold to Marshall, March 20, 1943, WA138 27, Marshall Papers, 56/41, George C. Marshall Research Library; Lexington, Virginia; Forrest C. Pogue, *George C. Marshall,* vol. 2, *Ordeal and Hope* (New York: Viking, 1966), 283; see also, Pogue, *George C. Marshall,* vol. 3, *Organizer of Victory* (New York: Viking, 1973), passim.
4. Thomas B. Buell, *Master of Sea Power: A Biography of Admiral Ernest J. King* (Boston: Little, Brown, 1980), 363–66; E. B. Potter, *Nimitz* (Annapolis, Md.: Naval Institute Press, 1975), 187; "Mitscher, Marc Andrew," in Alan Axelrod, *Profiles in Leadership* (New York: Prentice Hall, 2003), 366–68.
5. Ibid.
6. Parker, *Attendant Lords,* 24–34, 42–57, 118–21.
7. Alex Danchev, *Very Special Relationship: Field Marshal Sir John Dill and the Anglo-American Alliance, 1941–1944* (Washington, D.C.: Brassey's Defence, 1986), 23–32.
8. Hastings Ismay, "The Combined Chiefs of Staff Organization," Ismay Papers, 2/3/10/2A/1, LHC.
9. CCS 228/12, of July 4, 1944, is one of many CCS memoranda that has as a byline: "The *Representatives* of the British Chiefs of Staff." CAB 88/11/1, TNA [italics mine]. See also, Alex Danchev, "Being Friends: The Combined Chiefs of Staff and the Making of Allied Strategy in the Second World War," in *War, Strategy, and International Politics: Essays in Honour of Sir Michael Howard,* ed. Lawrence Freedman, Paul Hayes, and Robert O'Neill (New York: Oxford University Press, 1992), 199–200.

10. A. J. P. Taylor, *The First World War: An Illustrated History* (New York: Perigree Books/G. P. Putnam's Sons, 1980), 219–20.

11. For more on such combined command structures, see General Sir William Jackson and Field Marshal Lord Bramall, *The Chiefs: The Story of the United Kingdom Chiefs of Staff* (London: Brassey's, 1992), 245.

12. For additional information on such alliances, see Jackson and Bramall, *Chiefs,* 258–59; On Arnold retaining command of the B–29s, see Henry H. Arnold, *Global Mission* (New York: Harper and Brothers, 1949), 550.

13. King to Hopkins, September 17, 1942, King Collection, 37/5/12/1, Naval War College.

14. Wesley Frank Craven and James Lea Cate, eds. *The Army Air Forces in World War II,* vol. 6, *Men and Planes* (Washington, D.C.: Office of Air Force History, repr. 1983), 352; see also Craven and Cate, eds., *The Army Air Forces in World War II,* vol. 7, *Services around the World* (Chicago: University of Chicago Press, 1958), 24–29.

15. Grace Person Hayes, *The Joint Chiefs of Staff in World War II: The War against Japan* (Annapolis, Md.: Naval Institute Press, 1982), 4, 105.

16. John Kennedy Ohl, *Supplying the Troops: General Somervell and American Logistics in WWII* (DeKalb: Northern Illinois University Press, 1994), 98–116; Letter from Kevin Smith to me, January 6, 1999.

17. C. B. A. (Betty) Behrens, *Merchant Shipping and the Demands of War* (London: Her Majesty's Stationery Office and Longman's, Green, 1955), 442; Ohl, *Supplying the Troops,* 100; Ronald Hope, *A New History of British Shipping* (London: John Murray, 1990), 386, 387; Letter to me from Kevin Smith, January 6, 1999.

18. Hope, *New History of British Shipping,* 387; Behrens, *Merchant Shipping and the Demands of War,* 272.

19. Pogue, *Ordeal and Hope,* 296; John D. Millett, *The United States Army in World War II: The Organization and Role of the Army Service Forces* (Washington, D.C.: Office of the Chief of Military History, 1954), 62.

20. Parker, *Attendant Lords,* 1–11.

21. Ibid., 155–56, 175–94; Oliver Warner, *Admiral of the Fleet: Cunningham of Hyndhope—the Battle for the Mediterranean* (Athens: Ohio University Press, 1967), 177–79.

22. Warner, *Cunningham of Hyndhope,* 178.

23. King interview, July 30–31, 1949, King Collection, 37/7/25/1–2, Naval War College.

24. Parker, *Attendant Lords,* 175–94.

25. Dill to Churchill, July 15, 1942, as reprinted in Winston S. Churchill, *The Second World War,* vol. 4, *The Hinge of Fate* (Boston: Houghton Mifflin, 1948–1953), 396.

26. Parker, *Attendant Lords,* 175–94.

27. Ibid., 1–11, 180.

28. Joint Staff Mission to Hollis, November 21, 1942, LETOD 435, CAB 122/177/1–2, TNA.

29. Combined Staff planners, CCS 251/1. May 25, 1943, "Proposals for Improving Combined Planning," CAB 88/12/3, TNA.
30. Parker, *Attendant Lords,* 162–65; Danchev, *Very Special Relationship,* 50–65.
31. Combined Staff planners, "Proposals for Improving Combined Planning," 88/12/3–4.
32. See for example, Pogue, *Organizer of Victory,* passim; and Andrew Roberts, *Masters and Commanders: How Four Titans Won the War in the West, 1941–1945* (New York: HarperCollins, 2009), passim.
33. Roberts, *Masters and Commanders,* 76; Alex Danchev, "In the Back Room: Defence Co–operation," in *On Specialness: Essays in Anglo-American Relations* (New York: St. Martin's, 1998), 95; Pogue, *Organizer of Victory,* 70.
34. Danchev, *Very Special Relationship,* 133.
35. Danchev, "Being Friends," 202.
36. Ibid.; Roberts, *Masters and Commanders,* 31, 76–77; Buell, *Master of Sea Power,* 242.
37. Albert C. Wedemeyer, *Wedemeyer Reports!* (New York: Henry Holt, 1958), 165–67, 187–88; Danchev, "Being Friends," 200–201.
38. Pogue, *Organizer of Victory,* 32–35.
39. *Foreign Relations of the United States* [hereafter *FRUS*]: *The Conferences at Washington, 1941–1942 and Casablanca, 1943* (Washington, D.C.: U.S. Government Printing Office, 1968), 500–22, 613–47; Minutes CCS 101st Meeting, July 9, 1943, *Records of the JCS* Part 1, *1942–45: Meetings,* Microfilm (Frederick, Maryland: University Publications of America), reel 4, frame 0027, 1; minutes JCS 172nd Meeting, September 5, 1944, *Records of the JCS—Meetings,* reel 2, frame 0810; see also, Pogue, *Organizer of Victory,* 17.
40. Parker, *Attendant Lords,* 160.
41. Combined Chiefs of Staff, CCS 116/1, CAB 88/8/passim, TNA. See also, *FRUS: The Conferences at Washington, 1941–1942, and Casablanca, 1943,* 613–47.
42. Roberts, *Masters and Commanders,* 68–72, 339; Wedemeyer, *Wedemeyer Reports!,* 174, 179–80, 188, 191–92; Buell, *Master of Sea Power,* 267, 270.
43. Samuel Eliot Morison, *The Two–Ocean War: A Short History of the United States Navy in the Second World War* (Boston: Little, Brown, 1962), 238.
44. Pogue, *Organizer of Victory,* 27–30.
45. Buell, *Master of Sea Power,* 267, 279.
46. Pogue, *Organizer of Victory,* 30–31; Buell, *Master of Sea Power,* 279–80.
47. Pogue, *Organizer of Victory,* 31.
48. Wedemeyer, *Wedemeyer Reports!,* 192.
49. Kevin Smith, *Conflict over Convoys: Anglo–American Logistics Diplomacy in the Second World War* (Cambridge, UK: Cambridge University Press, 1996), 1–2.
50. Ibid., 3–4. See also, Robert W. Love Jr., *History of the U.S. Navy,* vol. 2, *1942–1991* (Harrisburg, Pa.: Stackpole Books, 1992), 119; Roberts, *Masters and Commanders,* 428.

51. Pogue, *Organizer of Victory,* 39; Millett, *United States Army in World War II,* 174; *FRUS: The Conferences at Washington, 1941–1942, and Casablanca, 1943,* 536, text and note.

52. Joint Staff Mission, "Extract of Minutes of M.M. (42) 1st Meeting," February 12, 1942, CAB 122/011/1, TNA; Joint Staff Mission, "Scale of British Effort in the Pacific after the Defeat of Germany," attached note, September 26, 1944, CAB 122/1095/passim, TNA. See invitation card dated January 12, 1944, CAB 122/941/1, TNA.

53. Pound to Churchill and COS Committee, February 10, 1943, First Sea Lord's Records, 1943–Part 1, ADM 205/27/1, TNA.

54. Pogue, *Organizer of Victory,* 38–39.

55. Noble to Cunningham, January 30, 1944, Cunningham Papers, ADD 52571, British Library [hereinafter BL]. See letterhead.

56. Joint Staff Mission, "Extract of Minutes of M.M. (42) 1st Meeting"; Joint Staff Mission, "Scale of British Effort in the Pacific after the Defeat of Germany."

57. "Office Accommodation in Washington," undated British Joint Staff Mission document, CAB 122/011/1, TNA.

58. Joint Staff Mission, "Extract of Minutes of M.M. (42) 1st Meeting"; Joint Staff Mission, "Scale of British Effort in the Pacific after the Defeat of Germany."

59. Danchev, *Very Special Relationship,* 23–32; Knox to King, March 10, 1944, "Navy Department Office Space in Washington, D.C.," King Papers, Man. Div., box 12, Knox file, LC.

60. Redman to Deane, June 8, 1943, CAB 122/011/1, TNA.

61. *FRUS: The Conferences at Washington, 1941–1942, and Casablanca, 1943,* 522.

62. *FRUS: The Conferences at Washington and Quebec, 1943.* (Washington, D.C.: U.S. Government Printing Office, 1970), vi–vii, 52–111, 152.

63. Dill to son John, September 14, 1944, Dill Papers, 5/6, LHC.

64. *FRUS: The Conferences at Washington and Quebec, 1943,* viii–ix, 870–81, 889–904.

65. Pogue, *Organizer of Victory,* 519.

66. Roberts, *Masters and Commanders,* 546; Pogue, *Organizer of Victory,* 520–22; Buell, *Master of Sea Power,* 484–85.

67. Pogue, *Organizer of Victory,* 520–21; Roberts, *Masters and Commanders,* 545–47.

68. Laurence Kuter, as quoted in Pogue, *Organizer of Victory,* 520.

Chapter 3. The Combined Chiefs of Staff and the War in the Pacific

1. Forrest C. Pogue, *George C. Marshall,* vol. 2, *Ordeal and Hope* (New York: Viking, 1966), 28.

2. Christopher Thorne, *Allies of a Kind: The United States, Britain and the War against Japan* (London: Hamish Hamilton, 1978), 134; Grace Person Hayes, *The Joint Chiefs of Staff in World War II: The War against Japan* (Annapolis, Md.: Naval Institute Press, 1982), 8–11. Hayes in particular provides a detailed account of the ABC talks.

3. British Joint Staff Mission, CCS 308/6, "Reorganization of Command in India and Southeast Asia," November 8, 1943, CAB 88/15/2, TNA.

4. Samuel Eliot Morison, *History of United States Naval Operations in World War II,* vol. 3, *The Rising Sun in the Pacific 1931–April 1942* (Boston: Little, Brown, 1955), 255–57.

5. Ibid., 256.

6. Mark A. Stoler, *Allies in War: Britain and America against the Axis Powers 1940–1945* (London: Hodder Arnold, 2005), 63–66; E. B. Potter, *Nimitz* (Annapolis, Md.: Naval Institute Press, 1975), 76–86; Robert William Love Jr., "Ernest Joseph King," in *The Chiefs of Naval Operations* (Annapolis, Md.: Naval Institute Press, 1980), 150; Samuel Eliot Morison, *History of United States Naval Operations in World War II,* vol. 4, *Coral Sea, Midway and Submarine Actions: May 1942–August 1942* (Boston: Little, Brown, 1949), 44–45n, 54–55, 59–60n, 79–82; John B. Lundstrom, *Black Shoe Carrier Admiral: Frank Jack Fletcher at Coral Sea, Midway, and Guadalcanal* (Annapolis, Md.: Naval Institute Press, 2006), 209–12, 215–16; Thomas B. Buell, *Master of Sea Power: A Biography of Admiral Ernest J. King* (Boston: Little, Brown, 1980), 199–202.

7. Stoler, *Allies in War,* 161–63; Potter, *Nimitz,* 264–66.

8. Thorne, *Allies of a Kind,* 144–47, 155–57, 163.

9. Ibid., 135–41, 163. See also, B. H. Liddell Hart, *History of the Second World War* (New York: G. P. Putnam's Sons, 1970), 298, 317, 365.

10. See General Sir William Jackson and Field Marshal Lord Bramall, *The Chiefs: The Story of the United Kingdom Chiefs of Staff* (London: Brassey's, 1992), 240; Andrew Roberts, *Masters and Commanders: How Four Titans Won the War in the West, 1941–1945* (New York: HarperCollins, 2009), 312.

11. COS Committee to Churchill, COS (44) 123 (0), "Plans for the Defeat of Japan," February 5, 1944, CAB 122/1072/1, TNA; Combined Chiefs of Staff, CCS 319/5, "Quadrant: Report to the President and Prime Minister of the Final Agreed Summary of Conclusions Reached by the Combined Chiefs of Staff," August 24, 1943, in *FRUS: The Conferences at Washington and Quebec, 1943* (Washington, D.C.: U.S. Government Printing Office, 1968), 1126–27.

12. For more on this, see Jackson and Bramall, *Chiefs,* 240.

13. Thorne, *Allies of a Kind,* 261–90; Samuel Eliot Morison, *The Two Ocean War: A Short History of the United States Navy in the Second World War* (Boston: Little, Brown, 1962), 305, 421.

14. Forrest C. Pogue, *George C. Marshall.* vol. 3, *Organizer of Victory* (New York: Viking, 1973), 21–32. See also, Ernest J. King and Walter Muir Whitehill, *Fleet Admiral King: A Naval Record* (New York: W. W. Norton, 1952), 424; Roberts, *Masters and Commanders,* 312.

15. JPS London to JPS Washington, Blue No. 59, December 23, 1942, Joint Staff Mission Papers, CAB 122/31/2, TNA.

16. U.S. Joint Chiefs of Staff, CCS 301, August 9, 1943, CAB 88/15/4, TNA.

17. King and Whitehill, *Fleet Admiral King,* 415–23. See also, Casablanca minutes, as reprinted in *FRUS: The Conferences at Washington, 1941–1942, and Casablanca, 1943,* 536.

18. Marshall to CCS, from Casablanca minutes, in *FRUS: The Conferences at Washington, 1941–1942, and Casablanca, 1943,* 620.

19. Ibid.

20. Ibid., 603.

21. For more on Brooke's tenacity, see Jackson and Bramall, *Chiefs,* 240.

22. Brooke to CCS, from Casablanca minutes, in *FRUS: The Conferences at Washington, 1941–1942, and Casablanca, 1943,* 619.

23. Alex Danchev, *Very Special Relationship: Field Marshal Sir John Dill and the Anglo-American Alliance, 1941–1944* (Washington, D.C.: Brassey's Defence, 1986), 124; Pogue, *Organizer of Victory,* 336.

24. Pogue, *Organizer of Victory,* 21–32; Sally Lister Parker, *Attendant Lords: A Study of the British Joint Staff Mission in Washington, 1941–1945* (PhD dissertation, University of Maryland, College Park, 1984), 160–62.

25. Combined Chiefs of Staff, CCS 94, "Operations in 1942/43, July 24, 1942, CAB 88/6/2, TNA. See also, Sir Michael Howard, *Grand Strategy,* vol. 4, *August, 1942–September, 1943* (London: Her Majesty's Stationery Office, 1972), 192.

26. Sir David Fraser, *Alanbrooke* (New York: Atheneum, 1982), 261–63; Kevin Smith, *Conflict over Convoys: Anglo–American Logistics Diplomacy in the Second World War* (Cambridge, UK: Cambridge University Press, 1996), 77–78; Alex Danchev and Daniel Todman, eds., *War Diaries 1939–1945: Field Marshal Lord Alanbrooke* (Berkeley: University of California Press, 2001), 267–68, 315. In particular, see Brooke's entries for June 20 and August 29, 1942.

27. British COS Committee, CCS 135/2, "American-British Strategy in 1943," January 3, 1943, CAB 88/8/2, TNA; Roberts, *Masters and Commanders,* 320.

28. Howard, *Grand Strategy,* vol. 4, 91.

29. Combined Chiefs of Staff, CCS 242/6—Enclosure, "Trident: Report to the President and Prime Minister of the Final Agreed Summary of Conclusions Reached by the Combined Chiefs of Staff," May 25, 1943, reprinted in *FRUS: The Conferences at Washington and Quebec: 1943,* 369; Combined Chiefs of Staff, CCS 308/6, "Report to the President and the Prime Minister," November 8, 1943 (Annex 1), CAB 88/15/7–8, TNA.

30. Howard, *Grand Strategy,* vol. 4, 450.

31. Winston S. Churchill, *The Second World War,* vol. 5, *Closing the Ring* (Boston: Houghton Mifflin, 1951), 274–76. See also Churchill, ibid., vol. 6, *Triumph and Tragedy* (Boston: Houghton Mifflin, 1953), 770.

32. Bernard C. Nalty, "The Gilberts and the Marshalls," in *Pearl Harbor and the War in the Pacific* (New York: Smithmark, 1991), 134.

33. Combined Chiefs of Staff, "Report to the President and the Prime Minister."

34. Joint Staff Mission to COS Committee, JSM 427 BIGOT, October 16, 1942, CAB 122/177/3, TNA.

35. Thomas Buell, *The Quiet Warrior: A Biography of Admiral Raymond A. Spruance* (Annapolis, Md.: Naval Institute Press, 1987), 240–44; Ronald H. Spector, *Eagle against the Sun: The American War with Japan* (New York: Free Press, 1985), 257; Nalty, "Gilberts and Marshalls," 139; Potter, *Nimitz,* 276. See also, King and Whitehill, *Fleet Admiral King,* 520–29.

36. Nalty, "Gilberts and Marshalls," 130–34; Hayes, *Joint Chiefs of Staff in World War II,* 3–6.

37. King and Whitehill, *Fleet Admiral King,* 387–88, 432–41.

38. Ibid., 441.

39. Ibid.

40. Hayes, *Joint Chiefs of Staff in World War II,* 310.

41. Ibid.

42. Thorne, *Allies of a Kind,* 295–96.

43. Spector, *Eagle against the Sun,* xiv, 257–71. See also, Nalty, "Gilberts and the Marshalls," 138.

44. Thorne, *Allies of a Kind,* 296.

45. Ibid., 296–97.

46. Hayes, *Joint Chiefs of Staff in World War II,* 145–47, 311–12; Potter, *Nimitz,* 211–12, 276–96; Barrie Pitt, ed., *The Military History of World War II* (New York: Military, 1986), 165.

47. U.S. Joint Chiefs of Staff, CCS 417/8, September 9, 1944, CAB 122/1072/1, TNA.

48. U.S. Joint Chiefs, CCS 417/5, "Overall Objective in the War against Japan," August 4, 1944, CAB 122/1072/1, TNA.

49. U.S. Joint Chiefs of Staff, CCS 219, "Conduct of the War in 1943–44," May 14, 1943, CAB 88/11/1–2, TNA. See also Howard, *Grand Strategy,* vol. 4, 561–70.

50. COS Committee to Churchill, "Plans for the Defeat of Japan."

51. Ibid. See also Fraser, *Alanbrooke,* 413–14.

52. Spector, *Eagle against the Sun,* xiii; MacArthur to Marshall, June 24, 1942, Marshall Papers, 73/12/1, George C. Marshall Research Library, Lexington, Va.; Potter, *Nimitz,* 212; John Toland, *The Rising Sun: The Decline and Fall of the Japanese Empire* (New York: Bantam, 1970), 530–36.

53. Hayes, *Joint Chiefs of Staff in World War II,* 122.

54. Ibid., 310.

55. Combined Chiefs of Staff, "Quadrant: Report to the President and Prime Minister."

56. Buell, *Master of Sea Power,* 358.

57. Potter, *Nimitz,* 276–96.

58. COS Committee, CCS (44) 396 (0), "War against Japan—Summary of Various Courses," May 4, 1944, CAB 122/1072/1, TNA.

59. Ibid.

60. COS Committee, "War against Japan—Summary of Various Courses," 122/1072/1 and passim.

61. P. Noble to A. B. Cunningham, April 2, 1944, Cunningham Papers, ADD 52571/1, BL. See also JSM to COS Committee, JSM 110, August 3, 1942, AIR 8/1050/1–2, TNA.

62. Cunningham, interview with M. C. Long, Alanbrooke Papers, 12/11/1/5/2–3, LHC.

63. Thorne, *Allies of a Kind*, 592.

64. Danchev, *Very Special Relationship*, 73.

65. H. L. Moore to Churchill, April 24, 1943, ADM 205/27/1, TNA.

66. Cunningham, interview, 12/11/1/5/2.

67. Ibid. See also, Churchill, *Triumph and Tragedy*, 152.

68. Ibid.; Cunningham, interview, 12/11/1/5/2.

69. Ibid.

70. Churchill, *Triumph and Tragedy;* 152–53; Sir Hastings Ismay, *The Memoirs of General Lord Ismay* (New York: Viking, 1960), 399–401; Michael Simpson, *A Life of Admiral of the Fleet Andrew Cunningham: A Twentieth Century Naval Leader* (London: Frank Cass, 2004), 199–200. See also, Fraser, *Alanbrooke*, 416–17.

71. Cunningham diary entry, July 14, 1944, Cunningham Collection, ADD 52577, 46, BL.

72. Ibid.

73. Thorne, *Allies of a Kind*, 592.

74. Cunningham diary entry, July 14, 1944; COS Committee, "War against Japan—Summary of Various Courses," 122/1072/4–5. See also, Fraser, *Alanbrooke*, 414.

75. See, for example, Fraser, *Alanbrooke*, 416.

76. Cunningham diary entry, August 10, 1944.

77. Ibid.

78. COS Committee to Churchill, "Plans for the Defeat of Japan"; Lambe to Cunningham, February 5, 1944, Cunningham Papers, ADD 52571, 2, BL.

79. Fraser, *Alanbrooke*, 420.

80. Ibid.

81. Potter, *Nimitz*, 347–49.

82. Hayes, *Joint Chiefs of Staff in World War II*, 433.

83. A. Doyle to R. Smeeton, undated, 1, attached to Noble to Cunningham, January 30, 1944, Cunningham Papers, ADD 52571, BL. See also, British Joint Planning Staff, JP (42) 1005, "Future Strategy," January 10, 1943, CAB 84/51/1, TNA.

84. Lambe to Cunningham, February 5, 1944.

85. Ibid.

86. Ibid. [italics mine].

87. Ibid., 2.

88. Clark G. Reynolds, *The Fast Carriers: The Forging of an Air Navy* (New York: McGraw-Hill, 1968), 310–39; Simpson, *Life of Admiral of the Fleet Andrew Cunningham*, 203.

89. Noble to Cunningham, January 30, 1944.

90. The best example is Thorne, *Allies of a Kind,* passim.

91. Ibid., 335.

92. See Fraser, *Alanbrooke,* 420. See also, Pogue, *Organizer of Victory,* 24–25.

93. Smeeton to Pott, January 10, 1944, 2, attached to Noble to Cunningham, January 30, 1944.

94. See Reynolds, *Fast Carriers,* 246–47, 334, 337.

95. Noble to Cunningham. January 30, 1944; Doyle to Smeeton, undated, 1–2.

96. Doyle to Smeeton, undated, 1–2.

97. COS Committee, "War against Japan—Summary of Various Courses," 122/1072/1.

98. Ibid., 122/1072 and passim.

Chapter 4. Related Advantages

1. Samuel E. Morison, *History of United States Naval Operations in World War II,* vol. 10, *The Atlantic Battle Won* (Boston: Little, Brown, 1956), 303; Karl Doenitz, *Memoirs: Ten Years and Twenty Days,* trans. R. H. Stevens and David Woodward (New York: World, 1959), 416–17.

2. Doenitz, *Ten Years and Twenty Days,* 416–17; Morison, *Atlantic Battle Won,* 275.

3. Erling Hunt, *America Organizes to Win the War* (New York: Harcourt Brace, 1942), 126, 364–65.

4. Ibid., 365.

5. Sally Lister Parker, *Attendant Lords: A Study of the British Joint Staff Mission in Washington, 1941–1945* (PhD dissertation, University of Maryland, College Park, 1984), 108–10.

6. Jeremy Noakes and Geoffrey Pridham, eds., *Nazism, 1919–1945: A History in Documents and Eyewitness Accounts,* vol. 2, *Foreign Policy, War and Racial Extermination* (New York: Schocken Books, 1988, 1990), 126–27.

7. Akira Iriye, *Power and Culture: The Japanese-American War, 1941–1945* (Cambridge, Mass.: Harvard University Press, 1981), 8, 11; Bernard C. Nalty, "Sources of Victory," in *Pearl Harbor and the War in the Pacific* (New York: Smithmark, 1991), 285.

8. Omer Bartov, *Hitler's Army: Soldiers, Nazis, and War in the Third Reich* (New York: Oxford University Press, 1992), 35, 127.

9. Leon Wolff, *In Flanders Fields: The 1917 Campaign* (New York: Viking, 1958), 53–55, 63–65.

10. A. J. P. Taylor, *The First World War: An Illustrated History* (New York: Perigree Books / G. P. Putnam's Sons, 1980), 195–96.

11. Wolff, *In Flanders Fields,* 241.

12. Newton D. Baker, as quoted in "Baker Sees Italy Now on Joint Front," *New York Times,* November 5, 1917, 10.

13. Hastings Ismay to Churchill, "The Combined Chiefs of Staff Organization," Ismay Papers, 2/3/10/2A/1–2, LHC.

14. Alan F. Wilt, *War from the Top: German and British Military Decision Making during World War II* (Bloomington: Indiana University Press, 1990), 218, 224.

15. Sir Michael Howard, *Grand Strategy,* vol. 4, *August, 1942–September, 1943* (London: Her Majesty's Stationery Office, 1972), 310. See table in Winston S. Churchill, *The Second World War,* vol. 5, *Closing the Ring* (Boston: Houghton Mifflin, 1951), 10. See also Robin Brodhurst, *Churchill's Anchor: Admiral of the Fleet Sir Dudley Pound, OM, GCB, GCVO* (Barnsley, South Yorkshire, UK: Leo Cooper, 2000), 275.

16. Churchill, *Closing the Ring,* 10.

17. Noakes and Pridham, *Nazism,* vol. 2, 837.

18. Ibid., 837–38.

19. Akira Iriye, *Origins of the Second World War in Asia and the Pacific* (New York: Longman, 1987), 140–41; John Lewis Gaddis, *Strategies of Containment: A Critical Appraisal of American Postwar National Security Policy* (New York: Oxford University Press, 1982), 7–8.

20. Gordon A. Craig, *Germany: 1866–1945* (New York: Oxford University Press, 1978), 725–26.

21. Mussolini to Ciano, October 12, 1940, as quoted in Noakes and Pridham, *Nazism,* vol. 2, 813.

22. Iriye, *Power and Culture,* 27; Noakes and Pridham, *Nazism,* vol. 2., 797, 830–31; Eric Larrabee, *Commander in Chief: Franklin Delano Roosevelt, His Lieutenants, and Their War* (New York: Harper and Row, 1987), 83.

23. Alex Danchev, "Great Britain: The Indirect Strategy," in *Allies at War: the Soviet, American, and British Experience, 1939–1945,* eds. David Reynolds, Warren F. Kimball, and A.O. Chubarian. (New York: St. Martin's, 1994): 6.

24. Wesley Frank Craven and James Lea Cate, eds., *The Army Air Forces in World War II,* vol. 6, *Men and Planes* (Chicago: University of Chicago Press, 1955), 302–4.

25. Paul Kennedy, *The Rise and Fall of the Great Powers: Economic Change and Military Conflict from 1500 to 2000* (New York: Vintage Books, 1987, 1989), 354; Julius Augustus Furer, *The Administration of the Navy Department in World War II* (Washington, D.C.: U.S. Government Printing Office, 1959), 855–57; Irving Brinton Holley Jr., *The United States Army in World War II: Buying Aircraft— Matériel Procurement for the Army Air Forces* (Washington, D.C.: Office of the Chief of Military History, 1954), 309, 518–29; Donald M. Nelson, *Arsenal of Democracy: The Story of American War Production* (New York: Harcourt Brace, 1946), 65; Craven and Cate, *Men and Planes,* 308.

26. Craven and Cate, *Men and Planes,* 308.

27. Ibid., 313; Holley, *Buying Aircraft,* 540–46; R. Elberton Smith, *The United States Army in World War II: The Army and Economic Mobilization* (Washington, D.C.: Office of the Chief of Military History, 1959), 480–82.

28. Kennedy, *Rise and Fall of the Great Powers,* 354; Furer, *Administration of the Navy Department in World War II,* 855–57; Holley, *Buying Aircraft,* 309, 518–29; Nelson, *Arsenal of Democracy,* 65. See David Rigby, "The Mobilization of the American Economy during the Second World War" (unpublished paper, December 1991), 22.

29. Craig, *Germany,* 627.
30. Richard Overy, *Why the Allies Won* (New York and London: W. W. Norton, 1995), 199–204.
31. Craig, *Germany,* 732.
32. Ibid., 732–33, 737.
33. Ibid., 733.
34. Overy, *Why the Allies Won,* 206.
35. Danchev, "Great Britain," 6; Kennedy, *Rise and Fall of the Great Powers,* 354. See also, United States Strategic Bombing Survey, "Over-All Report" (European Report 2), in *United States Strategic Bombing Survey* (New York: Garland, 1976), vol. 1, 14, 31; Bartov, *Hitler's Army,* 13, 15; Max Hastings, *Bomber Command* (New York: Dial / James Wade, 1979), 225; David Rigby, "The Effects of Strategic Bombardment on Germany During the Second World War" (unpublished paper, February 1992), 22, 37.
36. Overy, *Why the Allies Won,* 217–18.
37. Noakes and Pridham, *Nazism,* vol. 2., 730–31, 830; Craig, *Germany,* 733.
38. Samuel Eliot Morison, *History of United States Naval Operations in World War II,* vol. 15, *Supplement and General Index* (Boston: Little, Brown, 1962), 30–31; *The Aircraft Carrier* (Secaucus, N.J.: Chartwell Books, 1984), 29, 41, 49–55, 67, 80; Furer, *Administration of the Navy Department in World War II,* 879–80; Barrie Pitt, ed., *The Military History of World War II* (New York: Military, 1986), 202.
39. Parker, *Attendant Lords,* 1–10, 234–35.
40. *New York World-Telegram,* May 8, 1945, reprinted in *USA Today,* May 5, 1995, 6A, photo.
41. Winston S. Churchill, *The Second World War,* vol. 6, *Triumph and Tragedy* (Boston: Houghton Mifflin, 1953), 540; Maurice Matloff, *Strategic Planning for Coalition Warfare 1943–1944* (Washington, D.C.: Office of the Chief of Military History, 1959), vol. 2, 280.
42. John R. Deane, "Memorandum for the United States Chiefs of Staff: Present Relations between the United States Military Mission, Moscow and the Soviet Military Authorities," January 22, 1945, *Records of the Joint Chiefs of Staff,* part 1, *1942–1945: European Theater* (Frederick/Bethesda, Md.: University Publications of America, 1982), reel 2, frame 0186, 4.
43. Matloff, *Strategic Planning for Coalition Warfare 1943–1944,* vol. 2, 290.
44. British ambassador (Moscow) to Eden, November 9, 1943, CAB 122/941/1, TNA; Joint Staff Mission to War Cabinet, September 30, 1943, LETOD 1423, CAB 122/941/1, TNA; John R. Deane, *The Strange Alliance: The Story of Our Efforts at Wartime Co-operation with Russia* (New York: Viking, 1947), 6, 9, 11. See also, Keith Eubank, *Summit at Teheran* (New York: William Morrow, 1985), 67.
45. Matloff, *Strategic Planning for Coalition Warfare,* vol. 2, 289.
46. Ibid., 285.
47. John Lewis Gaddis, *The United States and the Origins of the Cold War 1941–1947* (New York: Columbia University Press, 1972), 73.

48. Deane, "Present Relations between the United States Military Mission, Moscow and the Soviet Military Authorities," 6.

49. Ibid., frame 0189, 7.

50. U.S. Chiefs of Staff, CCS 732, "Alleged Attacks by U.S. Lightning Planes on Soviet Troops," *Records of the Joint Chiefs of Staff*, part 1, *1942–1945: The Soviet Union* (Frederick/Bethesda, Md.: University Publications of America, 1981), reel 2, frame 0106, 2.

51. U.S. Chiefs of Staff, JCS Memo 260, "Coordination of Allied Air Operations with Soviet Authorities," *Records of the Joint Chiefs of Staff*, part 1, *1942–1945: The Soviet Union*, reel 2, frames 0030–0031.

52. U.S. Chiefs of Staff, CCS 732, "Alleged Attacks by U.S. Lightning Planes on Soviet Troops." *Records of the Joint Chiefs of Staff*, part 1, *1942–1945: The Soviet Union*, frame 0106, 2.

53. Ibid., frames 0109–0110, 5–6.

54. Winston S. Churchill, *The Second World War*, vol. 2, *The Grand Alliance* (Boston: Houghton Mifflin, 1950), 388. See also, Churchill, *Closing the Ring*, 264–66.

55. COS ad hoc committee, COS (42) 140, "Anglo–Russian Cooperation," February 26, 1942, AIR 8/617/1, TNA; Martel to COS Committee, COS (43) 204, "The Northern Ports in Russia," July 21, 1943, CAB 122/103/1, 3, 6–8, TNA. See also, No. 30 Mission to Air Ministry (rptd Embassy, Kuibyshev), WX.3129, "Liaison with U.S.S.R.," March 15, 1942, AIR 8/617/1, TNA.

56. Martel to COS Committee, "Northern Ports in Russia," 7.

57. Ibid., 2.

58. McFarlane to War Office (Chiefs of Staff Committee), WX.1273, February 4, 1942, AIR 8/617/1, TNA.

59. No. 30 Mission to Air Ministry, "Liaison with U.S.S.R."

60. Martel to COS Committee, "Northern Ports in Russia," 1–2.

61. Ibid., 1–2.

62. Ibid., 2.

63. Ibid., 5.

64. Baggallay to Foreign Office, with copies to Portal and to War Cabinet, February 11, 12, 13, 1942, AIR 8/617/1, TNA.

65. Gaddis, *Strategies of Containment*, 13–16.

66. Churchill, *Triumph and Tragedy*, 544, 546; Deane, *Strange Alliance*, 205–15.

67. Pitt, *Military History of World War II*, 244. See also, Nicholas V. Raisanovsky, *A History of Russia*, 4th ed. (New York: Oxford University Press, 1984), 525; Kennedy, *Rise and Fall of the Great Powers*, 353.

68. Pitt, *Military History of World War II*, 75, 289.

69. See, for example, Deane, *Strange Alliance*, 107–25.

70. U.S. Chiefs of Staff, JCS 527/5, "Procedure for the Release of Technical Information to the U.S.S.R.," *Records of the Joint Chiefs of Staff*, part 1, *1942–1945: The Soviet Union*, reel 1, frames 0730–0731, 24–25.

71. Combined Intelligence Committee, CIC 23/D, "Disclosure of Technical Information to the U.S.S.R." CAB 122/104/3, 6, 10, TNA; Representatives of the British Chiefs of Staff (JSM), CCS 187/12, July 11, 1944, CCS Papers, CAB 88/10/5–7, TNA.

72. Winston S. Churchill, *The Second World War*, vol. 4, *The Hinge of Fate* (Boston: Houghton Mifflin, 1950), 377–81.

73. Deane, *Strange Alliance*, 3, 7–8; Matloff, *Strategic Planning for Coalition Warfare*, vol. 2, 291.

74. Deane, *Strange Alliance*, 8.

75. Matloff, *Strategic Planning for Coalition Warfare*, vol. 2, 299–300.

76. Ibid., 301.

Chapter 5. The Combined Chiefs of Staff and Overlord

1. Alex Danchev, "Biffing: The Saga of the Second Front," in Danchev, *On Specialness: Essays in Anglo-American Relations* (New York: St. Martin's, 1998), 32–33.

2. Leonard Mosley, *Marshall: Hero for Our Times* (New York: Hearst Books, 1982), 505–7.

3. Forrest C. Pogue, *George C. Marshall*, vol. 2, *Ordeal and Hope* (New York: Viking, 1966), 162–63; Mark A. Stoler, *Allies in War, Britain and America against the Axis Powers 1940–1945* (London: Hodder Arnold, 2005), 75–76.

4. Forrest C. Pogue, *George C. Marshall*, vol. 3, *Organizer of Victory* (New York: Viking, 1973), 227, 272–73.

5. Forrest C. Pogue, *U.S. Army in World War II: The Supreme Command* (Washington, D.C.: Office of the Chief of Military History, 1954), 25–27.

6. Winston S. Churchill, *The Second World War*, vol. 5, *Closing the Ring* (Boston: Houghton Mifflin, 1951), 418.

7. Suggested by a reviewer who kindly provided feedback on this manuscript.

8. Churchill, *Closing the Ring*, 85, 418.

9. Andrew Roberts, *Masters and Commanders: How Four Titans Won the War in the West, 1941–1945* (New York: HarperCollins, 2009), 395–98.

10. Danchev, "Biffing," 33.

11. Stimson to FDR, as quoted in Roberts, *Masters and Commanders*, 394.

12. Pogue, *Organizer of Victory*, 273–74.

13. Dill to British Chiefs of Staff, JSM 814, March 16, 1943, CAB 122/1072, TNA; Pogue, *Organizer of Victory*, 117; British Joint Planning Staff, JP (43) 135 (Final), March 31, 1943, "Amphibious Operations in 1943 From United Kingdom--Revised Directive," CAB 84/53/1–3, TNA; Larry I. Bland, ed., Sharon Ritenour Stevens, assoc. ed., *The Papers of George Catlett Marshall*, vol. 3, *"The Right Man for the Job:" December 7, 1941–May 31, 1943* (Baltimore: Johns Hopkins University Press, 1991), 678.

14. Barrie Pitt, ed., *The Military History of World War II* (New York: Military, 1986), 244–47; Omer Bartov, *Hitler's Army: Soldiers, Nazis, and War in the Third Reich* (New York: Oxford University Press, 1992), 45.

15. Bartov, *Hitler's Army,* 29, 45.

16. Kevin Smith, *Conflict over Convoys: Anglo-American Logistics Diplomacy in the Second World War* (Cambridge, UK: Cambridge University Press, 1996), 1–4; Robert W. Love Jr., *History of the U.S. Navy,* vol. 2. *1942–1991* (Harrisburg, Pa.: Stackpole Books, 1992), 119.

17. Warren F. Kimball, *Forged in War: Roosevelt, Churchill, and the Second World War* (New York: William Morrow, 1997), 145.

18. John Colville, *The Fringes of Power: 10 Downing Street Diaries: 1939–1955* (New York: W. W. Norton, 1985), 583.

19. See Macmillan quote in Alex Danchev, "On Specialness: Anglo-American Apocrypha," in Danchev, *On Specialness,* 3–4.

20. For the quote, see Danchev, "On Specialness: Anglo-American Apocrypha," 5–6. See also, Kimball, *Forged in War,* 243–45.

21. Danchev, "Great Britain: The Indirect Strategy," in D. Reynolds, Warren Kimball, and A. O. Chubarian, eds., *Allies at War* (New York: St. Martin's, 1994), 4.

22. See Portal quote in Danchev, "Biffing," 42.

23. Maurice Matloff, *Strategic Planning for Coalition Warfare 1943–1944* (Washington, D.C.: Office of the Chief of Military History, 1959), vol. 2, 168. See also, Pogue, *Organizer of Victory,* 201–2.

24. U.S. Joint Staff planners, CCS 235, May 18, 1943, "Defeat of the Axis Powers in Europe," in *Records of the JCS,* part 1, *1942–45: European Theater,* Microfilm (Bethesda/Frederick, Md.: University Publications of America), reel 1, frame 0211, 6; Roberts, *Masters and Commanders,* 425.

25. Sir David Fraser, *Alanbrooke* (New York: Atheneum, 1982), 268. For more on Brooke's views about the cross-channel attack, see Maurice Matloff, "Wilmot Revisited: Myth and Reality in Anglo-American Strategy for the Second Front," in *D–Day 1944,* ed. Theodore A. Wilson (Abilene: Eisenhower Foundation and University Press of Kansas, 1971, 1994), 5.

26. Marshall to JCS, Minutes JCS 100th Meeting, August 6, 1943, *Records of the JCS,* part 1, *1942–45: Meetings* (Bethesda/Frederick, Md.: University Publications of America), reel 1, frame 1115, 8.

27. Joint Intelligence Committee, Memorandum for Information No. 134 (476-4), October 25, 1943, "Probabilities of a German Collapse," *Records of the JCS—European Theater,* reel 10, frames 0653–0655, 1–3.

28. Fraser, *Alanbrooke,* 270.

29. Brooke's undated late-1950s reply to letters from Butler and Howard, Alanbrooke Papers, 10/3/12: 1, LHC.

30. Paul Kennedy, *The Rise and Fall of the Great Powers: Economic Change and Military Conflict from 1500 to 2000* (New York: Vintage Books, 1987, 1989), 274.

31. Brooke's undated late-1950s reply to letters from Butler and Howard.

32. See Danchev, "Great Britain: The Indirect Strategy," in Reynolds, Kimball, and Chubarian, eds., *Allies at War,* 17–18.

33. Alex Danchev, "Being Friends: The Combined Chiefs of Staff and the Making of Allied Strategy in the Second World War," in *War, Strategy, and International Politics: Essays in Honour of Sir Michael Howard,* ed. Lawrence Freedman, Paul Hayes, and Robert O'Neill (New York: Oxford University Press, 1992), 196, 204.

34. Roberts, *Masters and Commanders,* 252.

35. Matloff, *Strategic Planning for Coalition Warfare,* vol. 2, 168.

36. Minutes of COS Committee Meeting—COS (43) 83rd Meeting (0), April 22, 1943, CAB 79/60/1–3, TNA; Combined Staff planners, CCS 250/1, May 25, 1943, "Implementation of Decisions Reached at the Trident Conference," CAB 88/12/6, TNA.

37. Pogue, *Organizer of Victory,* 242.

38. Matloff, *Strategic Planning for Coalition Warfare,* vol. 2, 167–70.

39. Combined Staff planners, "Implementation of Decisions Reached at the Trident Conference."

40. Matloff, *Strategic Planning for Coalition Warfare,* vol. 2, 168–69.

41. Ibid., 169.

42. Mark A. Stoler, *Allies and Adversaries: The Joint Chiefs of Staff, the Grand Alliance, and U.S. Strategy in World War II* (Chapel Hill: University of North Carolina Press, 2000), 171; Danchev, "Biffing," 38–39; R. J. Overy, *Why the Allies Won* (New York: W. W. Norton, 1995), 145–46.

43. Brooke Diary, April 9, 1942, Alanbrooke Papers, 5/5/92–93, LHC.

44. Ibid.

45. Combined Staff planners, CCS 72, May 16, 1942, "Bolero," CAB 88/6/2–3, TNA.

46. Brooke diary entry, April 14, 1942.

47. Fraser, *Alanbrooke,* 248–49.

48. Ibid., 248.

49. Brooke's undated late-1950s reply to letters from Butler and Howard. For more on the British view, see General Sir William Jackson and Field Marshal Lord Bramall, *The Chiefs: The Story of the United Kingdom Chiefs of Staff* (London: Brassey's, 1992), 222.

50. Brian Bond, "Alanbrooke and Britain's Mediterranean Strategy, 1942–1944," in Freedman et al., *War, Strategy, and International Politics,* 184; Denis Richards, *Portal of Hungerford* (London: Heinemann, 1977), 261, 265.

51. Stoler, *Allies in War,* 144.

52. Leahy to FDR, November 17, 1943, "Memorandum on Command," RG 218/127/20, NA; Pogue, *Organizer of Victory,* 318.

53. Leahy to FDR, "Memorandum on Command."

54. Roberts, *Masters and Commanders,* 14. See also Ian Jacob quote therein, ibid., 324.

55. Pogue, *Organizer of Victory,* 318–22; Sir Hastings Ismay, *The Memoirs of General Lord Ismay* (New York: Viking, 1960), 312.

56. Combined Staff planners, "Implementation of Decisions Reached at the Trident Conference."

57. Ibid., 3–4.

58. Roberts, *Masters and Commanders,* 369–70. See also, Stoler, *Allies in War,* 120.

59. Maurice Matloff and Edwin M. Snell, *Strategic Planning for Coalition Warfare 1941–1942* (Washington, D.C.: Office of the Chief of Military History, 1953), vol. 1, 294, 306.

60. Pogue, *Ordeal and Hope,* 344, 402; Stoler, *Allies and Adversaries,* 85; Roberts, *Masters and Commanders,* 233; Fraser. *Alanbrooke,* 259.

61. Matloff, "Wilmot Revisited," in Wilson, ed, *D–Day 1944,* 7.

62. Stoler, *Allies and Adversaries,* 86.

63. Matloff and Snell, *Strategic Planning for Coalition Warfare,* vol. 1, 294–95.

64. Smith, *Conflict over Convoys,* 77–78.

65. Alex Danchev and Daniel Todman, eds., *War Diaries 1939–1945: Field Marshal Lord Alanbrooke* (Berkeley: University of California Press, 2001), 267–68, 315. In particular, see Brooke's entries for June 20 and August 29, 1942.

66. Matloff and Snell, *Strategic Planning for Coalition Warfare,* vol. 1, 297.

67. Marshall to FDR, October 7, 1943, RG 218/127/20/73/1–2, NA.

68. Ibid.

69. Oliver Warner, *Admiral of the Fleet: Cunningham of Hyndhope—the Battle for the Mediterranean* (Athens: Ohio University Press, 1967), 181. For more on resources affecting Overlord planning, see Jackson and Bramall, *Chiefs,* 225–26.

70. Portal to AMSO, May 4, 1942, AIR 8/642, TNA.

71. Minutes of Monthly Meeting between Portal and his Commanders in Chief, June 9, 1942, AIR 8/620/2, TNA.

72. Portal Memorandum for COS Committee, COS (42) 351, July 21, 1942, "Continental Operations 1943: Operational Organisation and System of Command of the RAF," CAB 80/37/1, TNA.

73. Richards, *Portal of Hungerford,* 207, 261.

74. Matloff and Snell, *Strategic Planning for Coalition Warfare,* vol. 1, 280.

75. Joint Staff Mission, CCS 75, June 5, 1942, "System of Command for Continental Operations in 1943," annex 2 of COS (42) 439, October 26, 1942, CAB 80/38, TNA.

76. Matloff and Snell, *Strategic Planning for Coalition Warfare,* vol. 1, 212–15.

77. Pitt, *Military History of World War II,* 143, 240.

78. Roberts, *Masters and Commanders,* 215.

79. Alex Danchev, "God Knows: Civil-Military Relations with Allies," in Danchev, *On Specialness: Essays in Anglo-American Relations.* (New York: St. Martin's, 1998), 65; Bartov, *Hitler's Army,* 45.

80. Danchev, "God Knows: Civil-Military Relations with Allies," 65.

81. R. J. Overy, *The Air War: 1939–1945* (New York: Stein and Day, 1980), 57.

82. Pitt, *Military History of World War II,* 240, 246–47.

83. Omer Bartov, *The Eastern Front, 1941–1945: German Troops and the Barbarisation of Warfare* (New York: St. Martin's, 1986), 124–25; Bartov, *Hitler's Army,* passim.

84. Antony Beevor, *Stalingrad* (New York: Penguin, 1998), 56; Williamson Murray and Allan R. Millett, *A War to Be Won: Fighting the Second World War* (Cambridge, Mass.: Belknap Press of Harvard University Press, 2000), 141.

85. Jeremy Noakes and Geoffrey Pridham, eds., *Nazism, 1919–1945: A History in Documents and Eyewitness Accounts,* vol. 2, *Foreign Policy, War and Racial Extermination* (New York: Schocken Books, 1988, 1990), 1096.

86. Richard J. Evans, *The Third Reich at War* (New York: Penguin, 2009), 194–95, 490–92; Bartov, *Eastern Front, 1941–1945,* 107.

87. Bartov, *Hitler's Army,* 6; Andreas Hillgruber, *Germany and the Two World Wars,* trans. William C. Kirby (Cambridge, Mass.: Harvard University Press, 1981), 85–88, 92–93, 97; Hannes Heer, "How Amorality Became Normality: Reflections on the Mentality of German Soldiers on the Eastern Front," in Hannes Heer and Klaus Naumann, eds., *War of Extermination: The German Military in World War II, 1941–1944* (New York: Beghahn Books, 2000), 334.

88. Richard Rhodes, *Masters of Death: The SS-Einsatzgruppen and the Invention of the Holocaust* (New York: Alfred A. Knopf, 2002), 114.

89. Bartov, *Hitler's Army,* 183–85. Quotes from pages 185 and 183.

90. Danchev, "Biffing," 37; Eisenhower to Combined Chiefs of Staff, CCS 103, August 25, 1942, "Operation Torch," CAB 88/7/3, TNA.

91. King, as quoted in Thomas B. Buell, *Master of Sea Power: A Biography of Admiral Ernest J. King* (Boston: Little, Brown, 1980), 193 (and 265 for more on King's boxing analogy); King memo to FDR (page 2), King Papers, Ms. Collection 37, box 4, folder number 3, Naval War College.

92. Fraser, *Alanbrooke,* 269.

93. Joint Chiefs of Staff, CCS 215, May 13, 1943, "Invasion of the European Continent from the United Kingdom in 1943–44," CAB 88/11, TNA.

94. British Joint Planning Staff, CCS 167, January 22, 1943, "Continental Operations in 1943," CAB 88/9/1–6, TNA.

95. Winston S. Churchill, *The Second World War,* vol. 6, *Triumph and Tragedy* (Boston: Houghton Mifflin, 1953), 17, 24, 189, 193, 194. See also Churchill, *Closing the Ring,* 85.

96. British Joint Planning Staff, JP (43) 103 (Final), March 4, 1943, "Operations against the Continent," CAB 84/53, TNA.

97. Richards, *Portal of Hungerford,* 266; British Chiefs of Staff, CCS 304, August 10, 1943, "Operation 'Overlord'—Outline Plan," CAB 88/15/1–2, TNA; Joint Chiefs of Staff, CCS 423/1, December 4, 1943, CAB 122/1224/1, TNA.

98. Stoler, *Allies and Adversaries,* 166–70; Roberts, *Masters and Commanders,* 398, 432, 458; Michael Simpson, *A Life of Admiral of the Fleet Andrew Cunningham: A Twentieth Century Naval Leader* (London: Frank Cass, 2004), 176.

99. Eisenhower to Combined Chiefs of Staff, "Operation Torch."

100. Joint Staff Mission to British Chiefs of Staff, JSM 501, November 27, 1942, CAB 122/31/1, TNA.

101. Joint Chiefs of Staff, JCS 611, November 26, 1943, "'Overlord' and the Mediterranean," in *Records of the JCS—Meetings,* reel 1, frame 0292, appendix B, 4.

102. British Chiefs of Staff, CCS 409, "'Overlord' and the Mediterranean," November 25, 1943, *Records of the JCS—European Theater,* reel 1, frames 0285–0286, 1–2.

103. Joint Chiefs of Staff, "'Overlord' and the Mediterranean," 1.

104. British Chiefs of Staff, "'Overlord' and the Mediterranean," 1.

105. Ibid.

106. Roberts, *Masters and Commanders,* 369–70, 390, 395, 402.

107. British Chiefs of Staff, "'Overlord' and the Mediterranean," 1–2.

108. U.S. Joint Chiefs of Staff, "'Overlord' and the Mediterranean," 1–2.

109. Ibid., frame 0291, appendix A, 2.

110. Matloff, *Strategic Planning for Coalition Warfare,* vol. 2, 127–28; Roberts, *Masters and Commanders,* 579.

111. Churchill to FDR, Number 717, June 28, 1944, RG 218/4/16/Enclosure "A," NA.

112. FDR to Churchill, Number 573, June 28, 1944, RG 218/4/16/Enclosure "B," NA.

113. Ibid.

114. Joint Staff Mission, CCS 603/15, August 5, 1944, "Operations to Assist 'Overlord,'" in *Records of the JCS—European Theater,* reel 7, frame 1029, 1.

115. Joint Chiefs of Staff, CCS 603/16, August 5, 1944, "Operations to Assist 'Overlord,'" *Records of the JCS—European Theater,* reel 7, frame 1031, 1.

Chapter 6. Keeping the Armchair Strategists at Bay

1. Anonymous December 1941 letter, King Papers, Naval War College, Collection 37, box 6, folder 4.

2. King response to anonymous letter, ibid.

3. Samuel Eliot Morison, *The Two Ocean War: A Short History of the United States Navy in the Second World War* (Boston: Little, Brown, 1962), 109–10.

4. Ibid., 110–21, "happy time" quote as reprinted therein on page 110; Thomas B. Buell, *Master of Sea Power: A Biography of Admiral Ernest J. King* (Boston: Little, Brown, 1980), 282–90.

5. Michael Gannon, *Operation Drumbeat: The Dramatic True Story of Germany's First U-Boat Attacks along the American Coast in World War II* (New York: Harper and Row, 1990), 240, 412–15.

6. FDR to King, July 7, 1942, King Papers, Manuscript Division, box 14, "Franklin D. Roosevelt" file, LC.

7. Gannon, *Operation Drumbeat,* 391–95.

8. Brooke diary entry, September 10, 1944, as reprinted in Sir David Fraser, *Alanbrooke* (New York: Atheneum, 1982), 442.

9. Alex Danchev, *Very Special Relationship: Field Marshal Sir John Dill and the Anglo-American Alliance, 1941–1944* (Washington, D.C.: Brassey's Defence, 1986), 130.

10. Winston S. Churchill, *The Second World War,* vol. 5, *Closing the Ring* (Boston: Houghton Mifflin, 1951), vi.

11. Portal to Churchill, March 16, 1943, Portal Papers, 4/25, Christ Church, Oxford.

12. Denis Richards, as quoted in John Terraine, *The Right of the Line: The Royal Air Force in the European War 1939–1945* (London: Hodder and Stoughton, 1985), 254.

13. Churchill to Ismay and Bridges, COS (42) 443, October 31, 1942, CAB 80/38, TNA.

14. Brooke Diary, October 22, 1942, Alanbrooke Papers, 5/6A/59, LHC.

15. Ibid.

16. Brooke diary entry, June 26, 1942, 5/5/137.

17. Alex Danchev and Daniel Todman, eds., *War Diaries 1939–1945: Field Marshal Lord Alanbrooke* (Berkeley: University of California Press, 2001), 267–68. See particularly Brooke's entry for June 20, 1942.

18. Brooke diary entry, March 31, 1942, 5/5/87.

19. Col. Peter Earle, interview with M. C. Long, Alanbrooke Papers, 12/11/2/17/3, LHC.

20. Ibid.

21. Churchill to Lord Portal, Minister of Works, March 7, 1944, reprinted in Churchill, *Closing the Ring,* 697.

22. Winston S. Churchill, *The Second World War,* vol. 4, *The Hinge of Fate* (Boston: Houghton Mifflin, 1950), 865. See also, Churchill, *Closing the Ring,* 700.

23. P. J. Grigg, interview with M. C. Long, Alanbrooke Papers, 12/11/2/16/2, LHC.

24. Ibid.

25. Ibid.

26. Brooke diary entry, March 31, 1942, 5/5/87.

27. Grigg interview, 12/11/2/16/1–2.

28. Portal, interview with M. C. Long, 1952, Alanbrooke Papers, 12/11/1/1/3, LHC.

29. Ibid.

30. Ibid., 12/11/1/1/3–4.

31. Churchill to Portal, June 15, 1942, Portal Papers, 3/46, Christ Church, Oxford; Ismay, interview by Joan Bright Astley, Alanbrooke Papers, LHC, 12/XI/2/8, 1, King's College.

32. Portal to Churchill, July 31, 1942, AIR 8/451/1–2, TNA.

33. Portal to Sir Archibald Sinclair (Secretary of State for Air), July 7, 1942, AIR 8/451/1–5, TNA; Portal to Air Chief Marshal Sir Wilfrid Freeman, January 6, 1943, AIR 8/451/passim, TNA.

34. Stephen Roskill, *Churchill and the Admirals* (New York: William Morrow, 1978), 83, 95. Morton received a commission as an army major during the war.

35. Ibid., 83.

36. A. J. P. Taylor, *Beaverbrook* (New York: Simon and Schuster, 1972), 414–15.

37. Denis Richards, *Portal of Hungerford* (London: Heinemann, 1977), 194–95.

38. Earl of Birkenhead, *The Professor and the Prime Minister* (Boston: Houghton Mifflin, 1962), 220; R. F. Harrod, *The Prof: A Personal Memoir of Lord Cherwell* (London: Macmillan, 1959), 226–28.

39. Birkenhead, *Professor and the Prime Minister,* 230–31.
40. Ibid., 237–38.
41. Ibid.
42. C. P. Snow, *Science and Government* (Cambridge, Mass.: Harvard University Press, 1961), 67.
43. Birkenhead, *Professor and the Prime Minister,* 238.
44. Portal to Churchill, June 24, 1943, Portal Papers, 4/52B, Christ Church, Oxford.
45. Portal to Churchill, May 19, 1942, AIR 8/330/1–2, TNA.
46. Ibid., AIR 8/330/1.
47. Lindemann to Churchill, May 14, 1942, AIR 8/330, TNA.
48. Portal to Churchill, August 12, 1942, AIR 8/330/1–2, TNA.
49. Lindemann to Churchill, July 25, 1942, AIR 8/451, TNA.
50. Ibid.
51. Portal to Churchill. July 31, 1942, AIR 8/451/1–2.
52. Ibid., AIR 8/451/1.
53. Ibid.
54. Chaz Bowyer, *The Encyclopedia of British Military Aircraft* (New York: Bison, 1982), 138.
55. Ibid., 126.
56. Portal to Churchill, July 31, 1942, AIR 8/451/1.
57. Ibid., AIR 8/451/1–2.
58. Ibid., AIR 8/451/1.
59. Lindemann to Churchill, March 30, 1942, AIR 8/440, TNA.
60. Churchill, *Closing the Ring,* 518; Arthur Harris, *Bomber Offensive* (New York: Macmillan, 1947), 101, 134, 191, 201. See David Rigby. "The Effects of Strategic Bombardment on Germany during the Second World War" (unpublished paper, February 1992), 9–10; and Rigby, "American Strategy in the Second World War with Special Emphasis on the Pacific Theater of Operations" (unpublished paper, December 1990), 16.
61. United States Strategic Bombing Survey [hereafter USSBS], "Over-All Report" (European Report 2), in *United States Strategic Bombing Survey* (New York: Garland, 1976), vol. 1, 51, 58. See Rigby, "Effects of Strategic Bombardment on Germany during the Second World War," passim.
62. USSBS, "The Defeat of the German Air Force" (European Report 59), in *United States Strategic Bombing Survey* (New York: Garland, 1976), vol. 3, 9. See also, Barrie Pitt, ed., *The Military History of World War II* (New York: Military, 1986), 218–20; and Rigby, "Effects of Strategic Bombardment on Germany during the Second World War," passim.
63. Wesley Frank Craven and James Lea Cate, *The Army Air Forces in World War II,* vol. 3, *January 1944 to May 1945* (Chicago: University of Chicago Press, 1951), 62; USSBS, "Defeat of the German Air Force," 42. See also USSBS, "Over-All Report," 49; and Rigby, "Effects of Strategic Bombardment on Germany during the Second World War," 24–25.

64. USSBS, "Over-All Report," 10.

65. Harris, *Bomber Offensive*, 147, 194. See Hans Rumpf, *The Bombing of Germany*, trans. Edward Fitzgerald (New York: Holt, Rinehart and Winston, 1963), 130; also Rigby, "Effects of Strategic Bombardment on Germany during the Second World War," passim.

66. Pitt, *Military History of World War II*, 210. See Rigby, "Effects of Strategic Bombardment on Germany during the Second World War," passim.

67. Richards, *Portal of Hungerford*, 258–59, 314–15.

68. Churchill to Portal, October 7, 1941, AIR 8/440/1–2, TNA.

69. Ibid., AIR 8/440/2.

70. Combined Chiefs of Staff, CCS 166/1/D, in *Foreign Relations of the United States: The Conferences at Washington, 1941–1942 and Casablanca, 1943* (Washington, D.C.: U.S. Government Printing Office, 1968), 782.

71. Ibid., 781 [italics mine].

72. USSBS, "Over-All Report," 16; USSBS, "The German Anti-Friction Bearings Industry" (European Report 53), in *United States Strategic Bombing Survey* (New York: Garland, 1976), vol. 3, 1–2; USSBS, "Aircraft Division Industry Report" (European Report 4), in ibid., vol. 2, 7. See Rigby, "Effects of Strategic Bombardment on Germany during the Second World War," passim.

73. Forrest C. Pogue, *George C. Marshall*, vol. 3, *Organizer of Victory* (New York: Viking, 1973), passim; Knox to King, November 20, 1942, King Papers, Man. Div., box 12, Knox file, LC.

74. E. B. Potter, *Nimitz* (Annapolis, Md.: Naval Institute Press, 1975), 186.

75. Forrestal to King, May 29, 1944, King Collection, 37/7/20, Naval War College.

76. Ernest J. King, n.d., "Secretaries Knox and Forrestal," King Collection, 37/7/20/1–2, Naval War College.

77. Joint Chiefs of Staff to FDR, memorandum, "Operations against Burma," attached to JCS 162, December 7, 1942, *Records of the Joint Chiefs of Staff*, part 1, *1942–1945: European Theater* (Frederick/Bethesda, Md.: University Publications of America, 1982), reel 12, frames 0841–0842, 1–2.

78. King interview, "Comments of Joint Chiefs of Staff," July 30–31, 1949, King Collection, 37/7/25/2–3, Naval War College.

79. James MacGregor Burns, *Roosevelt: The Soldier of Freedom: 1940–1945* (New York: Harcourt Brace Jovanovich, 1970), 492–95.

80. Christopher Thorne, *Allies of a Kind: The United States, Britain and the War against Japan* (London: Hamish Hamilton, 1978), 165–66; Keith Eubank, *Summit at Teheran* (New York: William Morrow, 1985), 60–67.

81. Burns, *Roosevelt*, 41–42, 45–47, 210–12, 499–501; William Manchester. *American Caesar: Douglas MacArthur, 1880–1964* (Boston: Little, Brown, 1978), 146, 150; D. Clayton James, *The Years of MacArthur*, vol. 1, *1880–1941* (Boston: Houghton Mifflin, 1970), 352–54.

82. Timothy Maga, "Vision and Victory: Franklin Roosevelt and the Pacific War Council, 1942–1944," *Presidential Studies Quarterly* 21 (Spring 1991), 351–52.

83. Ibid., 352.

84. Ibid., 355–63.

85. Ibid., 352–55, 360–63.

86. British Chiefs of Staff Committee, COS (43) 220, July 30, 1943, "Meeting with Dr. T.V. Soong," CAB 80/41/1–3, TNA.

87. Burns, *Roosevelt*, 495–96; minutes COS (43) 75th Meeting (0), April 13, 1943, CAB 79/60, TNA.

88. Roskill, *Churchill and the Admirals*, 210, 295–99; Richards, *Portal of Hungerford*, 187; Andrew Roberts, *Masters and Commanders: How Four Titans Won the War in the West, 1941–1945* (New York: HarperCollins, 2009), 43.

89. Richards, *Portal of Hungerford*, 183–85.

90. Ibid., 185.

91. Ibid., 187.

92. Cunningham Diary, July 14, 1944, Cunningham Collection, ADD 52577, 46, BL.

93. Oliver Warner, *Admiral of the Fleet: Cunningham of Hyndhope—the Battle for the Mediterranean* (Athens: Ohio University Press, 1967), 244.

94. See, for example, Cunningham diary entry, August 10, 1944, ADD 52577, 58.

95. Brooke diary entry, September 15, 1942, 5/6A/40.

96. Ibid., 5/6A/41.

97. Fraser, *Alanbrooke*, 361.

98. British Joint Planning Staff, JP (43) 296 (Final), September 9, 1943, "Operations against Norway," CAB 84/55/1, TNA.

99. Robert E. Sherwood, *Roosevelt and Hopkins: An Intimate History* (New York: Harper and Brothers, 1950), 470–73.

100. King to Hopkins, September 28, 1945, King Papers, Man. Div., box 12, Hopkins file, LC.

101. Gerald T. White, *Billions for Defense: Government Financing by the Defense Plant Corporation during World War II* (University: University of Alabama Press, 1980), 18, 36, 67, 75; Rigby, "The Mobilization of the American Economy during the Second World War" (unpublished paper, December 1991), passim.

102. R. Elberton Smith, *The United States Army in World War II: The Army and Economic Mobilization* (Washington, D.C.: Office of the Chief of Military History, 1959), 146.

103. John D. Millett, *The United States Army in World War II: The Organization and Role of the Army Service Forces* (Washington, D.C.: Office of the Chief of Military History, 1954), 189–212, 218, 227, 229; Donald M. Nelson, *Arsenal of Democracy: The Story of American War Production* (New York: Harcourt Brace, 1946), 109–10, 201–2; Smith, *Army and Economic Mobilization*, 146; John Kennedy Ohl, *Supplying the Troops: General Somervell and American Logistics in WWII* (DeKalb: Northern Illinois University Press, 1994), 75. See Rigby, "Mobilization of the American Economy during the Second World War," passim; and Rigby, "American Strategy in the Second World War with Special Emphasis on the European Theater and Logistics" (unpublished paper, May 1991), passim.

104. Ohl, *Supplying the Troops,* 75.

105. Norman Beasley, *Knudsen: A Biography* (New York and London: Whittlesey House McGraw-Hill, 1947), 343.

Chapter 7. Delegation versus Control from the Center

1. R. J. Overy, *Why the Allies Won* (New York: W. W. Norton, 1995), 255–56.

2. See chapter 6. See also ibid., 21–22.

3. Brooke diary, August 6, 1942, Alanbrooke Papers, 5/6B/20, LHC.

4. Ibid., 5/6B/21.

5. Ibid., 5/6B/22.

6. Alex Danchev and Daniel Todman, eds., *War Diaries 1939–1945: Field Marshal Lord Alanbrooke* (Berkeley: University of California Press, 2001), 259, 290–96.

7. Ibid., 295.

8. E. B. Potter, *Nimitz* (Annapolis, Md.: Naval Institute Press, 1975), 191.

9. Ibid., 191–92, 196–97, 207–8, 222; Henry H. Arnold, *Global Mission* (New York: Harper and Brothers, 1949), 340–43; Thomas B. Buell, *Master of Sea Power: A Biography of Admiral Ernest J. King* (Boston: Little, Brown, 1980), 225.

10. Potter, *Nimitz,* 191–92, 196–97, 207–8, 222; Buell, *Master of Sea Power,* 225.

11. Potter, *Nimitz,* 197.

12. Buell, *Master of Sea Power,* 225; Robert William Love Jr., "Ernest Joseph King," in *The Chiefs of Naval Operations* (Annapolis, Md.: Naval Institute Press, 1980), 156–57.

13. Buell, *Master of Sea Power,* 225, 478.

14. Edward P. Stafford, *The Big E: The Story of the USS* Enterprise (Annapolis, Md.: Naval Institute Press, 1962, 1988), 177.

15. Potter, *Nimitz,* 191–92, 196–98, 206–8, 222; Arnold, *Global Mission,* 340; Buell, *Master of Sea Power,* 225, 478.

16. Forrest C. Pogue, *George C. Marshall,* vol. 3, *Organizer of Victory* (New York: Viking, 1973), 330–33; Carlo D'Este, *World War II in the Mediterranean 1942–1945* (Chapel Hill, N.C.: Algonquin Books of Chapel Hill, 1990), 139–46, 154–56; Barrie Pitt, ed., *The Military History of World War II* (New York: Military, 1986), 276–79.

17. See Andrew Roberts, *Masters and Commanders: How Four Titans Won the War in the West, 1941–1945* (New York: HarperCollins, 2009), 235.

18. Larry I. Bland, ed., Sharon Ritenour Stevens, assoc. ed., *The Papers of George Catlett Marshall,* vol. 3, *"The Right Man for the Job:" December 7, 1941–May 31, 1943* (Baltimore: Johns Hopkins University Press, 1991), 472, 473n; Walter Muir Whitehill, afterword, in Ernest J. King and Whitehill, *Fleet Admiral King: A Naval Record* (New York: W. W. Norton, 1952), 651.

19. Douglas Southall Freeman, *Lee's Lieutenants: A Study in Command,* vol. 1, *Manassas to Malvern Hill* (New York: Charles Scribner's Sons, 1942), 621–28.

20. Ibid., 627.

21. Ibid., 664–68.

22. Bland and Stevens, *Papers of George Catlett Marshall*, vol. 3, 472.

23. Ibid., 472

24. Freeman, *Lee's Lieutenants*, 605–14, 628–29; Bruce Catton, *The Civil War* (Boston: Houghton Mifflin, 1987), 348.

25. See quote from Marshall to Freeman above.

26. Winston S. Churchill, *The Second World War*, vol. 4, *The Hinge of Fate* (Boston: Houghton Mifflin, 1950), 262–66; Stephen Roskill, *Churchill and the Admirals* (New York: William Morrow, 1978), 130, 210.

27. Peter Kemp, "Admiral of the Fleet: Sir Dudley Pound," in *Men of War: Great Naval Leaders of World War II*, edited by Stephen Howarth (New York: St. Martin's, 1992), 34–35; Robin Brodhurst, *Churchill's Anchor: Admiral of the Fleet Sir Dudley Pound, OM, GCB, GCVO* (Barnsley, South Yorkshire, UK: Leo Cooper, 2000), 248.

28. Roskill, *Churchill and the Admirals*, 130.

29. Robin Brodhurst, *Churchill's Anchor*, 238, 245, 248.

30. Pound to Naval Staff, July 18, 1943, ADM 205/27, TNA.

31. Portal to COS Committee, COS (42) 341, "Provision of Long Range Aircraft for Anti-Submarine Patrols," July 14, 1942, CAB 80/37/1–3, TNA; Pound to COS Committee, COS (42) 342, "Provision of Long Range Aircraft for Anti-Submarine Patrols," July 14, 1942, CAB 80/37, TNA.

32. Kemp, "Admiral of the Fleet Sir Dudley Pound," 21–22, 39; Brodhurst, *Churchill's Anchor*, 180.

33. Pound to Churchill and British Chiefs of Staff, February 10, 1943, ADM 205/27, TNA.

34. Denis Richards, *Portal of Hungerford* (London: Heinemann, 1977), 306.

35. Portal to Harris, June 14, 1942, Portal Papers, 9/31A/1–2, Christ Church, Oxford; Richards, *Portal of Hungerford*, 306.

36. Richards, *Portal of Hungerford*, 140.

37. Portal to Leigh-Mallory, July 21, 1944, Portal Papers, 12/7D, Christ Church, Oxford.

38. Buell, *Master of Sea Power*, 361.

39. Potter, *Nimitz*, 241.

40. Ibid., 265–66.

41. Martin Stephen, *The Fighting Admirals: British Admirals of the Second World War* (Annapolis, Md.: Naval Institute Press, 1991), 185.

42. Cunningham diary, April 13, 1944, ADD52577, 7, BL.

43. Cunningham diary entry, April 14, 1944, 7.

44. Combined Staff planners, CCS 496, March 3, 1944, "Policy as to the Organization and Employment of Airborne Troops," attached to COS (44) 230 (0), March 6, 1944, AIR 8/662/1–3, TNA.

45. Ibid., 1 (of CCS 496).

46. Pogue, *Organizer of Victory*, 378–83.

47. Brooke to COS Committee, COS (42) 426, October 10, 1942, "The Value of Airborne Forces," CAB 80/38/1–5, TNA.

48. Brooke to COS Committee, COS (43) 81 (0), "Airborne Forces for North Africa and the United Kingdom," February 24, 1943, AIR 8/661/1, TNA; Portal to COS Committee, Minutes of COS (43) 87th Meeting (0), April 28, 1943, AIR 8/661, 1 of extract, TNA.

49. Portal to JSM (RAFDEL), Webber W395, April 15, 1943, AIR 8/661/1, TNA.

50. Ibid.

51. Wesley Frank Craven and James Lea Cate, *The Army Air Forces in World War II*, vol. 6, *Men and Planes* (Chicago: University of Chicago Press, 1955), 352, 354.

52. Portal to COS Committee, COS (42) 417, September 28, 1942, "Airborne Forces," CAB 80/38/1–4, TNA.

53. Ibid., 2.

54. Ibid.

55. Ibid., 3.

56. Combined Staff planners, "Policy as to the Organization and Employment of Airborne Troops," AIR 8/662/2.

57. Ibid.

58. Ibid., 1–2.

59. Combined Staff planners, COS (44) 230 (0).

60. Combined Chiefs of Staff, CCS 252, June 3, 1943, CAB 88/12/1–3, TNA. See also, CCS 252/1, June 8, 1943, CAB 88/12, TNA.

61. Marshall to Eisenhower, CCS 103/2, September 14, 1942, CAB 88/7, TNA. See also, Joint Staff Mission to British Chiefs of Staff, JSM 465, November 6, 1942, CAB 122/177, TNA.

62. Dill to COS Committee, November 2, 1942, JSM 455, CAB 122/177, TNA.

63. Ibid.

64. Churchill, *Hinge of Fate*, 620–47. See also, Gordon Wright, *The Ordeal of Total War: 1939–1945* (New York: Harper Torchbooks, 1968), 186–87.

65. Halifax to Eden, telegram 5933, December 7, 1942, CAB 122/180, TNA.

66. Ibid.

67. Churchill, *Hinge of Fate*, 620–47; Wright, *Ordeal of Total War*, 186–87.

68. Eden to Halifax, telegram 8255, December 29, 1942, CAB 122/180/1, TNA.

69. Commander R. D. Coleridge, RN, to William G. Hayter of British Embassy, Washington, D.C., November 14, 1942, CAB 122/180, 1–2, and enclosure, TNA.

70. Marshall to Eisenhower, as reprinted in JSM 626, from Joint Staff Mission to British Chiefs of Staff, December 28, 1942, CAB 122/180/1, TNA.

71. Winston S. Churchill, *The Second World War*, vol. 6, *Triumph and Tragedy* (Boston: Houghton Mifflin, 1953), 172–86.

Chapter 8. Production and Diplomatic Tasks for the Combined Chiefs

1. *The Aircraft Carrier* (Secaucus, N.J.: Chartwell Books, 1984), 76–77; Barrie Pitt, ed., *The Military History of World War II* (New York: Military, 1986), 201.

2. Land to War Production Board, April 12, 1945, attached to letter from Land to King, July 26, 1946, King Papers, Man. Div., box 18, Stark file, LC.

3. Munitions Assignment Board to Combined Chiefs of Staff, CCS 62, "Auxiliary Aircraft Carriers," April 9, 1942, CAB 88/6/1–2, TNA; Combined Chiefs of Staff, CCS 62/1, "Auxiliary Aircraft Carriers," April 24, 1942, CAB 88/6/2, TNA. See also Thomas B. Buell, *Master of Sea Power: A Biography of Admiral Ernest J. King* (Boston: Little, Brown, 1980), 309–10.

4. Admiralty to BAD August 8, 1942, Salor 4392, CAB 122/172/1–7, TNA.

5. Sir Charles Webster and Noble Frankland, *The Strategic Air Offensive against Germany, 1939–1945,* vol. 2, *Endeavor* (London: Her Majesty's Stationery Office, 1961), part 4, 231, 250. See also United States Strategic Bombing Survey, "Defeat of the German Air Force," in *United States Strategic Bombing Survey* (New York: Garland, 1976), 3, 6; and David Rigby. "The Effects of Strategic Bombardment on Germany during the Second World War" (unpublished paper, February 1992), 31–33, 38–39.

6. FDR to Joint Chiefs of Staff, October 1, 1942, enclosure to JCS 124, "Production of Combat Aircraft for 1943," October 7, 1942, *Records of the Joint Chiefs of Staff,* part 1, *1942–1945: Strategic Issues* (Frederick/Bethesda, Md.: University Publications of America, 1982), reel 8, frame 0626, 1.

7. Ibid.

8. Ibid., frames 0626–0627, 1–2.

9. Joint Chiefs of Staff to FDR, enclosure to JCS 134/1, "U.S. War Production Objectives, 1943," October 22, 1942, *Records of the Joint Chiefs of Staff,* part 1, *1942–1945: Strategic Issues,* reel 8, frame 0629, 1 [my italics].

10. Ibid.

11. Ibid., frames 0629–0630, 1–2.

12. Ibid., frame 0630, 2.

13. Ibid.

14. Wesley Frank Craven and James Lea Cate, eds. *The Army Air Forces in World War II,* vol. 6, *Men and Planes* (Chicago: University of Chicago Press, 1955), 352; Paul Kennedy, *The Rise and Fall of the Great Powers: Economic Change and Military Conflict from 1500 to 2000* (New York: Vintage Books, 1987, 1989), 354.

15. Portal to Sinclair, July 17, 1942, AIR 8/451/2–4, TNA.

16. Portal to Freeman, January 6, 1943, AIR 8/451, TNA. Background on Freeman is from a telephone interview I conducted with Mr. Sebastian Cox, Head of the Air Historical Branch at the Ministry of Defence, London, June 25, 1997. See also, Sebastian Ritchie, *Industry and Air Power: The Expansion of British Aircraft Production, 1935–1941* (London: Frank Cass, 1997), 51–52, 188, 223, 228–29.

17. Portal to Sinclair, July 17, 1942, AIR 8/451/5.

18. Portal to Freeman, March 9, 1943, AIR 8/451, TNA.

19. Ibid.

20. Portal to Sinclair, July 17, 1942, AIR 8/451/5.

21. Portal to Freeman, January 6, 1943.

22. Freeman to Portal, December 19, 1942, AIR 8/451/1–2, TNA.

23. Ibid., 2.

24. William Green and Gordon Swanborough, *The Complete Book of Fighters* (New York: Smithmark, 1994), 288–89.

25. Portal to Freeman, November 18, 1942, AIR 8/451/1, TNA.

26. Portal to Freeman, December 13, 1942, AIR 8/451/1, TNA.

27. Denis Richards, *Portal of Hungerford* (London: Heinemann, 1977), 218–23.

28. Thomas M. Coffey, *HAP: The Story of the U.S. Air Force and the Man Who Built It, General Henry H. "Hap" Arnold* (New York: Viking, 1982), 182, 257–58, 314–15, 322–23.

29. Portal to Sinclair, December 10, 1940, AIR 8/452/1, TNA.

30. Sinclair to Beaverbrook, December 2, 1940, AIR 8/452/2, TNA.

31. Richards, *Portal of Hungerford,* 219.

32. Joint War Production Staff to COS Committee, "Combined Production Requirements for 1943," annex to JWPS (42) 77 (Final), October 3, 1942, CAB 80/38/1, TNA.

33. Ibid., 2.

34. Ibid.

35. Joint War Production Staff to COS Committee, "Combined Production Requirements for 1943," CAB 80/38/2.

36. Ibid.

37. Ibid.

38. Leahy (for JCS) to FDR, July 20, 1943, "Logistics Planning," RG 218/127/20/9/2, NA.

39. Ibid.

40. Ibid.

41. Reeves and Dorling to Combined Staff planners, June 4, 1942, attached to CCS 80, June 12, 1942, CAB 88/6/3–6, TNA.

42. Clark G. Reynolds, *The Fast Carriers: The Forging of An Air Navy* (New York: McGraw-Hill, 1968), 127–28.

43. Ibid., 19.

44. Reeves and Dorling to Combined Staff planners, June 4, 1942, attached to CCS 80, June 12, 1942, CAB 88/6/3–6, TNA.

45. King to Combined Chiefs of Staff, CCS 80/1, June 16, 1942, "Balanced Building Program of Cargo and Combat Shipping," CAB 88/6/1–2, TNA.

46. Ibid., 1.

47. Ibid., 2.

48. Ibid.

49. Pound to Naval Staff, July 18, 1943, ADM 205/27, TNA.

50. Leahy to Combined Production and Resources Board, January 2, 1943, attached to CCS 137/1, January 8, 1943, "Construction Program of Escort Vessels," CAB 88/8/Enclosure B, TNA.

51. Ibid.

52. King to Vice Chief of Naval Operations, C-in-C Pacific Fleet, and C-in-C Atlantic Fleet, February 11, 1943, King Papers, 7/5/9/1, Naval War College.

53. Ibid., 2.

54. Samuel Eliot Morison, *The Two Ocean War: A Short History of the United States Navy in the Second World War* (Boston: Little, Brown, 1962), 108–21.

55. Buell, *Master of Sea Power,* 309–10.

56. Robert E. Sherwood, *Roosevelt and Hopkins: An Intimate History* (New York: Harper and Brothers, 1950), 745–93.

57. Joint Staff Mission, CCS 270/8, September 20, 1943, "Land Airport Facilities in the Azores," CAB 88/13/1–2, TNA.

58. Ibid., CAB 88/13/1–3, 5, 12, and appendix B.

59. Ibid., 4–5.

60. See George F. Kennan, *Memoirs: 1925–1950* (Boston: Little, Brown, 1967), 151.

61. Joint Chiefs of Staff. CCS 270/7, September 7, 1943, "Plans for the Use of the Azores," CAB 88/13/2, TNA.

62. Joint Staff Mission, CCS 270/8, September 20, 1943, "Land Airport Facilities in the Azores," CAB 88/13/2–3, TNA.

63. Joint Chiefs of Staff, "Plans for the Use of the Azores."

64. Joint Staff Mission, "Land Airport Facilities in the Azores," CAB 88/13.

65. Ibid., 3.

66. Kennan, *Memoirs,* 145–63.

67. Frank O. Braynard (FRS) and William H. Miller, *Fifty Famous Liners 2* (New York: W. W. Norton, 1985), 103–6. See also, Nicholas T. Cairis, *North Atlantic Passenger Liners: Since 1900* (London: Ian Allan, 1972), 199.

68. Braynard and Miller, *Fifty Famous Liners 2,* 103.

69. Ibid., 106.

70. Ibid., 103.

71. Joint Chiefs of Staff, CCS 228, June 7, 1943, CAB 88/11/1, TNA. See also, Combined Chiefs of Staff, Series CCS 228/1–12, June 7, 1943–July 4, 1944, CAB 88/11, TNA.

72. Marshall to Joint Chiefs of Staff, 714-1 (JCS 504), September 17, 1943, "Japanese Atrocities—Reports of by Escaped Prisoners," *Records of the Joint Chiefs of Staff,* part 1, *1942–1945: The Pacific Theater* (Frederick/Bethesda, Md.: University Publications of America, 1982), reel 1, frames 0001–0003, 1–3; P. Scott Corbett, *Quiet Passages: The Exchange of Civilians between the United States and Japan during the Second World War* (Kent, Ohio: Kent State University Press, 1987), 57, 64–65, 93–94.

73. FDR to Stimson and Knox, September 9, 1943, "Japanese Atrocities—Reports of by Escaped Prisoners," *Records of the Joint Chiefs of Staff,* part 1, *1942–1945: The Pacific Theater,* reel 1, frame 0004, 4.

74. Leahy to FDR, September 17, 1943, enclosure B, "Japanese Atrocities—Reports of by Escaped Prisoners," *Records of the Joint Chiefs of Staff,* part 1, *1942–1945: The Pacific Theater,* reel 1, frames 0005–0006, 5–6.

75. Ibid., frame 0005, 5.
76. Marshall to Joint Chiefs of Staff, 714–1 (JCS 504), September 17, 1943. "Japanese Atrocities—Reports of by Escaped Prisoners," *Records of the Joint Chiefs of Staff*, part 1, *1942–1945: The Pacific Theater*, reel 1, frames 0002–0003, 2–3.
77. Joint Chiefs of Staff, CCS 228, June 7, 1943, CAB 88|11, TNA passim.
78. Ibid., CAB 88/11/1.
79. Joint Chiefs of Staff, CCS 228/11, June 27, 1944, CAB 88/11/1–2, TNA. See also, Joint Staff Mission, CCS 228/12, July 4, 1944, CAB 88/11/1–3, TNA.
80. Christopher Thorne, *Allies of a Kind: The United States, Britain and the War against Japan* (London: Hamish Hamilton, 1978), 620.
81. British Chiefs of Staff Committee, COS (43) 212, July 26, 1943, "Trial of Service and Merchant Navy Personnel for Offences in Russia," CAB 80/41/Annex, TNA [my italics].
82. Winston S. Churchill, *The Second World War*, vol. 6, *Triumph and Tragedy* (Boston: Houghton Mifflin, 1953), 551–61.
83. British Joint Staff Mission, CCS 739/8, May 19, 1945, "Relations with Yugoslav Forces in Austria and Venezia Giulia," *Records of the Joint Chiefs of Staff—The European Theater* (Frederick/Bethesda, Md.: University Publications of America, 1982), reel 5, frame 0407, 2.
84. Churchill, *Triumph and Tragedy*, 551–61.

Conclusion

1. Mark A. Stoler, *Allies and Adversaries: The Joint Chiefs of Staff, the Grand Alliance, and U.S. Strategy in World War II* (Chapel Hill: University of North Carolina Press, 2000), 166–70; Andrew Roberts, *Masters and Commanders: How Four Titans Won the War in the West, 1941–1945* (New York: HarperCollins, 2009), 398, 432, 458; Michael Simpson, *A Life of Admiral of the Fleet Andrew Cunningham: A Twentieth Century Naval Leader* (London: Frank Cass, 2004), 176.
2. See chapter 2.
3. Sally Lister Parker, *Attendant Lords: A Study of the British Joint Staff Mission in Washington, 1941–1945* (PhD dissertation, University of Maryland, College Park, 1984), 117–18.
4. Omar Bradley, *A Soldier's Story* (New York: Henry Holt, 1951), 195.
5. Ibid.
6. Alex Danchev and Daniel Todman, eds., *War Diaries 1939–1945: Field Marshal Lord Alanbrooke* (Berkeley: University of California Press, 2001), 23–32. See also, Alex Danchev, "Good Boy: Field Marshal Sir John Dill," in *On Specialness: Essays in Anglo-American Relations* (New York: St. Martin's, 1998), 86.
7. A. W. DePorte, *Europe between the Superpowers: The Enduring Balance* (New Haven, Conn.: Yale University Press, 1986), 47–48.
8. E. B. Potter, *Nimitz* (Annapolis, Md.: Naval Institute Press, 1975), 324–25.
9. Ibid, 325.

BIBLIOGRAPHY

In regard to primary source material, the exact words of the Combined Chiefs of Staff as recorded at their formal meetings at Casablanca, Teheran, Yalta, and the other major wartime conferences are available in published form in the *Foreign Relations of the United States* (or *FRUS*) series. The minutes of such meetings, while illuminating and comprehensive, do not fully explain the decisions taken and the compromises reached informally by the Combined Chiefs outside of their formal meetings. This is where the unpublished primary source material relating to the Combined Chiefs of Staff becomes an invaluable resource.

Primary Sources

Archives

AMERICAN

Naval War College, Newport, Rhode Island
   King Collection
Library of Congress
   King Papers
   Leahy Papers
U.S. National Archives and Records Administration
   Record Group 218: Records of the Joint Chiefs of Staff
George C. Marshall Research Library, Lexington, Virginia
   Marshall Papers

BRITISH

The National Archives (TNA), Kew
   CAB 88: Papers of the Combined Chiefs of Staff
   CAB 122: Papers of the British Joint Staff Mission in Washington
   AIR 8: Air Ministry Papers
   ADM 205: First Sea Lord Papers
Liddell Hart Centre for Military Archives, King's College London
   Brooke Papers
   Dill Papers
   Ismay Papers

Christ Church, Oxford
  Portal Papers
Churchill College, Cambridge
  Pound Papers
British Library
  Cunningham Papers

Published Primary Sources

Bland, Larry I., ed. Sharon Ritenour Stevens, assoc. ed. *The Papers of George Catlett Marshall*. Vol. 3. *"The Right Man for the Job:" December 7, 1941–May 31, 1943*. Baltimore: Johns Hopkins University Press, 1991.

———. *The Papers of George Catlett Marshall*. Vol. 4. *"Aggressive and Determined Leadership:" June 1, 1943–December 31, 1944*. Baltimore: Johns Hopkins University Press, 1996.

Danchev, Alex, and Daniel Todman, eds. *War Diaries 1939–1945: Field Marshal Lord Alanbrooke*. Berkeley: University of California Press, 2001.

United States Strategic Bombing Survey. "The Defeat of the German Air Force," (European Report 59). In *United States Strategic Bombing Survey*. Vol. 3. New York: Garland, 1976.

———. "Over-All Report" (European Report 2). In *United States Strategic Bombing Survey*. Vol. 1. New York: Garland, 1976.

———. "The German Anti-Friction Bearings Industry" (European Report 53). In *United States Strategic Bombing Survey*. Vol. 3. New York: Garland, 1976.

———. "Aircraft Division Industry Report" (European Report 4). In *United States Strategic Bombing Survey*. Vol. 2. New York: Garland, 1976.

Foreign Relations of the United States: The Conferences at Washington, 1941–1942 and Casablanca, 1943. Washington, D.C.: U.S. Government Printing Office, 1968.

———. *The Conferences at Washington and Quebec, 1943*. Washington, D.C.: U.S. Government Printing Office, 1970.

Microfilm Primary Sources

The following microfilm collections are available in the Government Documents Department of the Lamont Library, Harvard University:

PRO CAB 79: British Chiefs of Staff Committee—Minutes of Meetings
PRO CAB 80: British Chiefs of Staff Committee—Memoranda and Reports
PRO CAB 84: British Joint Planning Staff—Papers
PREM 3: Official Papers of the Minister of Defence
[Please note: The above microfilms that reference "PRO" collections are using the old British archival name "Public Record Office." This entity is now known as "The National Archives (TNA)."]
Records of the Joint Chiefs of Staff. Part 1. *1942–1945: European Theater*. Frederick/Bethesda, Md.: University Publications of America, 1982.

Records of the Joint Chiefs of Staff. Part 1. *1942–1945: Strategic Issues.* Frederick/
Bethesda, Md.: University Publications of America, 1982.

Records of the Joint Chiefs of Staff. Part 1. *1942–1945: The Soviet Union.* Frederick/
Bethesda, Md.: University Publications of America, 1982.

Records of the Joint Chiefs of Staff. Part 1. *1942–1945: The Pacific Theater.* Frederick/
Bethesda, Md.: University Publications of America, 1982.

Records of the Joint Chiefs of Staff. Part 1. *1942–1945: Meetings.* Frederick/Bethesda,
Md.: University Publications of America, 1982.

Secondary Sources
Books

The Aircraft Carrier. Secaucus, N.J.: Chartwell Books, 1984.

Arnold, Henry H. *Global Mission.* New York: Harper and Brothers, 1949.

Axelrod, Alan. *Profiles in Leadership.* New York: Prentice Hall, 2003.

Bartov, Omer. *The Eastern Front, 1941–1945: German Troops and the Barbarisation of
Warfare.* New York: St. Martin's, 1986.

———. *Hitler's Army: Soldiers, Nazis, and War in the Third Reich.* New York: Oxford
University Press, 1992.

Beasley, Norman. *Knudsen: A Biography.* New York: Whittlesey House McGraw-Hill,
1947.

Beevor, Antony. *Stalingrad.* New York: Penguin, 1998.

Behrens, C. B. A. (Betty). *Merchant Shipping and the Demands of War.* London: Her
Majesty's Stationery Office and Longman's, Green, 1955.

Bialer, Seweryn, ed. *Stalin and His Generals: Soviet Military Memoirs of World War II.*
New York: Pegasus, 1969.

Birkenhead, Earl of. *The Professor and the Prime Minister.* Boston: Houghton Mifflin,
1962.

Bond, Brian. *The First World War and British Military History.* New York: Macmillan,
1991.

Bowyer, Chaz. *The Encyclopedia of British Military Aircraft.* New York: Bison, 1982.

Bradley, Omar. *A Soldier's Story.* New York: Henry Holt, 1951.

Braynard, Frank O. (FRS), and William H. Miller. *Fifty Famous Liners 2.* New York:
W. W. Norton, 1985.

Brodhurst, Robin. *Churchill's Anchor: Admiral of the Fleet Sir Dudley Pound, OM,
GCB, GCVO.* Barnsley, South Yorkshire, UK: Leo Cooper, 2000.

Bryant, Arthur. *The Turn of the Tide: 1939–1943.* London: Collins, 1957.

Buell, Thomas B. *Master of Sea Power: A Biography of Admiral Ernest J. King.* Boston:
Little, Brown, 1980.

———. *The Quiet Warrior: A Biography of Admiral Raymond A. Spruance.* Annapolis,
Md.: Naval Institute Press, 1987.

Burns, James MacGregor. *Roosevelt: The Soldier of Freedom: 1940–1945.* New York:
Harcourt Brace Jovanovich, 1970.

Cairis, Nicholas T. *North Atlantic Passenger Liners: Since 1900*. London: Ian Allen, 1972.

Catton, Bruce. *The Civil War*. Boston: Houghton Mifflin, 1987.

Chant, Christopher. *Encyclopedia of World Aircraft*. New York: Mallard, 1990.

Chisholm, Ann, and Michael Davie. *Lord Beaverbrook: A Life*. New York: Alfred A. Knopf, 1993.

Churchill, Winston S. *The Second World War*. 6 Vols. Boston: Houghton Mifflin, 1948–1953.

Coffey, Thomas M. *HAP: The Story of the U.S. Air Force and the Man Who Built It, General Henry H. "Hap" Arnold*. New York: Viking, 1982.

Colville, John. *The Fringes of Power: 10 Downing Street Diaries: 1939–1955*. New York: W. W. Norton, 1985.

Corbett, P. Scott. *Quiet Passages: The Exchange of Civilians between the United States and Japan during the Second World War*. Kent, Ohio: Kent State University Press, 1987.

Craig, Gordon A. *Germany: 1866–1945*. New York: Oxford University Press, 1978.

Craven, Wesley Frank, and James Lea Cate, eds. *The Army Air Forces in World War II*. Vol. 3. *January 1944 to May 1945*. Chicago: University of Chicago Press, 1951.

———. *The Army Air Forces in World War II*. Vol. 6. *Men and Planes*. Chicago: University of Chicago Press, 1955.

———. *The Army Air Forces in World War II*. Vol. 7. *Services around the World*. Chicago: University of Chicago Press, 1958.

Cunningham, Andrew B. *A Sailor's Odyssey*. London: Hutchinson, 1951.

Danchev, Alex. *On Specialness: Essays in Anglo-American Relations*. New York: St. Martin's, 1998.

———. *Very Special Relationship: Field Marshal Sir John Dill and the Anglo-American Alliance, 1941–1944*. Washington, D.C.: Brassey's Defence, 1986.

———, ed. *Establishing the Anglo-American Alliance: The Second World War Diaries of Brigadier Vivian Dykes*. London: Brassey's, 1990.

Deane, John R. *The Strange Alliance: The Story of Our Efforts at Wartime Co-operation with Russia*. New York: Viking, 1947.

Delgado, James P., ed. *Encyclopedia of Underwater and Maritime Archaeology*. New Haven, Conn.: Yale University Press, 1997.

DePorte, A. W. *Europe between the Superpowers: The Enduring Balance*. New Haven, Conn.: Yale University Press, 1986.

D'Este, Carlo. *World War II in the Mediterranean 1942–1945*. Chapel Hill, N.C.: Algonquin Books of Chapel Hill, 1990.

Doenitz, Karl. *Memoirs: Ten Years and Twenty Days*. Translated by R. H. Stevens and David Woodward. New York: World, 1959.

Dunlop, Richard. *Donovan: America's Master Spy*. New York: Rand-McNally, 1982.

Ehrman, John. *Grand Strategy*. Vol. 5. *August 1943–September 1944*. London: Her Majesty's Stationery Office, 1956.

Eubank, Keith. *Summit at Teheran*. New York: William Morrow, 1985.

Evans, Richard J. *The Third Reich at War*. New York: Penguin, 2009.

Fox, Stephen. *Transatlantic: Samuel Cunard, Isambard Brunel, and the Great Atlantic Steamships*. New York: HarperCollins, 2003.

Fraser, David, Sir. *Alanbrooke*. New York: Atheneum, 1982.

Freedman, Lawrence, Paul Hayes, and Robert O'Neill, eds. *War, Strategy, and International Politics: Essays in Honour of Sir Michael Howard*. New York: Oxford University Press, 1992.

Freeman, Douglas Southall. *Lee's Lieutenants: A Study in Command*. Vol. 1. *Manassas to Malvern Hill*. New York: Charles Scribner's Sons, 1942.

Furer, Julius Augustus. *The Administration of the Navy Department in World War II*. Washington, D.C.: U.S. Government Printing Office, 1959.

Gaddis, John Lewis. *Strategies of Containment: A Critical Appraisal of American Postwar National Security Policy*. New York: Oxford University Press, 1982.

———. *The United States and the Origins of the Cold War 1941–1947*. New York: Columbia University Press, 1972.

Gannon, Michael. *Operation Drumbeat: The Dramatic True Story of Germany's First U-Boat Attacks along the American Coast in World War II*. New York: Harper and Row, 1990.

Gilbert, Martin. *Churchill: A Life*. New York: Henry Holt, 1991.

———. *Winston S. Churchill*. Vol. 7. *Road to Victory: 1941–1945*. Boston: Houghton Mifflin, 1986.

Green, William, and Gordon Swanborough. *The Complete Book of Fighters*. New York: Smithmark, 1994.

Harris, Arthur. *Bomber Offensive*. New York: Macmillan, 1947.

Harrison, Gordon. *United States Army in World War II: Cross-Channel Attack*. Washington, D.C.: Office of the Chief of Military History, 1951.

Harrod, R. F. *The Prof: A Personal Memoir of Lord Cherwell*. London: Macmillan, 1959.

Hastings, Max. *Bomber Command*. New York: Dial / James Wade, 1979.

Hayes, Grace Person. *The Joint Chiefs of Staff in World War II: The War against Japan*. Annapolis, Md.: Naval Institute Press, 1982.

Heer, Hans, and Klaus Naumann, eds. *War of Extermination: The German Military in World War II, 1941–1944*. New York: Berghahn Books, 2000.

Hillgruber, Andreas. *Germany and the Two World Wars*. Translated by William C. Kirby. Cambridge, Mass.: Harvard University Press, 1981.

Holley, Irving Brinton, Jr. *The United States Army in World War II: Buying Aircraft— Matériel Procurement for the Army Air Forces*. Washington, D.C.: Office of the Chief of Military History, 1954.

Hope, Ronald. *A New History of British Shipping*. London: John Murray, 1990.

Hough, Richard. *Mountbatten*. New York: Random House, 1981.

Howard, Sir Michael. *Grand Strategy*. Vol. 4. *August, 1942–September, 1943*. London: Her Majesty's Stationery Office, 1972.

Hunt, Erling. *America Organizes to Win the War.* New York: Harcourt Brace, 1942.

Iriye, Akira. *Origins of the Second World War in Asia and the Pacific.* New York: Longman, 1987.

———. *Power and Culture: The Japanese-American War, 1941–1945.* Cambridge, Mass.: Harvard University Press, 1981.

Ismay, Hastings, Sir. *The Memoirs of General Lord Ismay.* New York: Viking, 1960.

Jackson, General Sir William, and Field Marshal Lord Bramall. *The Chiefs: The Story of the United Kingdom Chiefs of Staff.* London: Brassey's, 1992.

James, D. Clayton. *The Years of MacArthur.* Vol. 1. *1880–1941.* Boston: Houghton Mifflin, 1970.

Jones, Jesse H., with Edward Angly. *Fifty Billion Dollars: My Thirteen Years with the RFC—1932–1945.* New York: Macmillan, 1951.

Keegan, John, ed. *Churchill's Generals.* New York: William Morrow, 1992.

Kemp, Peter. "Admiral of the Fleet: Sir Dudley Pound." In *Men of War: Great Naval Leaders of World War II,* edited by Stephen Howarth. New York: St. Martin's, 1992.

Kennan, George F. *Memoirs: 1925–1950.* Boston: Little, Brown, 1967.

Kennedy, Paul. *The Rise and Fall of the Great Powers: Economic Change and Military Conflict from 1500 to 2000.* New York: Vintage Books, 1987, 1989.

Kimball, Warren F. *Forged in War: Roosevelt, Churchill, and the Second World War.* New York: William Morrow, 1997.

King, Ernest J., and Walter Muir Whitehill. *Fleet Admiral King: A Naval Record.* New York: W. W. Norton, 1952.

Langley, Susan B. M. "Habbakuk." In *Encyclopedia of Underwater and Maritime Archaeology,* edited by James P. Delgado. New Haven, Conn.: Yale University Press, 1997.

Larrabee, Eric. *Commander in Chief: Franklin Delano Roosevelt, His Lieutenants, and Their War.* New York: Harper and Row, 1987.

Leahy, William D. *I Was There.* New York: Whittlesey House / McGraw-Hill, 1950.

Liddell Hart, B. H. *History of the Second World War.* New York: G. P. Putnam's Sons, 1970.

Lord Moran. *Churchill at War: 1940–45.* New York: Carroll and Graf, 2002.

Love, Robert William, Jr., ed. *The Chiefs of Naval Operations.* Annapolis, Md.: Naval Institute Press, 1980.

———. *History of the U.S. Navy.* Vol. 2. *1942–1991.* Harrisburg, Pa.: Stackpole Books, 1992.

Lundstrom, John B. *Black Shoe Carrier Admiral: Frank Jack Fletcher at Coral Sea, Midway, and Guadalcanal.* Annapolis, Md.: Naval Institute Press, 2006.

Manchester, William. *American Caesar: Douglas MacArthur, 1880–1964.* Boston: Little, Brown, 1978.

Massie, Robert K. *Castles of Steel: Britain, Germany, and the Winning of the Great War at Sea.* New York: Random House, 2003.

Matloff, Maurice. *Strategic Planning for Coalition Warfare 1943–1944.* Vol. 2.

Washington, D.C.: Office of the Chief of Military History, 1959.

———, and Edwin M. Snell. *Strategic Planning for Coalition Warfare 1941–1942*. Vol. 1. Washington, D.C.: Office of the Chief of Military History, 1953.

Menaul, Stewart, ed. *Russian Military Power*. New York: Bonanza Books, 1982.

Merryman, Molly. *Clipped Wings: The Rise and Fall of the Women Airforce Service Pilots (WASPs) of World War II*. New York: New York University Press, 1998.

Millett, John D. *The United States Army in World War II: The Organization and Role of the Army Service Forces*. Washington, D.C.: Office of the Chief of Military History, 1954.

Milward, Alan. *War, Economy, and Society: 1939–1945*. Berkeley: University of California Press, 1977.

Morison, Samuel Eliot. *History of United States Naval Operations in World War II*. Vol. 4. *Coral Sea, Midway and Submarine Actions: May 1942–August 1942*. Boston: Little, Brown, 1950.

———. *History of United States Naval Operations in World War II*. Vol. 3. *The Rising Sun in the Pacific 1931–April 1942*. Boston: Little, Brown, 1955.

———. *History of United States Naval Operations in World War II*. Vol. 10. *The Atlantic Battle Won: May 1943—May 1945*. Boston: Little, Brown, 1956.

———. *History of United States Naval Operations in World War II*. Vol. 15. *Supplement and General Index*. Boston: Little, Brown, 1962.

———. *The Two Ocean War: A Short History of the United States Navy in the Second World War*. Boston: Little, Brown, 1962.

Mosley, Leonard. *Marshall: Hero for Our Times*. New York: Hearst Books, 1982.

Murfrett, Malcolm, ed. *The First Sea Lords: From Fisher to Mountbatten*. Westport, Conn.: Praeger, 1995.

Murray, Williamson, and Allan R. Millett. *A War to Be Won: Fighting the Second World War*. Cambridge, Mass.: Belknap Press of Harvard University Press, 2000.

Nalty, Bernard C. "The Gilberts and the Marshalls." In *Pearl Harbor and the War in the Pacific*. New York: Smithmark, 1991.

Nelson, Donald M. *Arsenal of Democracy: The Story of American War Production*. New York: Harcourt Brace, 1946.

Noakes, Jeremy, and Geoffrey Pridham, eds. *Nazism, 1919–1945: A History in Documents and Eyewitness Accounts*. Vol. 2. *Foreign Policy, War and Racial Extermination*. New York: Schocken Books, 1988, 1990.

Ohl, John Kennedy. *Supplying the Troops: General Somervell and American Logistics in WWII*. DeKalb: Northern Illinois University Press, 1994.

Overy, R. J. *The Air War: 1939–1945*. New York: Stein and Day, 1980.

———. *Why the Allies Won*. New York: W. W. Norton, 1995.

Pitt, Barrie, ed. *The Military History of World War II*. New York: Military, 1986.

Pogue, Forrest C. *George C. Marshall*. Vol. 1. *Education of a General*. New York: Viking, 1963.

———. *George C. Marshall*. Vol. 2. *Ordeal and Hope*. New York: Viking, 1966.

————. *George C. Marshall*. Vol. 3. *Organizer of Victory*. New York: Viking, 1973.

————. *U.S. Army in World War II: The Supreme Command*. Washington, D.C.: Office of the Chief of Military History, 1954.

Potter, E. B. *Nimitz*. Annapolis, Md.: Naval Institute Press, 1975.

Raisanovsky, Nicholas V. *A History of Russia*. 4th ed. New York: Oxford University Press, 1984.

Reynolds, Clark G. *The Fast Carriers: The Forging of An Air Navy*. New York: McGraw-Hill, 1968.

Reynolds, David, Warren Kimball, and A. O. Chubarian, eds. *Allies at War: the Soviet, American, and British Experience, 1939–1945*. New York: St. Martin's, 1994.

Rhodes, Richard. *Masters of Death: The SS-Einsatzgruppen and the Invention of the Holocaust*. New York: Alfred A. Knopf, 2002.

Richards, Denis. *Portal of Hungerford*. London: Heinemann, 1977.

Ritchie, Sebastian. *Industry and Air Power: The Expansion of British Aircraft Production, 1935–41*. London: Frank Cass, 1997.

Roberts, Andrew. *Masters and Commanders: How Four Titans Won the War in the West, 1941–1945*. New York: HarperCollins, 2009.

Rosen, S. McKee. *The Combined Boards of the Second World War: An Experimentation in International Administration*. New York: Columbia University Press, 1951.

Roskill, Stephen. *Churchill and the Admirals*. New York: William Morrow, 1978.

Rumpf, Hans. *The Bombing of Germany*. Translated by Edward Fitzgerald. New York: Holt, Rinehart and Winston, 1963.

Sherwood, Robert E. *Roosevelt and Hopkins: An Intimate History*. New York: Harper and Brothers, 1950.

Simpson, Michael. *A Life of Admiral of the Fleet Andrew Cunningham: A Twentieth Century Naval Leader*. London: Frank Cass, 2004.

Smith, Kevin. *Conflict over Convoys: Anglo-American Logistics Diplomacy in the Second World War*. Cambridge, UK: Cambridge University Press, 1996.

Smith, R. Elberton. *The United States Army in World War II: The Army and Economic Mobilization*. Washington, D.C.: Office of the Chief of Military History, 1959.

Snow, C. P. *Science and Government*. Cambridge, Mass.: Harvard University Press, 1961.

Spector, Ronald H. *Eagle against the Sun: The American War with Japan*. New York: Free Press, 1985.

Stafford, Edward P. *The Big E: The Story of the USS* Enterprise. Annapolis, Md.: Naval Institute Press, 1962, 1988.

Stephen, Martin. *The Fighting Admirals: British Admirals of the Second World War*. Annapolis, Md.: Naval Institute Press, 1991.

Stoler, Mark A. *Allies and Adversaries: The Joint Chiefs of Staff, the Grand Alliance, and U.S. Strategy in World War II*. Chapel Hill: University of North Carolina Press, 2000.

————. *Allies in War: Britain and America against the Axis Powers 1940–1945*. London: Hodder Arnold, 2005.

————. *George C. Marshall: Soldier Statesman of the American Century*. Boston: Twayne, 1989.

Sturton, Ian, ed. *Conway's All the World's Battleships: 1906 to the Present*. Annapolis, Md.: Naval Institute Press, 1987.

Taylor, A. J. P. *Beaverbrook*. New York: Simon and Schuster, 1972.

————. *The First World War: An Illustrated History*. New York: Perigree Books / G. P. Putnam's Sons, 1980.

Terraine, John. *The Right of the Line: The Royal Air Force in the European War 1939–1945*. London: Hodder and Stoughton, 1985.

The National Archive. *Records Information. 73. The Records of the Cabinet Office*. Kew Gardens, UK: TNA, 1995.

Thorne, Christopher. *Allies of a Kind: The United States, Britain and the War against Japan*. London: Hamish Hamilton, 1978.

Toland, John. *The Rising Sun: The Decline and Fall of the Japanese Empire*. New York: Bantam, 1970.

Van Wagenen Keil, Sally. *Those Wonderful Women in Their Flying Machines: The Unknown Heroines of World War II*. New York: Rawson, Wade, 1979.

Von Clausewitz, C. *On War*. Translated by M. Howard and P. Paret. Princeton, N.J.: Princeton University Press, 1976.

Warner, Oliver. *Admiral of the Fleet: Cunningham of Hyndhope—the Battle for the Mediterranean*. Athens: Ohio University Press, 1967.

Webster, Sir Charles, and Noble Frankland. *The Strategic Air Offensive against Germany, 1939–1945*. Vol. 2. *Endeavor*. London: Her Majesty's Stationery Office, 1961.

————. *The Strategic Air Offensive against Germany, 1939–1945*. Vol. 3. *Victory*. London: Her Majesty's Stationery Office, 1961

Wedemeyer, Albert C. *Wedemeyer Reports!* New York: Henry Holt, 1958.

White, Gerald T. *Billions for Defense: Government Financing by the Defense Plant Corporation during World War II*. University: University of Alabama Press, 1980.

Wilson, Theodore A., ed. *D-Day 1944*. Abilene: Eisenhower Foundation and University Press of Kansas, 1971, 1994.

Wilt, Alan F. *War from the Top: German and British Military Decision Making during World War II*. Bloomington: Indiana University Press, 1990.

Wolff, Leon. *In Flanders Fields: The 1917 Campaign*. New York: Viking, 1958.

Wright, Gordon. *The Ordeal of Total War: 1939–1945*. New York: Harper Torchbooks, 1968.

Ziegler, Philip. *Mountbatten*. New York: Harper and Row, 1985.

Articles

Maga, Timothy. "Vision and Victory: Franklin Roosevelt and the Pacific War Council, 1942–1944." *Presidential Studies Quarterly* 21 (Spring 1991).

Villa, Brian Loring. "Mountbatten, the British Chiefs of Staff, and Approval for the Dieppe Raid." *Journal of Military History* (formerly *Military Affairs*) 54, no. 2 (April 1990).

Newspapers
New York Times
New York World-Telegram
Times of London
USA Today

Unpublished Papers, Dissertations, Correspondence, and Conversations
Cox, Sebastian. Head of the Air Historical Branch at the Ministry of Defence. Telephone interview, London, June 25, 1997.
Parker, Sally Lister. *Attendant Lords: A Study of the British Joint Staff Mission in Washington, 1941–1945.* PhD dissertation, University of Maryland, College Park, 1984.
Rigby, David. "American Strategy in the Second World War with Special Emphasis on the European Theater and Logistics." Unpublished paper, May 1991.
———. "American Strategy in the Second World War with Special Emphasis on the Pacific Theater of Operations." Unpublished paper, December 1990.
———. "The Effects of Strategic Bombardment on Germany during the Second World War." Unpublished paper, February 1992.
———. "The Mobilization of the American Economy during the Second World War." Unpublished paper, December 1991.
Smith, Kevin. Letter to author, January 6, 1999.

INDEX

ABOUT THE AUTHOR

David Rigby holds a PhD in comparative history from Brandeis University. He has worked as a K–12 textbook editor. He teaches history as an adjunct instructor at Boston-area colleges and universities.